IMMIGRANTS UNDER THREAT

LATINA/O SOCIOLOGY SERIES

General Editors: Pierrette Hondagneu-Sotelo and Victor M. Rios

FOUR WEATHERCOCKS

. . . as they bade
to the eight different winds

THE OLIO (1830)

ABOUT THE AUTHOR

Greg Prieto is Assistant Professor of Sociology at the University of San Diego.

Immigrants under Threat

Risk and Resistance in Deportation Nation

Greg Prieto

NEW YORK UNIVERSITY PRESS

New York

NEW YORK UNIVERSITY PRESS
New York
www.nyupress.org

References to Internet websites (URLs) were accurate at the time of writing. Neither the author nor New York University Press is responsible for URLs that may have expired or changed since the manuscript was prepared.

Library of Congress Cataloging-in-Publication Data
Names: Prieto, Greg, author.
Title: Immigrants under threat : risk and resistance in deportation nation / Greg Prieto.
Description: New York : New York University Press, [2018] | Series: Latina/o sociology series | Includes bibliographical references and index.
Identifiers: LCCN 2017034391 | ISBN 9781479823925 (cl : alk. paper) | ISBN 9781479821464 (pb : alk. paper)
Subjects: LCSH: United States—Emigration and immigration—Government policy. | Mexicans—Government policy—United States. | Illegal aliens—Government policy—United States.
Classification: LCC JV6483 .P75 2018 | DDC 325.73—dc23
LC record available at https://lccn.loc.gov/2017034391

New York University Press books are printed on acid-free paper, and their binding materials are chosen for strength and durability. We strive to use environmentally responsible suppliers and materials to the greatest extent possible in publishing our books.

Manufactured in the United States of America

10 9 8 7 6 5 4 3 2 1

Also available as an ebook

For Michelle

CONTENTS

Introduction

Agency, Action, and the Material Moorings
of Immigrant Movements

La participación es la unica cosa que nos va a salvar.
—Esmeralda, primary informant

Power is everywhere, not because it embraces everything,
but because it comes from everywhere.
—Foucault, *History of Sexuality*

De-escalation, Nonparticipation, and Everyday
Immigrant Politics

The immigrant rights marches of 2006 were a historic touchtone in the evolution of Latino and immigrant political power.[1] Replenished by waves of predominately Mexican immigration after 1965,[2] the political power of Latino immigrants is illuminated in these massive displays of social movement activism. And yet immigrant collective action on the scale of the *primavera del inmigrante* had not been witnessed before and has not been seen since that historic outpouring of immigrant protest. And whatever electoral faith Latinos placed in the Obama administration to address the immigration issue was dashed by the record numbers of deportations executed under his watch.[3] We have before us a question not only about the escalation of immigrant politics, but also about their rapid *de-escalation*.[4] What explains this oscillation? How do we make sense of Latino immigrants' participation or lack thereof in these spectacular manifestations of collective resistance?

I think the answer lies in the everyday. Social movement organizing and the marches of 2006 are but the tip of the iceberg. These enormous displays of political power are both enabled and constrained by the material exigencies of immigrants' everyday lives as low-wage laborers whose exploitation is sustained by the most extensive immigration enforcement regime in US history. The metaphor is meant to illustrate not the relationship of something small to something large, but rather the way that the submerged portion of the iceberg both anchors and buoys the visible tip. This necessary and daily work of sustaining self and family inspires a set of widely shared grievances that become fertile ground for collective action. To protect what material gains they have reaped, immigrants, as a matter of necessity, avoid and insulate themselves from local police, immigration enforcement, and the unfamiliar. They avoid risk to protect their gains. And yet, their risk aversion simultaneously forms a counterweight against participation in protest. Their first priorities remain family and work.

In this study of two Mexican immigrant communities on California's Central Coast, the periodicity of immigration participation was a central dilemma for La Unión community organizers who sought to cultivate an immigrant political constituency. In both North City and South City,[5] organizers were regularly met with reticence and reluctance from the Mexican immigrants, undocumented and documented alike, whom they sought to recruit to social movement work. These were not insurmountable barriers for many potential immigrant activists. Collective mobilization emerged when it was organized by activists who were organically connected to the communities they sought to mobilize, when those activists were supported by robust organizations, and when they drew upon narrative frames that stressed immigrants' linked fate,[6] the efficacy of political action,[7] and their responsibility to act on their own behalves. And still, the action that emerged remained moored to the urgent material pressures of work and family.

Consider this exchange at the first La Unión house meeting that I attended just before the start of the new year in December 2011. The house meeting is a classic organizing strategy widely used during the farmworker struggle that began in the early 1960s and was led by the cofounders of the United Farmworkers (UFW), Dolores Huerta and César Chávez. The idea is simple: the activist asks a volunteer, friend, or family member to host a gathering at her home to which she invites neighbors, family, friends, and coworkers of her own. The community organizer will typically offer some combination of know-your-rights training and legislative updates, followed by a question-and-answer session and a call to participate in a future action. Three major goals are advanced: organizers share reliable and up-to-date information, personal networks become the springboard for political community, and, in a step-by-step fashion, a base of immigrant activists in waiting is cultivated with an eye toward future mass mobilizations and strategic efforts to influence legislators (e.g., lobbying, telephone campaigns, marches and rallies, etc.). The house meeting is an ideal site for observing the linkage between the everyday and social movement organizing because it is where the pain of precarity is made political, where the quotidian is remapped in historical terms.[8]

Primary informant and La Unión volunteer organizer Esmeralda organized this first house meeting. Dissatisfied with dwindling attendance at La Unión meetings, she decided that we should go out into the community instead of asking the community to come to us. I met Esmeralda at Vicky's home on the predominately Mexican eastside of South City. It was her daughter's 18th birthday, and so Esmeralda decided to piggyback on the occasion by scheduling this house meeting at the start of the birthday party. When I arrive, I'm greeted by a group of young girls, maybe 14 or 15 years old, who open the door and stare at me. I introduce myself as a friend of Esmeralda's here to meet our host Vicky. Of this group of four girls at the door, a young lady at the rear breaks an increasingly awkward silence by stepping forward and inviting me inside. As I move into the small living room, I am reminded that Christmas has just passed. A decorated Christmas tree stands in one corner. Two large couches are placed together in the shape of an L. An end table, bookshelves, and a television complete the living room furniture. In the kitchen around the corner, Esmeralda and her husband Ernesto are sitting at a dining table. Esmeralda introduces me to Vicky, who is busy making enchiladas for the party, serving them to us as they finish cooking, one plate at a time, so that we can eat before we begin the meeting.

As we eat and exchange pleasantries, Esmeralda peppers the young people in the room with questions. She asks a young man who is attending an alternative school about how things are going. He is clearly nervous, offering clipped responses. She isn't forceful though, signaling care and confidence. She commands the room by assuming the role of interlocutor.

As we finish our food, Esmeralda asks Ernesto and me to move chairs into a circle in the living room so that the other guests, adult neighbors and family members who are arriving, can sit. As people settle into the chairs that encircle the living room, Esmeralda begins the meeting by talking about why we are all here, turning first to the issue of car impoundments that has affected the immigrant community for quite some time. Esmeralda knows that having a car confiscated because they are undocumented and driving without a license, more than the fear of deportation, is the most common grievance in South City. She hooks the audience by leading with the topic she thinks will capture their attention. She also asks me to explain La Unión's mission to support working-class and immigrant families by building political power and cultivating leaders from within the community.

Esmeralda follows by running down a list of the major issues that affect immigrants locally and at the state and national levels. She talks about the California Dream Act, which had recently been signed into law by Governor Jerry Brown, allowing undocumented students to apply for private scholarships and state-funded financial aid. She also discusses the local-federal deportation program Secure Communities, E-Verify, the possibility of city identification for undocumented residents, and the national movement for immigration reform. The group asks questions. Will local police offer a grace period at checkpoints (*reténes*) for a licensed driver to retrieve an undocumented driver's vehicle? Not unless state legislation passes that mandates officers offer one. Do local police work with Immigration and Customs Enforcement (ICE)? Not directly, but Secure Communities operates at the local jail, so if you get into trouble you can be deported. Will there be immigration reform? Unless we demand change and get involved, we will never see reform.

In the final part of the meeting, Esmeralda turns to the recruitment of testimonies for an upcoming community forum with the police chief where we plan to ask for relief from car impoundments for undocumented drivers. As she solicits testimonials, she coaches attendees to deliver their accounts with confidence and precision. One middle-aged man in his 40s, husky, bald, and sitting in the corner of the room, raises his hand and shares that he has had no fewer than five cars impounded. He is soft-spoken, and I notice other attendees lean forward in their chairs to hear him. The last time police impounded his car he was parked briefly, but illegally, on the street while he collected bottles that he would later recycle to earn a little money. When the police stopped him, they confirmed it was his car that was parked illegally and asked for his identification—standard operating procedure for South City police. He turned over his passport. The officer asked if he had a driver's license. The man handed over his *matrícula consular*, a form of identification issued by the Mexican consulate to its expatriates living abroad. The officer repeated his question: "How can you drive without a license?" The man responded, "Well I need to work."

As he is telling this story, Regina interrupts him, "You say you've had five cars impounded ['*cinco cinco!*']." She tells him to raise his hand, hold all five fingers out, and in a clear, loud voice say, "I've had five cars impounded." She is encouraging him to be assertive and confident in the face of authority, to clearly communicate the extent of the damage wrought by impoundment after impoundment. Esmeralda collects three testimonials in all. Meeting participants write down a brief description of the events on a one-page form that she has created: name, date, officer's name, description of events.

As the meeting draws to a close another attendee sitting to my right, in his late 30s and sporting a hat, says that he's heard around town that people don't come to these forums or attend immigration committee meetings because they're afraid that immigration enforcement (*la migra*) will be there. Regina forcefully responds that ICE would never be at one of our meetings because that is the group that we are working against.

Esmeralda solicits hosts for future house meetings by going around the room, asking almost person by person, focusing on women in particular, whether they could commit to hosting the next house meeting. She repeats several times that the meeting can be at a time that is convenient for them. She understands everyone works, so she is happy to plan around schedules. Participants often respond that they cannot commit to hosting a house meeting because they have children or a job. Esmeralda responds that everybody has kids and a job and yet Vicky, tonight's host, is managing very well. In some cases, she seems to know when to stop pressing. One woman, in particular, gives more vague excuses like she has a lot going on with her family right now. Regina pushes her a bit, saying she can adjust the time to whenever works best for her. The woman responds stoically, repeating that she cannot. Esmeralda does not press any further.

We end the house meeting in the same way that we end most gatherings with La Unión: a practice sometimes called the unity clap, a rhythmic clap that starts slowly and increases in tempo. The unity clap was a common ritual employed during the farmworker struggle and continues to be used among organizers, especially those working in Latino communities. Esmeralda explains that it is a tool for demonstrating solidarity and for communicating between Filipino and Mexican farmworkers during the time of the UFW. We clap together as a group. The clapping synchronizes, growing louder and faster and ending in *gritos*, whistles, and whoops.

Those immigrants who toil under the weight of global capitalism and the most extensive deportation regime in US history are also those least available to combat their oppression. This dilemma lies at the heart of immigrant political action in the present: potentially transformative, but also moored to the pressing material needs of life as a Mexican immigrant. The house meeting is an ideal site to observe the confluence of the everyday and the historic. Here organizers work to translate individual grievances as a group condition best addressed through collective action. That the house meeting occurs just before Vicky's daughter's 18th birthday party reveals the central role of networks of kin, coworkers, comadres, and compadres in the cultivation of a political constituency.[9] The everyday is both the seat of grievance and the place where collective redress may begin.

But note also the way that party attendees balked at invitations to future movement work like hosting a house meeting or showing up to a community forum. Widespread fear of *la migra* and the more mundane priorities of work and family trump movement participation. For working-class Mexican immigrants, especially those without documentation, their social movements cannot be understood without attention to the quotidian conditions of their everyday lives, which simultaneously enable and constrain their political expression.

This proposition can be specified further. The dynamics of the house meeting are linked to broader demographic, political, and legal shifts begun in earnest in the mid-1960s. A major unanticipated consequence of the Immigration and Nationality Act of 1965 (Hart-Celler), which replaced the racist national origins system with the system that we have today,[10] was that migration from Asia, Africa, and especially Latin America increased dramatically.[11] Now privileging family reunification and employer preferences, this shift in immigration policy and the waves of immigration that followed spurred the "browning of America." In 1960, the US immigrant population was approximately 84 percent European and Canadian, 4 percent Asian, 10 percent Latin American, and 3 percent from other regions. By 2015, these figures had changed drastically, with 13 percent of immigrants coming from Europe and Canada, 27 percent from Asia, 51 percent from Latin America, and 9 percent from other regions.[12]

This transformation in the demographic composition of immigration translated into a broader shift in the United States in general. Consider that in 1965 Latinos represented 4 percent of the US population, Asian Americans less than 1 percent, and African Americans 11 percent, with the remaining 84 percent white. Driven by the historic shift in immigration policy, by 2015 Latinos represented 18 percent of the population, Asian Americans 6 percent, African Americans 12 percent, and whites 62 percent (with 2 percent from "other" groups).[13] Fall 2015 marked the first time the majority of all K–12 public school students were racial minorities.[14]

Consequently, Latinos have become an increasingly important electoral constituency that regularly gives the majority of its vote share to the Democratic Party.[15] Growing numbers of Latinos have produced new political constituencies whose growing political power has destabilized political arrangements related not only to immigration law and policy (e.g., Deferred Action for Childhood Arrivals), but also to education (e.g., bilingual education and in-state tuition), public safety (e.g., the California Values Act, limiting cooperation with ICE and driver's licenses for undocumented immigrants in California and 11 other states), health care (e.g., undocumented immigrants' access to the benefits of the Affordable Care Act in California), and current policing strategies (e.g., prosecutorial discretion and the rebranding of Secure Communities as the Prioritized Enforcement Program, focusing solely on serious and violent convicts).

At the same time, the issue of immigration generally and undocumented immigration specifically has reached crisis proportions.

Ramped up enforcement, beginning in the early 1990s with Operations Hold the Line in El Paso, Safeguard in Tucson, and Gatekeeper in San Diego,[16] interrupted what were previously cyclical migration patterns in which predominantly Mexican immigrants would come to the United States for the harvest season and then return home. As the border was fortified, clandestine crossing became both more dangerous and more expensive, thereby encouraging migrants to settle permanently in the United States.[17] Consequently, the numbers of undocumented immigrants skyrocketed from 3.5 million in 1990 to a peak of 12.2 million in 2007, then declining slightly and stabilizing at approximately 11 million through the present. In the post-9/11 moment, the Department of Homeland Security has doubled down on enforcement by bringing state and local governments into the work of immigration enforcement through a series of collaborative programs, a development referred to as devolution.[18]

As a consequence of these dual movements—greater numbers of migrants beleaguered by a more extensive immigration enforcement apparatus—immigrants' grievances have become both more urgent and more important to American politics. Though a powerful and bipartisan "anti-migrant bloc" has thwarted many attempts at immigration reform,[19] the growing political power of immigrants in the ballot box and in the streets represents a potential watershed in American politics. This situation, in which immigrants are economically necessary but socially undesirable, sustains their exploitation in the present, producing both a broadly shared set of grievances, as well as the conditions for redressing them.

How immigrants choose to confront their grievances brings us to the heart of this book. I am interested in the *relationship* between what I call the shell, or private strategies of avoidance and isolation, and immigrants' instrumental activism, or their public and collective mobilization for material change. Considering the link between the everyday and the collective, between private and public contention, a different dilemma comes into view than the one signaled by the simultaneity of immigrants' economic necessity and social undesirability. Though this theme has come to dominate the sociology of immigration, especially studies of migrant illegality,[20] I am interested in a rather different question. How do immigrants' primary strategies for avoiding dispossession, detention, and deportation by isolating themselves from risk both inspire and constrain their social movement organizing? Not simply the fact of their economic precarity, the material moorings of immigrant activism refer to the way that their activism is inspired and constrained by an imposed vulnerability that is sustained by increasingly greater numbers of state actors enforcing immigration law over larger swaths of geographic space. These historical forces create a context in which this gathering of Mexican immigrants at Vicky's home to discuss their grievances and their hopes for the future becomes possible, even probable. Turning inward, avoiding risk and isolating oneself and one's family from danger, is a necessary private strategy that simultaneously inspires and constrains the broadest expression of their resistance: social movement organizing. Everyday and individual acts of resistance exist on a continuum with collective mobilization. How are immigrants' strategies for managing their imposed vulnerability connected to what they do about it? Under what conditions do immigrants oscillate from reticence in private to resistance in public?

This tension between the everyday and the historic produces a certain periodicity of participation in social movements. The escalation and de-escalation of immigrant social movements, both in 2006 and in this study of local immigrant activism in California, reflect a choice between coping with dispossession, detention, and deportation in private versus in public. When Mexican immigrants are not taking to the streets or organizing legislative visits with their local congressional representatives, they have not forgone resistance. Rather the form of that resistance has slid to the other end of this continuum: toward private strategies of coping with risk by avoiding it in the first place. While the social movement literature offers useful tools for understanding when potential activists are moved to participate in social movements, such an account is incomplete without attending to the conditions of their everyday lives that both create the potential for public contention and form a counterweight against it. In this way, the material moorings of immigrant daily life enable and constrain their activism. When collective mobilization emerges, as we know it does, the result is an immigrant politics anchored in the material conditions of their lives that seek not to transcend but to burrow into the institutions of work and family that attend legal status and substantive belonging.

Power and Precarity

This dilemma of recruiting immigrants to social movement work is as historical as it is biographical. Immigrant action is tethered to the economic, political, and social history of migration out of which it arises: a history that I detail in the next chapter. That the effects of these historical transformations echo into the present teaches us that the past is not past. It is a "seething presence," conditioning the present and shaping the horizons of their expectations for the future. This is a question of agency: purposive human action, individual and collective, undertaken from a particular social location.[21] Given its central place in this text, how might we make sense of it?

In *Ghostly Matters*, Gordon describes the abiding grip of the past on present arrangements and its influence on the horizons of our expectations.[22] Immigrant agency, arising as it does from a history of dispossession and the threat of future displacement, is not the opposite of subjection exactly. Instead it is both enabled and constrained by it. To understand the double bind of precarity and power, we must first define power and clarify its relationship to agency. Power is typically defined negatively as domination or oppression. Power can certainly take this form, but Foucault famously countered this popular notion, arguing instead that power refers to networked relations of force that are as productive and disciplinary as they are repressive.[23] Power does not weigh down on us from above. Instead, it produces subjects from below. Power is not an object to be acquired or wielded, but a name for the complex ways that these relations of force unfold all around us, producing in us desires, orientations, and commitments that we come to understand as uniquely our own. In this formulation, power and agency are not counterposed to one another. Because there is no "out" to power, no a priori standpoint that is not inflected by these relations of force, we can think of agency not as opposed to power, but instead as arising from it. Agency arises from the histories, structures, and situated desires of subjects for whom we must reserve in our analyses a "complex personhood":

> Complex personhood means that people suffer graciously and selfishly too, get stuck in the symptoms of their troubles, and also transform themselves. Complex personhood means that even those called "Other" are

never never that. Complex personhood means that the stories people tell about themselves, about their troubles, about their social worlds, and about their society's problems are entangled and weave between what is immediately available as a story and what their imaginations are reaching toward. Complex personhood means that people get tired and some are just plain lazy. Complex personhood means that groups of people will act together, that they will vehemently disagree with and sometimes harm each other, and that they will do both at the same time and expect the rest of us to figure it out for ourselves, intervening and withdrawing as the situation requires.[24]

Because immigrant power arises from conditions of precarity, a diversity of responses is assured. Whether individual or collective, aimed at transforming institutions or simply inhabiting them, immigrant action is both inspired and constrained by the asymmetric relations of power that mark the Mexican immigrant experience in the United States. The politics that emerge from this double bind of precarity and power are at once liberatory and pragmatic. To hold to such an expansive (and also limited) notion of immigrant power is to eschew both romanticizing and underestimating immigrant agency, haunted as it is by a long history of exploitation, dispossession, and displacement. By embracing situated agency and complex personhood, this book offers a novel consideration of the way immigrants' lives form both the aspirational basis for their politics and their material mooring.

From Social Control to Situated Resistance

The notion that immigrants are economically essential but socially expendable constitutes one of the defining features of the Mexican immigrant experience. This contradiction is sustained by legal violence that hampers the life chances of immigrants[25]—documented, undocumented, and quasi-documented alike—in the deportation nation.[26] Deportability, or the threat of deportation, sustains the exploitation of undocumented immigrants:[27] a dynamic amplified by the growing overlap between criminal and immigration law (crimmigration)[28] and the increasing involvement of state and local government in immigration enforcement (devolution). This focus on social control, what is done to immigrants, is evident in studies of the many facets of the immigrant subordination, whether related to deportation,[29] detention,[30] sentencing,[31] border control,[32] global capitalism,[33] devolution,[34] everyday life,[35] work,[36] terrorism,[37] education,[38] or the family.[39] And yet, how immigrants who are caught in this contradictory situation manage and respond to their imposed vulnerability, individually and collectively, has received far less attention in the immigration literature.

Though the structure of immigrant subordination provides indispensable context for this study, it is not its focus. Josiah Heyman has called on immigration scholars "to shift our thinking about migration illegality from what is done to people, a certain status imposed upon them, to how they experience and act on it."[40] And, indeed, immigration scholars have increasingly examined what immigrants do in response to their marginalization.

Organized in a typology, immigrants' responses to precarity can be described as (1) "slantwise" activity, (2) "everyday" resistance, (3) advocacy and civic participation, and (4) social movement organizing. Slantwise, as Campbell and Heyman define it, refers to behaviors and actions that may either obstruct or reinforce existing relations of power and that are engaged in out of necessity, survival, or convenience, but do not *intend* resistance.[41] Everyday resistance, or "weapons of the weak,"[42] by contrast, includes strategies such as ignoring a deportation order or burning off one's fingertips in order to avoid deportation.[43] Advocacy refers to working within and against legal systems to contest a deportation order or otherwise advance the social standing and political power of immigrants from within institutional channels, like elections or participation in civic organizations.[44] Collective mobilization includes participation in social movement organizing that seeks to alter legal and political structures from their outside and in a significant and lasting way.[45]

The focus of a particular scholar's work from slantwise to social movement organizing produces varied empirical portraits of the scope and efficacy of immigrant agency and action. In Angela García's "Hidden in Plain Sight," for instance, she argues that undocumented immigrants, who have settled in restrictive locales that have embraced local immigration enforcement, strategically pass as US-born Latinos by performing assimilation—remaining calm in the presence of a police officer, speaking

English, keeping their cars clean and without dents—in order to avoid the scrutiny of police.[46] Contrast García's focus on passing and assimilation to Kim Voss and Irene Bloemraad's examination of immigrant social movements in their edited volume *Rallying for Immigrant Rights*.[47] In their introductory chapter, Bloemraad, Voss, and Lee draw on the social movement literature to explain the escalation and de-escalation of immigrant rights movements.[48] To explain those historic marches, they highlight the importance of mobilizing structures like civic and community organizations, threats to immigrants' rights and resources, and compelling narrative frames related to work and family. These important studies produce rather different expressions of immigrant agency ranging from reticence to resistance. And while some scholars have examined the relationships between different forms of immigrant agency, such as the way civic participation in schools, churches, and hometown associations undergirds collective mobilization,[49] this book distinguishes itself by centering the relationship between the most dissimilar forms of immigrant agency: everyday avoidance or insulation and social movement organizing.

Respondents' narratives illustrate the difference in the scope of and motivation for immigrant action individually in private versus collectively in public. Consider the experience of Xiomara, housekeeper and undocumented single mother of three. Xiomara is the kind of person toward whom many people gravitate. Short in stature with her tight curls tied back in a short ponytail, she radiates positivity and warmth. She exudes an indefatigable energy made all the more impressive in spite of, or perhaps because of, all that she has endured. And endured she has, largely for her three sons, one of whom, like her, is undocumented. When I sat with Xiomara in the light-filled kitchen of her small first-floor apartment, she shared openly, pausing thoughtfully before she answered a question.

Xiomara fled to the United States because of the domestic violence she faced from her husband in Zacatecas. She encountered a similar situation when she arrived in the United States in 2001. Afraid to call the police because of her status, she called them for help only after her abuser began threatening her young son. Until that point, she had made a habit of avoiding police and other authority figures to ward off the threats of car impoundment and deportation.

When I asked her about her previous interactions with police officers, she said, "I know and understand that I don't have a license and I'm breaking the law, but it is purely out of necessity. Purely out of necessity." She understands her relationship to the law, but knowingly violates it out of necessity. Garcia documents a similar sentiment in an exchange between an undocumented immigrant and an immigration judge in the mid-1950s in the midst of the deportation program pejoratively dubbed "Operation Wetback": "'The judge asked the man: Don't you respect the laws of this country?' To which he replied, 'Our necessities know no law.'"[50] These examples reveal knowing violation of the law, but done as a matter of necessity, not intentional defiance. Similar strategies emerged in my conversations with other respondents: avoiding driving when it was not absolutely necessary for fear of having their cars impounded, locking their children in the bathroom when ICE came knocking, and generally avoiding contact with those outside their networks of immediate family and close friends.

The question of whether these actions "count" as resistance hinges, in large part, on intent,[51] or knowing defiance even when the action is motivated, primarily or in part, by necessity or survival.[52] In Scott's seminal *Weapons of the Weak*, peasants in Sedaka, Malaysia, during the green revolution engaged in "everyday" resistance, such as poaching from private land.[53] In Campbell and Heyman's study, by contrast, the immigrants living in an impromptu *colonia* along the US-Mexico border developed unconventional housing arrangements and generally distrusted census takers, making their enumeration difficult and confounding the state's attempt to identify these migrants.[54] While the peasants in Sedaka knew they were defying the law in order to survive, the migrants in this colonia did not clearly understand the law or its role in their lives. For Scott, peasants in Sedaka intended to resist. For Campbell and Heyman, immigrants living in this colonia did not *intend* to resist and, moreover, did not often *know* that they were impeding the efforts of the state or violating the law.

The Mexican immigrants with whom I worked, by contrast, *knew* that they were breaking the law, but did not *intend* to. They used avoidance—hiding when ICE was nearby, limiting their driving all the while knowing that they needed a license but did not qualify for one—to insulate themselves from the risks that they knew they ran as undocumented immigrants, but did not do so intentionally in order to defy the state. Instead, they did so as a matter of necessity. These strategies compose the shell: to turn inward in an effort to limit exposure to risk. As I argue in Chapter 3, these strategies mitigate risk at the same time as they form a barrier against broader civic and political engagement.

The risk management that Xiomara must undertake is markedly different from the work of a community organizer. Esmeralda—primary informant and longtime volunteer organizer with La Unión—is also small in stature, but brimming over with charisma. She speaks with a pronounced Mexican accent that lends her fluent English a certain rhythm and also a certain self-possession. A longtime South City resident and naturalized citizen, she recounts the story of her late father who immigrated to the United States from Mexico City under the Bracero Program during World War II. Sitting across from her desk at a local elementary school where she works as a community liaison, she recalls a story that her father used to tell around the dinner table. Just shy of 20 years old, he worked laying railroad ties. As injured soldiers returned from war, the Red Cross held blood drives nearby. The *capataces* or foremen demanded that the braceros participate. Esmeralda recounts her father's challenge to the bosses: "'That's funny because, see, I cannot drink from the same water fountains, I cannot sit in the same places that they do on the bus, I cannot get into a bar.'" He ultimately convinced many of his fellow braceros not to give blood. As a child, Esmeralda thought these were just stories, all bombast. Later, taking Chicano studies courses in college, she realized:

> Oh my God [she'd often exclaim "OMD," short for "Oh my Dios"], my father, it was bigger than that, bigger than that, so that's why I totally believe in what I do. Because since my father passed away a few years ago, but he would be very upset if I'm here doing this and not doing it properly, you know, so it's like, "I have to do it, I have no choice."

A family legacy of activism incubated by the protections of citizenship and her role as a community leader suggest the way the confluence of biography, law, and place animates Esmeralda's commitment to community organizing.[55] This orientation is markedly different from Xiomara's relationship to politics and contention. Their overlapping social locations as Mexican immigrant women are differentiated by the varying class, legal, and occupational spaces that they inhabit. Their motivation for activism is inflected by these differences.

Xiomara, with Esmeralda's encouragement, participates actively in La Unión campaigns, but her motivation remains inspired and constrained by the material urgency of making life as a single undocumented mother of three children. By contrast, Esmeralda's motivation for activism is driven by a necessity of a rather different kind. The example of her father, her secure legal status, and her position as a community leader to whom many immigrants turn to for support inform an expansive sense responsibility for others. She is also not beleaguered by the deportation regime that proliferates an immobilizing fear and uncertainty among her undocumented counterparts, nor is she beset by the material insecurities that are sustained by that regime.

These two examples of immigrant agency provide useful bookends for the spectrum of immigrant agency I observed over the course of my fieldwork: avoidance and insulation, on the one hand, and social movement organizing, on the other. The former is individual in scope and immediate in term, engaged in out of necessity and not necessarily intending resistance, while the latter is collective, future-oriented, and intent on the transformation of those exploitative structures that have hemmed in immigrants. The material moorings of immigrant activism refer to the way the former type of agency both motivates and constrains the latter. It is here that scholars of social movements and resistance more broadly provide a springboard for theorizing this relationship between everyday risk management and historic collective action.

Continuums of Contention

Social movement scholars have long recognized that grievances alone do not spur collective action. Immigrants' grievances are many and widespread, while collective action is a far rarer thing. So, under what conditions is grievance addressed collectively? When do immigrant expressions of agency slide along this continuum of contention from the private risk management characteristic of the shell to the public and collective resistance that defines a social movement?[56]

Over several generations of study, social movement scholars have offered various theories that explain the emergence of social movements, moving through breakdown and strain theories to resource mobilization and political process theory. The last of these is the dominant approach today. Pioneered by Charles Tilly and Doug McAdam, political process theory explains social movements with three factors: mobilizing structures, political opportunities, and framing processes.[57] Social movement organizations cultivate both the economic and human capital needed to sustain social movements. Mobilization emerges when cues in the broader political environment signal that an opportunity to press a claim may be successful or when threats to vulnerable communities' rights and resources motivate people to come together to protect them (as with the marches of 2006, which were largely a response to the Sensenbrenner Bill [H.R. 4437] that would have funded 700 miles of double-layered fencing along the US-Mexico border, among other things). Participants are drawn to social movements when organizers use narrative frames that resonate with activists.[58]

Political process theory emphasizes structures and institutions. Scholars focused on "micromobilization,"[59] by contrast, offer a corrective to this structural emphasis by focusing on the way movements develop cultures and build collective identity through ongoing interactions between organizers and potential activists. Threats must be interpreted as such and attributed to responsible parties, opportunities for action must be perceived, and motivation for participation must be cultivated, sustained, and channeled. In conversations between organizers and local residents, they stressed both the broadly shared quality of their grievances and their collective responsibility for redressing those grievances. The cultivation of this social movement culture leverages already existing immigrant networks to enhance participation by reinforcing and politicizing already existing ties among neighbors, family members, and friends.

While networks and frames have long been a part of social movement theory, the social movement organization itself is very often the locus of these inquires. And rightfully so given that organizations are so often the site where consciousness is raised, collectivity is fostered, and strategy is devised. And yet, so much of what undocumented Mexican immigrants specifically and vulnerable populations generally do to manage what threatens them happens outside the purview of social movement organizations and so the social movement literature. The avoidance and isolation that make up the bulk of immigrants' responses to the deportation regime and its abettors inform and constrain their social movement work. Though attention to the everyday is not new to the social movement scholars,[60] it is not only the disruption of the quotidian that inspires social movement participation. Immigrants' primary strategy for managing risk in everyday life—the shell—encumbers, inspires, and shapes the tactics and demands of their social movements. The interview data, in particular, allow for this attention to everyday forms of agency outside my observations at La Unión.

The everyday, in other words, is prior to the organization. And it is in the everyday practices of the shell that we find the bulk of immigrant agency, which seeks not to transform their surroundings, but to manage and cope with its risks. My point is not simply to highlight the diversity of immigrants' responses to their imposed precarity. The *relationship* between these two distinct forms of immigrant agency must be theorized if we are to understand the concrete barriers immigrants face to political engagement, as well as the scope of their activism when those barriers are overcome.

The Everyday and the Historic

In my view, then, this link between the everyday and the historic, between the shell and collective mobilization, is a crucial piece of the immigrant social movement puzzle. Working both within and across disciplines, several scholars have looked closely at the relationship between quotidian survival and mass movements. In Vicki Ruiz's study of women cannery workers in 1930s southern California, for example, she argues that Mexican women's labor organizing was successful, in part, because it was sustained by a cannery *culture*. "The extension of family and friend networks inside southern California food processing plants," she explains, "nurtured the development of a closely-knit work environment" that supported later labor organizing efforts.[61] A similar network of kin and neighbors was evident in the house party that opens this book.

Asef Bayat offers perhaps the most elaborated theory of this connection with the "quiet encroachment of the ordinary,"[62] which he defines as a "silent, patient, protracted, and pervasive advancement of ordinary people on the propertied and powerful in order to survive hardships and better their lives."[63] Bayat goes on to argue that largely leaderless and unstructured episodic collective action emerges when their gains are threatened.[64] Bayat's explicit consideration of the relationship between individual and collective modes of survival and politics is an especially useful touchstone because, as with Mexican immigrants in this study, it moors the politics that emerge from this encroachment to the daily struggle to better oneself and one's family. In both cases, we see the agency of subordinated groups in their gradual transformation of the demographic and political composition of the nation, claiming rights and resources commensurate with their contributions to community and economy.

Unlike the collective action Bayat describes, however, immigrant social movement organizing is not leaderless and unstructured. In line with emerging scholarship on immigrant collective action,[65] their mobilization is not simply spontaneous or reactive, but cultivated in fairly traditional social movement organizational settings and emerges under conditions of both threat and growing political opportunity (see Chapter 5).[66] Importantly, Bayat's argument is set against the backdrop of an assault on civil society by authoritarian regimes in the Middle East and abetted by Western states, which requires the development of a new vocabulary for agency and politics. Civil society in the United States may well be under siege by the forces of neoliberalism, and still Central California is not Baghdad. Formal social movement organizing is still possible, so the challenge in the context of US immigration is to rethink not "life as politics," but rather the way that life tethers politics to its exigencies. Immigrant participants engaged in the collective work of making history are both enabled and constrained by the necessary work of making life, of erecting some bulwark of stability in the face precarity.

The material moorings of immigrant activism that I propose are much closer to Richard Flacks's analysis that he lays out in *Making History: The American Left and the American Mind*.[67] There he argued "the individual is best understood as acting politically out of a commitment to his or her everyday life."[68] Daily life is marked by a dialectic relationship between our egocentrism and our capacity for "cooperation, coordination, and harmony."[69] He refines this proposition by noting that those members of the power elite, whose everyday lives are engaged in the work of making history, like engineering social policy, guiding economic development, and so on, will feel as though these two realms overlap substantially. For those on the margins of social life, like (undocumented) Mexican immigrants, these realms will feel rather more distant from one another. For this latter group, then, to intervene in the historic requires a disruption or a break from the routines of the everyday. In the context of a broadly shared American culture that stresses individual liberty (in exchange for often alienating, boring, and unfulfilling labor) over collective democratic practice, troubles are often resolved or managed in private. And unless we experience strong positive attachment to an ethnic group or party, we cope with grievances through the expansion and enjoyment of time and resources in the private realm.[70]

So, when do movements emerge? Flacks, echoing political process theory, argues that major and minor disruptions to everyday life can lead to collective action when those communities have the space to physically gather, to communicate and attribute their grievances in a shared language, and to lay out credible lines of action that might reasonably result in the reduction or elimination of that threat. Resistance, therefore, begins with the "*conservative* impulse to preserve the ways of life that are felt to be endangered."[71] Which is to say that movement actors will engage in the work of making history out of a commitment to their daily lives. De-escalation will follow mobilization when those threats are reduced or when the organizations that sustain these movements are weakened by either internal mismanagement or reductions in funding as a consequence, for instance, of the Great Recession of 2008 (see Chapter 5).

The idea of the material moorings of immigrant activism builds on these insights by examining the way this dialectic relationship between the everyday and the historic informs both the hopes immigrants have for themselves in the future and their motivations for participation in social movement work, as well as in the tactics that participants and organizers adopt to pursue those goals. Moreover, the break from routine that participation in social movement work necessitates is not simply a break from the routines of daily life, but a break from a habituated response to deportation and dispossession (in the case of undocumented immigrants) and the expenditure of what scarce free time Mexican immigrants have for activities beyond the reproduction of the family. The tension between the everyday and the historic is exacerbated by a formal and informal immigration enforcement regime that sustains immigrants' exploitation and necessitates these protective strategies of avoidance and isolation. In other words, this tension between the everyday and the historic is both more acute for Mexican immigrants than for other activists and carried through to their motivation for activism. This relationship between the everyday (the shell) and the historic (social movement organizing) produces an instrumental politics that engages in protest to the extent that the small treasures that immigrants have secured through the travails of everyday life may be shored up by participating in historic collective action. The central contribution of this book, therefore, is a conceptualization of the way immigrant politics are both animated and limited by their social location as a racialized and economically subordinated group: what I refer to as the material moorings of immigrant action.

The Study

Before conceiving of the research study that forms the basis of this book, I was a volunteer for La Unión. My experience there raised a series of questions about immigrant incorporation and politics. As I sat in local immigrant families' living rooms, attended know-your-rights workshops, marched and rallied with coalitions of community leaders, the broad questions that were raised in my work with La Unión narrowed and came into conversation with the academic literature on immigration and social movements. First, what are the barriers to participation in social movement organizing and civic engagement for Mexican immigrants in these two cities? How are these barriers connected to wider structures of apprehension, deportation, and dispossession, which Mexican immigrants, especially the undocumented, must manage on a daily basis? Second, what are the micro-interactional processes among community members and community organizers that bring people into the social movement work of La Unión? And when they decide to become involved in this work, how can we conceptualize their activism? Finally, if we take a comparative meso-level view of these two communities, under what political conditions does immigrant mobilization emerge?

What is the relationship between broader political conditions and the social form of immigrant mobilization? In general, I examine the barriers to social movement participation and ask how they are overcome, at both the micro level of interaction and the meso level of social movement organizing.

The data for this study were collected using a multi-sited ethnography that included three years of participant observation from November 2009 through August 2012, but most intensively in the eight-month period between January and August 2012, and in depth, semistructured interviews with 61 respondents. Broadly, the goal for this fieldwork was to understand the challenges immigrants faced to incorporation in their local communities; how they encountered and negotiated the risks of apprehension, deportation, and property loss in their daily lives; and whether and when they were moved to act collectively. To collect these data, I volunteered with and eventually became a board member of La Unión: a small immigrant advocacy organization on California's Central Coast.

In the early 2000s, La Unión emerged out of a local living wage campaign and later evolved into a formal, multi-issue, social movement organization focused on workers' rights, public housing, and immigrant rights. La Unión operated as an advocacy organization and did not offer direct services, except to refer their immigrant constituents to places that did. A central part of La Unión's organizing strategy involves cultivating organic leadership by providing its constituents with the tools, training, and resources to advocate for themselves. Using a committee structure, organizers identified and worked closely with core community leaders who were then responsible for gathering neighbors, friends, and family members together for a variety of activities related to the particular issue they were working on. These activities included house meetings, know-your-rights workshops, precinct walks, legislative visits, and so on. Campaigns were developed with the input of the community and addressed local issues related to improved access to public transit, for instance, and dovetailed with national efforts for immigration reform. During moments of national mobilization, for example, we hosted local press conferences in support of immigration reform but also traveled to nearby large cities to join in solidarity with larger, regional organizations. During the bulk of my observations, however, no opportunity existed for national reform. Consequently, organizing efforts focused on local and sometimes state-level targets.

The fieldwork began as I helped to organize house meeting campaigns in South City and then in North City. It immediately became clear that the support of primary informants would be essential in this study. Organizers in both North City and South City urged meeting participants to "tell their stories" and vouched for my trustworthiness. Having unsuccessfully tried to approach immigrant residents on my own in other community settings, I was acutely aware of the importance of the word of a trusted community leader in securing their participation in this project. Over time and with the essential help of primary informants, I slowly developed trust with members of the Mexican immigrant community, which enabled me to build a snowball sample and to expand the number of participants, most of whom were not previously involved with the social justice work of La Unión.

Comparative Ethnography

One of the distinguishing features of the contemporary immigration enforcement apparatus is that state and local governments have gotten in on the act. As I describe in greater detail in the next chapter, programs like the Criminal Alien Program,[72] composed of Secure Communities (rebranded as the Prioritized Enforcement Program) and 287(g), among others, have shouldered local police with the responsibilities typically reserved for ICE.

But these programs have been rolled out unevenly and met by resistance from many immigrant rights social movement organizations (SMOs) and some local police. The resultant geography of local immigration enforcement is "multilayered" and "patchwork."[73] Given the uneven quality of the contemporary deportation regime, I chose two cities that capture the empirical variation in local political climates that exists from city to city across the United States: from the conservative and restrictive attitudes and policies typical in places like Hazelton, Pennsylvania, and Maricopa County, Arizona, to the relatively more progressive typical of places like San Francisco and Bell, California. The two cities I consider are located at the southern and northern ends of one county in Central California; South City represents the more progressive case, North City the repressive case. Though immigrant respondents in both North City and South City shared grievances in common—fear of detention, deportation, and car impoundments—the distinctly conservative climate in North City incubated anti-immigrant sentiment and made life more challenging for immigrant residents there. As I recount at the beginning of Chapter 5, for instance, the mayor of North City barred the Mexican consulate from hosting "mobile consulate" events, in which the consul would offer various services to those Mexican expatriates living several hours north of the consul's Los Angeles office. At about the same time, in South City the mayor had made a public statement of support for the TRUST Act, which was ultimately signed into state law and mandated local police noncooperation with the Secure Communities deportation program (except in cases where an individual was charged with a "serious" offense).

These cities are also characterized by different immigrant demographics: South City, home to long-term immigrants with families and working in service work, home care, and local restaurants, and North City, home to a larger population of seasonal agricultural laborers. Organizers and community members themselves often compared the cities. La Unión maintained offices in both places, and some North City residents attended the university in South City. Because these cities were both situated in one county jurisdiction and shared some elected officials, their comparison emerged from residents' and organizers' own conceptualization of their sphere of influence. I adopt this comparison here not only because it reflects the empirical variation in local political climates and threat for immigrants, but also because the contrast was often drawn in the minds of Mexican immigrants living in either place.

In my observations, these differences in climate mattered most not in the daily work of avoidance and insulation in which immigrants in both cities engaged, but in the social movement tactics adopted when collective mobilization emerged. Though the chapters in this book are meant to be read in order, for readers interested in the comparative quality of the data and social movement theory, Chapter 5 will be of particular interest.

The Role of the Researcher

Participants were initially cordial to me, a biracial Mexican American and white graduate student collecting data in Mexican immigrant communities, but were far from trusting. Despite several years working with La Unión, I was unfamiliar with many members of the community, especially the majority of participants who had not worked with La Unión prior to these house meetings. It was not until well-known and respected organizers in North City and South City vouched for me that immigrant residents began speaking to me, agreed to be interviewed, and shared their stories. I believe that over time respondents began to regard me less as a categorical outsider and more as a tenuously trustworthy ally whom they could support and even regard as a role model.

My proficient, but still formal, Spanish became less of a boundary marker of my outsider status and was increasingly regarded as an admirable (but perhaps still tragicomic) effort to reclaim language and culture after generations of assimilationist pressure. After interviews, respondents often commented that they were glad to see me working toward an advanced degree, something several respondents mentioned they wanted for their own children. While I was never regarded as an insider, my relationships with respected community leaders and my ongoing work with La Unión transformed the way respondents viewed my educational background, racial identity, and language skills. At a minimum, respondents came to regard me as a well-meaning, albeit awkward, ally and, at best, as a model of the kind of occupational and educational mobility they wanted for their own children.

For the sake of brevity, readers interested in an expanded discussion of the methodology—including details related to access to the community, the study timeline, respondent demographics, additional sampling considerations, and the interview process—can turn to the appendix.

Limitations

The dynamic interplay of the everyday and the historic that I attempt to capture with the material moorings of Mexican immigrant action begs a question about whether this same dynamic is present in the social movement work of other immigrant groups, especially the DREAMers. Comprising the 1.5 generation, or the generation of immigrants who came to the United States as children, the DREAMers initially adopted anonymous and more subdued forms of activism only to later become more radical in their tactics and their demands: engaging in civil disobedience, calling for executive action in the face of stymied reform, and expanding their claims to legalization for their parents. Leisy Abrego explains that this difference between the limited activism of first-generation immigrants compared to the contentious activity of the 1.5 generation stems from their differing legal consciousness.[74] The first-generation experience is distinguished by an abiding fear of deportation instilled at the time of their crossing. Their illegal status remains salient at work: the primary institution in which they are socialized. This fear leads to the sense that collective mobilization is too risky or ineffective. Members of the 1.5 generation, by contrast, do not viscerally recall the experience of their clandestine crossing as children and are therefore less culpable for their status than their parents. They are often unaware of their legal status while they are in school: an institution that lends them a sense of safety and stimulates their political consciousness. This alternate socialization leads to a willingness and availability for protest that is not shared by their parents.

This study is of the former, first-generation group. Consequently, the material moorings of immigrant activism are likely to apply to the first generation and not to 1.5-generation immigrant youth, a small minority in my sample. Most respondents were between 40 and 60 years old and were first-generation immigrants of varying statuses who were married, working, and raising children. Their social location was one of biographical unavailability for protest, to reverse Doug McAdam's proposition,[75] and not only because they were fearful of deportation, though this was a powerful disincentive. First-generation undocumented Mexican immigrants managed that fear through the avoidance and isolation characteristic of the shell and thereby shored up the fragile economic gains they have made since their migration. In this way, fear is not a monolithic force that stands outside of them, but is threaded through their own sense of agency. Their default mode is to avoid and isolate themselves and their loved ones for whom they are responsible in order to protect them from deportation and dispossession and to ward off the material precarity that attends life as a working-class immigrant in California.

Material Moorings and the Horizons of Latino Politics

"We want your labor, but we don't want you": observers critical of the current immigration enforcement regime have long highlighted the untenability of a political and economic system dependent on immigrant labor, yet unwilling to provide reasonable pathways to full membership. Immanent to this dilemma of economic necessity, on the one hand, and social marginalization, on the other, is also the possibility of renewed democratic practice, an invitation to politics as a consequence of migration. Much of the immigration literature does not account for immigrants' individual or collective expressions of agency as they negotiate this dilemma, nor the link between them. Among social movement scholars, an overreliance on organizations as the point of entry for understanding movement emergence risks ignoring the everyday. And not only its disruption, but the way the quotidian inspires and constrains movement participation, producing a certain periodicity of participation and an orientation to collective mobilization for the sake of securing the gains made in the realm of the everyday.

Decades of sustained Latin American migration, predominated by Mexican immigrants, from the margins of the global economy back to one of its imperial centers has transformed community and country. Immigrants alter the landscape and rhythm of the communities where they settle. Performing cultural citizenship,[76] they speak their native languages, worship, engage in leisure, create art, open businesses, and labor in formal and informal economies, all the while contributing to and utilizing local, state, and national resources.[77] These demographic and cultural transformations are accompanied by political change. As the "browning of America" proceeds apace, Latinos, many of whom are or are related to immigrants, exercise their growing political power at the ballot box and in the streets. This growing constituency, which breaks to the left, introduces a potentially transformative element to the American political scene. Evidenced in the most recent election returns, the May Day marches of 2006, the activism of the DREAMers and their parents, and state- and local-level struggles unfolding around the nation, the emergence of a broad and vigorous Latino politics may represent a watershed in American politics more generally.

From immigration reform to bilingual education, these battles have consolidated a Latino constituency whose aspirations are tethered to their quotidian struggle to *adelantarse*. This is a rather different dilemma than the one signaled by the scholarly refrain that "we want your labor, but we don't want you." Their condition is not only one of deportability and marginalization, but also one of latent political power. The historical and political dynamic by which decades of immigration have ushered in a new and potentially transformative political constituency raises questions about opportunities for and barriers to immigrant social movement organizing. When immigrant activism does emerge, as we know it does, what motivates immigrants' participation and what claims do they articulate? What can immigrant social movements teach us about power and resistance?

Over the course of my fieldwork, I have been struck by the pragmatic scope of immigrant demands: for driver's licenses, a social security number, access to credit, better educational opportunities, and basic economic mobility. The material moorings of the immigrant rights movement reflect this oscillation from the everyday to the historic not for the sake of making history itself, but in an effort to secure through collective action those material gains that inspired their migration in the first place. The scope of immigrant political claims—the horizons of their expectations—is shaped by the urgency of their material demands: demands made urgent as a consequence of the racialization of their communities and the subordination of their labor.

Here, I counter the claims of some scholars who have observed in immigrant politics a radical challenge to nationalism, the liberal state, territorial borders, emphasizing freedom of movement over immigrants' incorporation into US cultural and economic life.[78] To make this counterclaim, however, is not to argue that such radical politics are necessarily at odds with the pragmatic claims making I observed in this study. It is rather to assert the empirical variation that exists among immigrants as they engage the complex calculus of naming injury, blaming actors or institutions, and claiming rights.[79] What explains these differing portrayals of immigrant agency and activism? Different SMOs embrace different organizing philosophies and strategies, shaping the tenor and content of the immigrants' claims.[80] Scholars must also reckon with the irreducible variation that will always be present in a community as large as the one denoted by the useful fiction of the terms "Latino" and "Latino immigrant." Powerful and revolutionary constituencies, moreover, can be built out of campaigns making more modest and reformist claims. And yet, the de-escalation and fragmentation of the immigrant rights struggle after 2006, as well as my own observations of the reluctance that organizers regularly faced trying to recruit immigrant community members to social movement activism, suggest that while a more radical politics might be possible, it does not often emerge. Why not?

The notion of material moorings is meant to explain why immigrant activism emerges despite obstacles, and, when it does, why immigrants adopt certain claims and not others. To do this, I situate immigrant activism both in a broader historical context marked by massive demographic change and unprecedented enforcement, as well as in relationship to those other forms of everyday agency, like avoidance and insulation, that reflect the material exigencies of daily life as a Mexican immigrant in California and that moor their activism to those exigencies. My claim is not that a radical immigrant politics is not possible, but that those portrayals circulating in academic texts diverge from my observations in Central California. Immigrant respondents were less interested in transcending or undermining the nation-state than in burrowing more deeply into it so that they might avail themselves of the material resources and dignity that attend full membership.[81]

My observations illuminate what I see as a central dilemma in immigrant politics. Immigrant activism is linked to immigrants' lived experience of legal and material precarity, and specifically to their everyday strategies for mitigating that precarity. When immigrant activism emerges, it remains tethered to its material inspiration, which, in turn, shapes immigrants' goals. To inhabit the norms of citizenship, to avail themselves of those resources denied noncitizens, is to engage in a transformative immigrant politics whose focus remains instrumental in its effort to make history so that they might make life unburdened by the national hypocrisy of recruiting labor without expanding membership.[82] The historian Walter Johnson argues that "collective resistance is, at bottom, a process of everyday organization, one that, in fact, depends upon connections and trust established in everyday actions."[83] When organizers and community leaders build upon connections established among family and neighbors and when politics are introduced as a potential remedy, then their grievances may be framed not as shame or solitary hardship, but as evidence of their "linked fate"[84] and the "political efficacy"[85] that can animate collective action.

What political action that emerges is not simply a counterpoint to the forces of social control and immiseration: state-guided global capitalism; immigration enforcement at all levels of government; myriad mechanisms of class subordination from wage theft to illegality as a bar to occupational mobility; and a Latino threat narrative buoyed by a long-standing American culture of racism and xenophobia.[86] These elements of global political economy and American law and culture themselves shape the social location out of which immigrant politics emerge. As with the "American letters" of a previous generation's immigrants, today's Mexican immigrants circulate the promise that abundant work opportunities can transform their quality of life: that hard work trumps the many impairments of inequality, that the wealth generated will be shared, that risks pay off. These material and cultural contexts powerfully shape the scope and character of immigrant agency in its many forms.

With the idea of material moorings, I wish to offer a complex and empirically grounded framework for understanding the way that resistance is not power's counterpoint. Instead, relations of power shape resistance in profound ways. Consequently, the strategies for survival and contestation that emerge are better conceptualized as tethered to the everyday and historical forces that have brought large numbers of immigrants to the United States and created the conditions of inequality from which a pragmatic and potentially liberatory immigrant politics emerges. Born of the exigencies of material deprivation and the urgent work of stewarding family, the Mexican immigrants in this study largely sought to capture those benefits that attend citizenship, including a fair wage, access to credit, property, and education (especially their children's), and to exit this life knowing they have provided those around them with a certain material comfort. These desires are born of the experience of precarity and inform immigrant agency in its various manifestations, big and small.

Chapter Outline

In Chapter 1, I provide a brief historical overview of immigration and immigration policy. I argue that early American history was marked by the categorical exclusion of certain racialized immigrant groups, while the 20th century witnessed the emergence of a new hegemony under which immigrants and their descendants were "included through exclusion." This transformation is coextensive with the shifting meaning of race and new geopolitical and domestic policy interests. While US industry has long relied upon and recruited immigrant labor, these economic trends chafe up against nativist forces of exclusion at all levels of social life from local and popular opposition to national and legal restriction. Immigrants' economic necessity coupled with their political and social exclusion sustains their exploitability in a segmented labor market.

If Chapter 1 offers a broad historical overview of immigrant marginalization, Chapter 2 hones in on one contemporary and informal practice of immigrant subordination: the car impoundment. Impoundment is an informal technology of immigration enforcement that impoverishes undocumented, unlicensed drivers and constitutes an instance of what Devon Carbado terms "racial naturalization."[87] This local police practice, while nominally about traffic safety, constitutes a ritual of humiliation that impedes the economic and physical mobility of undocumented Mexican immigrants and naturalizes them not to US citizenship but to US racial hierarchy. This chapter also examines immigrants' assessments of police in general. These range from the strongly positive to the strongly negative, revealing important variation in immigrants' experience of police. Interestingly, even when immigrants' assessments of police were strongly negative, they still reported an ambivalence about whether police can be trusted. While negative regard of police by working-class people of color is certainly not a new phenomenon, I argue that this ambivalence indicates an ongoing normative investment in the police as an institution despite the widespread understanding that they are engaged in racial profiling.

In Chapter 3, I argue that Mexican immigrants (both documented and undocumented alike) employ savvy strategies of avoidance and insulation to mitigate the threat of deportation and the confiscation of their vehicles. Extending a metaphor passed down from Max Weber and Derek Sayer, I conceptualize these strategies and the general sense of fear and isolation articulated by many of my respondents as a "shell": something that both protects Mexican immigrants from these risks, and serves as a barrier to participation in social movement organizing and the wider civic life of the communities in which they live and work. In other words, the same strategies engaged in as a form of protection also function as a barrier to civic engagement.

In Chapter 4, I argue that Mexican immigrants "come out of the shell" when they are engaged consistently by trusted community leaders supported by sustainable SMOs. These community leaders use a range of rhetorical strategies at the micro-interactional level to draw immigrants into social movement organizing. Immigrants themselves contribute to this process, often articulating a sophisticated understanding of their personal troubles and the wider social issues to which their troubles are connected. I describe those immigrants who decide to become involved in community organizing as "instrumental activists" who are willing to participate in social movement organizing, not due to a broad sense of social justice or a commitment to radical politics, but in order to secure the quotidian makings of a dignified and decent life composed of good work opportunities for themselves and educational and social mobility for their children.

Local political opportunity structures play an important role in shaping immigrants' social movements, particularly the tactics they choose to press their claims. The comparative quality of the data comes into focus most clearly in Chapter 5. I compare one relatively progressive city to one relatively conservative city. Given the geographic expansion of immigration enforcement to state and local governments, I draw primarily on social movement theory to illustrate the way that the local political environment shapes the tactics that immigrants use to press their claims. I argue that growing threat does not repress mobilization, but leads to more confrontational social movement tactics. In the comparatively less threatening site, tactics took on a more collaborative tone.

In the conclusion, I explore three ways that immigrant politics, from the everyday to the collective, dovetail with and three ways they diverge from the expectations of neoliberal citizenship and its attendant emphases on individualism, self-reliance, flexibility, and self-discipline.

The notion of material moorings is presented here as a name for the dilemma in which many immigrants find themselves: inspired to action by urgent material grievances, but also constrained by that same quotidian urgency. I characterize these politics as neither wholly conformist nor radical, but as embodying both pragmatic and liberatory elements. This simultaneity suggests that immigrant politics contain within them a renewed democratic practice at the same time as they seek to inhabit the norms of hardworking, law-abiding, family-oriented citizens in waiting in order to erect a bulwark against the churn of precarity that inspired their migration in the first place.

1

Ghost in the Deportation Machine

A Brief History of Immigrant Inclusion through Exclusion

We Want Your Labor, but We Don't Want You

Héctor is soft-spoken and measured, choosing his words carefully. He keeps his hands, slightly weathered and the color of mahogany, folded on the table in front of him as we talk. His was the single interview I conducted in my apartment. He had insisted it was not inconvenient to come to me. Without my eyes moving over the intimate topography of someone else's interior life, I focused squarely on Héctor. He wore dark jeans and a button-down, thick dark hair combed to one side. Having interviewed other respondents immediately after a shift, I note that he has not come directly from work. He cleaned up and dressed for the interview. As we talked he exuded a sense of reliability and purpose born of an unwavering commitment to provide for his daughter whom he raises alone. His wife died when his daughter was two years old, motivating him to make the journey northward. He came to Central California from Oaxaca, Mexico, without authorization in the early 1990s. He describes what happened to his job prospects when, as a consequence of Proposition 187, California law changed to begin requiring that Californians demonstrate proof of legal residence in order to obtain a driver's license. Faced with this new requirement, Héctor, undocumented, was unable to renew his license: a legal shift that had profound consequences for his ability to earn a living.

> Well, in the first place I lost my job, and I was earning a lot of money because I was a driver with a company and I had several years in that company, I was established there and that was a job that . . . a requirement of my two jobs were to have a driver's license. So, I had several years there and I had a good salary and I was full-time in these two jobs and when I lost my driver's license I couldn't work. I was really affected because I

had to learn other occupations. I had to learn about construction, painting and carpentry, now I'm a handyman and I work a part-time job in a restaurant, too. I get some money as a handyman because I work as an independent contractor. I'm my own boss, but I had to spend a lot of years to learn my new occupation and that was an obstacle. That situation was difficult for me. I think that has affected everyone, and I only have one daughter, but there are people with three children and a wife and parents to support, too.

—Héctor, Mexican, undocumented, South City, 40–50, handyman and restaurant employee

Héctor's job loss evidences the way that immigrants are simultaneously included and excluded in the United States. This contradiction lies at the heart of the Mexican immigrant experience. US immigration policy has long suffered from a kind of political schizophrenia: while immigrant labor is critical to the functioning of the US economy and global capitalism, and has been actively recruited by the state and by industry, immigrants are nonetheless targeted as undeserving interlopers. They are portrayed in the media and in politics as undeservedly availing themselves of America's largesse, a portrayal that erases their contributions to American prosperity in the first place. They find work, but not broader social acceptance; they are permitted employment, but not membership. Consequently, Mexican immigrants find their economic mobility stunted and their avenues for meaningful social and political integration blocked.

In Héctor's case, a change in state law jeopardized his fragile and hard-won economic stability. He cherished this stability in no small part because it allowed him to support his only daughter to whom he is devoted. This law does not exclude him exactly. Instead, the socially necessary labor that he provides is subordinated by various exclusionary campaigns, like Proposition 187, that stunt his physical and socioeconomic mobility. Héctor's experience throws into relief the central theme of this brief history of immigration policy: what Nicholas de Genova has called "inclusion through exclusion."[1]

While certain racialized groups were utterly excluded in early American history—black slaves, Chinese, Japanese, etc.—Mexican immigrants are better understood as simultaneously included and excluded: a historical condition that sustains their vulnerability and shapes their politics in the present. Mexican immigrants are incorporated into the socioeconomic life of the nation, but at its lowest rungs. The US economy from the settler period forward has relied on the labor of immigrants, a relationship often explicitly facilitated by state-sponsored labor-importation schemes. But to the extent that immigrants are incorporated into the economic, social, and political life of the nation, their "incorporation is persistently beleaguered with exclusionary campaigns that ensure that this inclusion is itself a form of subjugation."[2] This exploitative relationship, this condition of inclusion through exclusion, sustains a pool of cheap and mobile immigrant labor on which global capitalism relies to reproduce itself.

The subordination of immigrant labor and the marginalization of immigrant communities are not, as I stressed in the introduction, the centerpiece of this book. And yet, tracing the contours of their exploitation is critical for defining the social location out of which immigrant agency and immigrant social movements arise. Immigrants are indeed haunted by the collective political choices of the past, and the horizons of their expectations for the future, as with a palimpsest, bleed through this history. Significant transformations occur, and yet the residue of what has come before abides. So it goes with the history of immigration to the United States. What has come before—ideology, politics, and law—continues to exert an influence on what happens and what is thought possible in the present. While the general thrust of this book is toward a consideration of situated agency and resistance, this necessary genealogy of exploitation aids in denaturalizing taken-for-granted assumptions about the US "immigrant problem" and outlining the historical conditions that produce immigrants' precarity and their power.

Historical Transformations in Immigration and Enforcement in Four Waves

The history of US immigration policy unfolds in cycles of repression and liberalization that are inspired, in large part, by domestic and foreign policy priorities of the United States. Drawing on Martin's periodization,[3] I briefly summarize four key transformations in US immigration policy from 1780 through the present, culminating in a "deportation regime" that is historically unprecedented in its geographical reach and enforcement capacity.[4] I emphasize the history of Mexican immigration specifically, given the focus of this ethnography.

Beginning with the period from 1780 to 1875, a laissez-faire approach to immigration policy dominated. States, private business, and railroad companies actively recruited immigrants. This immigration was facilitated by the federal government, which provided subsidies for railroad construction and maintained high tariffs on European goods, spurring demand for labor on railroads and in US factories. Immigrants represented a significant proportion of soldiers in the army. They were also recruited as a part of the settler colonialist project and helped to push the American frontier westward.

Some immigrant groups, however, were completely barred from participation in this American expansionist project. For instance, while Mexicans after the Treaty of Guadalupe Hidalgo (1848) and blacks after the enactment of the Fourteenth Amendment could become naturalized citizens, the 1790 Naturalization Act as amended in 1870 created a special legal designation for Asian immigrants: "aliens ineligible for citizenship." The law effectively created a class of immigrants who could only be temporary workers. While this period was marked by fewer and less stringent immigration restrictions than in subsequent periods, the earliest versions of US immigrant policy were marred by racial exclusion.

During the 1840s, following a large influx of Irish and Catholic immigrants to the United States, the first organized anti-immigrant group, the American Native ("Know Nothing") Party, emerged. The moniker referred to the response that members of the movement were instructed to give when asked about their activities: "I know nothing about it." While the Know Nothing Party made a strong showing in the congressional elections of 1854, it was not enough to enact their anti-immigrant program. Slavery soon came to dominate the political agenda, eclipsing the immigration issue.

Beginning in the 1870s, *qualitative* restrictions were introduced to halt the migration of groups deemed undesirable by the state, including convicts and prostitutes. "Paupers" and "mental defectives" were added to the list with the Immigration Act of 1882. And, for the first time, an entire country was barred from entry: China. The infamous Chinese Exclusion Act of 1882 remained in place until its repeal in 1943.

Regarded as "not fit for our society,"[5] these early immigrant groups were perceived as "the dregs"—criminals, morons, paupers—of the countries from which they hailed, incapable of playing a role in fulfilling the destiny of an emerging United States. "Driven to the New World by their misfortunes or their misconduct," Alexis de Tocqueville wrote in the 1840s, these immigrants were variously perceived as savior and scourge.[6] They helped build the new capitalist economy and fulfill America's manifest destiny,[7] and yet nativists believed "that some influence originating abroad threatened the very life of the nation from within."[8]

At the turn of the century, the growing congressional concern with the influx of immigrants from Southern Europe seeking economic opportunity and immigrants from Eastern Europe fleeing religious persecution, in particular Jews fleeing a wave of pogroms, sparked another wave of restriction. Beginning in 1897, Congress attempted three times to pass a law requiring literacy tests for entry, but these were vetoed by three successive presidents, beginning with Grover Cleveland. President Woodrow Wilson vetoed the bill twice, but his veto was overridden in 1917, passing into law the Immigration Act of 1917. Thereafter, anyone over the age of 16 who could not read in any language was refused entry. The law further established the "Asiatic Barred Zone," barring immigration from much of Asia and the Pacific Islands, but not the Philippines or Japan (already voluntarily barred by the Japanese government as part of the Gentlemen's Agreement of 1907).

The early 1900s were characterized by the first set of *quantitative* restrictions, inaugurated by the passage of the National Origins Act of 1924, also known as the Johnson-Reed Act (and its precursor, the Emergency Quota Act of 1921). This legislation functionally excluded migrants from Southern and Eastern Europe, preserving an "imagined community"[9] of US whites who viewed themselves as descended from Northern and Western Europeans.

The act did three things. First, it excluded all immigration from countries whose inhabitants were "ineligible to citizenship": a euphemism for Japanese exclusion.[10] Second, in deference to the labor needs of southwestern agriculture and due to US trade and diplomatic interests with Mexico, it placed no numerical limits on immigration from the Western Hemisphere. Third, it effectively capped immigration from Southern and Eastern Europe and privileged Northern and Western European immigrants by applying a discriminatory quota formula.

This final element lies at the centerpiece of the legislation. In the wake of increased immigration from Southern and Eastern Europe at the turn of the 20th century, restrictionists were eager to curb any further inflow from these countries, whose inhabitants they regarded as mentally inferior and, consequently, incapable of full membership. The national origins formula mandated that no country could send more than 2 percent of the total number of immigrants already residing in the United States in 1890. The National Origins Act, passed in 1924, could have used the 1920 census as its baseline, but Congress chose instead to use the 1890 census because, at that time, US citizens of Northern and Western European descent predominated. Consequently, the quota for Northern and Western Europeans was quite large, while that for Southern and Eastern Europeans was much smaller.

While the Johnson-Reed Act put in place a hierarchy of desirability among European nations, those undesirable Europeans were still eligible for citizenship, while other groups, Asians in particular, were indefinitely barred from citizenship. The effect was the consolidation of whiteness in immigration law. As Ngai argues, the law constructed a white American race, in which persons of European descent shared a common whiteness distinct from those deemed to be not white. In the construction of that whiteness, "the legal boundaries of both white and nonwhite acquired sharper definition."[11] The 1924 act was a key moment in a genealogy of racial formation that brightened the boundaries of whiteness, even as whiteness itself contained its own internal strata.[12]

Notably, no country-based restrictions were placed on the Western Hemisphere since legislators from the West and Southwest insisted on the ready availability of Mexican immigrants to perform agricultural labor:[13] a relationship established at the turn of the 20th century and reinforced during World War I, which largely halted European immigration to the United States, deepening American dependence on Mexican immigrant labor. Indeed, the Immigration Act of 1917 permitted the secretary of labor to waive the restrictive provisions of the act, including the literacy test, for temporary agricultural laborers from the Western Hemisphere. One month after the United States declared war on Germany in April 1917, the secretary exercised this power in response to petitions from agricultural interests in the Southwest who predicted labor shortages.[14]

During the 19th century, immigration from Mexico was relatively light. The flow of migration from Mexico changed dramatically at the turn of the 20th century in response to economic development both in northern Mexico and in the southwestern United States, labor shortages that stemmed from the bars on Asian immigration established at the end of the previous century, and the increased numbers of war refugees and political exiles fleeing the Mexican Revolution (1910–20). In 1900, the number of Mexican nationals living in the United States reached 100,000 for the first time, and ballooned to 639,000 in 1930, at the beginning of the Great Depression. Growing migration entangled further the economies and peoples of the United States and Mexico as Mexican immigrants swelled the ranks of the US labor force.

While labor shortages generated by a world war and racist policy making created the historical conditions for an increased reliance on Mexican immigrant labor, this should not be taken to mean that Mexican immigrants were welcomed with open arms. Though the Western Hemisphere was exempt from the numerical restrictions of national origins, consular officials used immigration policies that were already in place to limit legal migration from Mexico, including a ban on contract labor, a literacy test, and a provision excluding persons "likely to become a public charge."[15] In addition, head taxes established in 1917 and 1924 encouraged immigrants to cross the border clandestinely. By the late 1920s these policies made more rigid the distinction between legal and "illegal" immigration and produced the figure of the Mexican "illegal immigrant" who was out of place by virtue of his or her "unauthorized entry" into a region that belonged to Mexico some 70 years earlier.

As a result, the 20th century was marked by the emergence of "illegal immigration" as the central dilemma in immigration policy, for which deportation was the primary remedy. Spurred by the economic catastrophe of the Great Depression, the criminalization and racialization of Mexican "illegal immigrants" intensified, culminating in the "mass repatriation" of Mexicans out of the Southwest to Mexico. This repatriation effort was nominally "voluntary"; however, many Mexican immigrants and Mexican Americans were driven out of their homes and communities under the threat of violence. Balderrama and Rodriguez report that the Immigration and Naturalization Service (INS) regularly conducted raids of immigrant *colonias* all over the Southwest, rounding up both Mexican nationals and Mexican Americans for deportation.[16] They recount the "infamous" La Placita raid, which occurred on February 26, 1931. Hundreds of INS agents, police officers, and sheriff's deputies were brought in from surrounding jurisdictions to execute the raid. Officers and agents surrounded a park, chosen for its "maximum psychological impact" on the Mexican community, blocking all entrances, and proceeded to comb through the crowd of approximately 400 people, detaining and deporting anyone who could not produce proof of legal immigration status.[17] News of the raid spread rapidly and with it the specter of deportation. These raids crystallized in the public imagination the threat that "illegal immigrants" purportedly posed to the nation.

Over the period of the early 1900s, Mexican immigration was buoyed by a growing reliance on their labor as a consequence of war, revolution, and US domestic and foreign policy, and, at the same time, was threatened by anti–(undocumented) Mexican immigrant sentiment that resonated with a well-established tradition of American xenophobia.

The repatriation campaigns of the 1930s were not meant to last, however. As the United States moved into the middle of the 20th century and became embroiled in another world war, economic and political realities shifted. Labor shortages in the wake of World War II led to the implementation of the Bracero Program (1942–64), which provided temporary work authorization for Mexican immigrant laborers. Barbara Driscoll notes that other groups that had provided agricultural labor in the past were no longer available to meet the shortage.[18] A burgeoning war industry absorbed many of the white tenant farmers who had moved west during the Great Depression and had been laboring in the California fields. Japanese immigrants and Japanese Americans had also worked as agricultural laborers, but their internment precluded their recruitment. The Great Migration, during which many black Americans migrated out of the South to the North, eliminated the option to employ black Americans to address the shortage.[19] High school graduates were also out, since they were being conscripted into the war effort.[20] Consequently, farmers looked to Mexican "braceros" to fill this growing demand. Mexico City was, however, reluctant to facilitate a temporary work program since the mass repatriation of Mexican immigrants and Mexican Americans was still fresh in Mexicans' collective memory. Eventually a binational deal was struck, but despite extensive negotiations with Mexico City, poor working and living conditions persisted, inspiring various strikes by braceros. These forces of inclusion and exclusion together generate the condition of deportability[21]—not deportation per se, but the threat of deportation—that does not fully exclude Mexican immigrants, but sustains their subordinate economic and social position as simultaneously necessary and unwanted. The cyclicality of their recruitment and rejection, their inclusion through exclusion, demonstrates the profound influence of domestic and foreign policy priorities on immigration law and policy.[22]

This pattern is evident even in those periods of historic immigration reform. Of various liberalizing policies,[23] the Immigration and Nationality Act of 1965 is the most significant because it abolished national origins. The system that took its place imposed hemispheric caps and later per country and worldwide caps, as well as privileged family reunification and employer preferences. In 1965, 170,000 visas were allotted to the Eastern Hemisphere and 120,000 to the Western Hemisphere, with the additional restriction that no more than 20,000 visas could be issued to a single country in the Eastern Hemisphere in a given year. In a 1976 amendment, the country cap was extended to the Western Hemisphere, and in 1978 the hemispheric caps were removed in favor a global visa cap of 290,000. These visas were distributed across seven preference categories related to family reunification and employer preferences. No numerical limit was applied to the spouses, unmarried minor children, or parents of naturalized citizens: an exemption that remains in place today.

The Hart-Celler Act, passed alongside a host of other landmark civil rights legislation and hailed as a progressive victory over the overtly racist National Origins Act, was lauded for its use of presumably more equitable hemispheric caps. But even these liberalizing policies contained within them elements of restriction. The 120,000 quota slots reserved for all of the Western Hemisphere were less than the known number of migrants coming from Mexico alone. Largely a concession to immigration restrictionists, this cap was instituted at a historical moment in which Mexico was sending the largest number of immigrants to the United States and represented the first ever quantitative limit on migration from the Western Hemisphere. This cap, coupled with the termination of the Bracero Program in 1964, demonstrated that the avenues for legal entry were quickly closing. In 1968, the year the new law went into effect, apprehensions for Mexican nationals shot up 40 percent to 151,000.[24] When the country cap went into effect in 1976, that number jumped to 781,000.

Today the global cap is 226,000 for family categories and 140,000 for employer categories. The per country quota cap stands at 25,620 or 7 percent of the global total. This one-size-fits-all approach *creates* substantive inequality despite the law's formally equal treatment of immigrants.[25] In this arrangement, immigrant groups coming from undersubscribed countries enjoy ready access to legal migration, while others hailing from oversubscribed countries, Mexican immigrants for instance, are subject to 10- to 20-year waiting periods (depending on the visa category to which they are applying). The structural pressure to immigrate without authorization is produced, in significant part, by a visa system established in the mid-1960s that artificially constricts legal avenues for migration. Immigration restrictionists call for undocumented Latino immigrants to "get in line" and "do it the right way," arguing "we are a nation of laws." What these arguments fail to acknowledge is the way past political choices, mutable as they are, haunt the legal avenues the immigrants might travel today, making them narrower and more difficult to traverse than those encountered by previous generations of immigrants. Even in the wake of this transformative and liberalizing policy reform, the dynamic of inclusion through exclusion continues to define the Mexican immigrant experience that at once welcomes and rejects them.

The fourth and final transformation in immigration policy occurs in the wake of global capitalist development and neoliberal economic policy marked by lowered barriers to trade, austerity, and the exploitation of labor on a global scale.[26] As a consequence, global migration increased dramatically. Congress responded with a flurry of immigration laws,[27] of which I highlight two. The Immigration Reform and Control Act of 1986 (IRCA) aimed to reduce unauthorized immigration by imposing employer sanctions and provided "amnesty" for some undocumented immigrants by creating a pathway to regularize their status if they had been unlawfully and continuously present in the United States prior to

January 1, 1982. Approximately 3 million immigrants did so. This bill did not, as Ngai argues, reform any of the underlying immigration laws, like the visa allotment system, that produced an enormous undocumented population in the first place.[28] Consequently, the amnesty only temporarily reduced the numbers of undocumented immigrants. IRCA's passage marked the last successful effort at reform.

The Personal Responsibility and Work Opportunity Reconciliation Act of 1996 (PRWORA) made most legal immigrants arriving after August 22, 1996 ineligible for welfare benefits unless they were refugees or veterans or had worked for 10 years in the United States. The act created a sharp distinction between citizens' and immigrants' ability to access the social safety net. Scholars have called PRWORA the third major change in immigration policy in the 20th century after national origins in 1924 and their elimination in 1965. These three historic policy shifts reflect the major political dilemmas of the time: "isolationism after WWI, the civil rights era of the 1960s, and the quest for a balanced budget in the 1990s."[29]

Immigration reform in the present has remained an elusive goal. A failed reform attempt occurred in 2007 under the Bush administration: an attempt foiled by well-organized and well-funded nativist groups like the Federation for Immigration Reform and America Counts. In June 2013 the latest reform attempt, the Border Security, Economic Opportunity, and Immigration Modernization bill, sponsored by the bipartisan "Gang of Eight," passed the Senate, but died in the Republican-controlled house. Warnings from party leaders like Karl Rove and Senator Marco Rubio, a Latino of Cuban descent and rising star within the party, cautioned that failure to enact reform would alienate a Latino voting bloc that would only become more powerful over time: a constituency that gave upward of 70 percent of their votes to Barack Obama during the 2012 election. Many in the Republican Party, however, continue to enjoy strong support from their mostly white and heavily gerrymandered congressional districts, and so are unmoved by the call from within their party to pander to Latinos by granting legalization to undocumented immigrants.

As the Republican Party wrangles with its tentative obsolescence, many observers on the political left, including national immigration organizations like the National Day Labor Organizing Network and

Presente, faulted Democrats for capitulating to Republican demands for greater enforcement, as well as President Obama for treating increased enforcement as a down payment on future reform that would never materialize.[30] The failure of reform is a "seething presence"[31] in the lives of undocumented immigrants who daily cope with the uncertainty that attends deportability.

The Deportation Nation Today

In the absence of reform, the state's primary response to the "immigrant problem" has been ever more enforcement. Of course, deportation is the most serious consequence that immigrants, documented and undocumented alike, face. The current deportation regime is historically unprecedented in its reach and intensity, and the scope of the problem is attributable to two recent transformations. The intensification of what Daniel Kanstroom calls "post-entry social control" is the first of these.[32] Since the mid-1990s, the grounds for the deportation of noncitizens—documented and undocumented—have expanded, the deportation process itself has become faster, and the avenues for judicial redress have narrowed.[33]

Second, there has been a geographic shift in the *place* of immigration enforcement. In the post-9/11 period, this "post-border turn" refers to the fact that immigration enforcement takes place no longer solely at the territorial boundaries of the United States, but within states, counties, and cities: in "show me your papers" laws, in county jails, and in everyday police work, like traffic stops.[34] The growing involvement of state and local governments in the work of federal immigration enforcement—a process referred to as devolution—has meant that local police have, willingly or unwittingly, become part-time immigration enforcement agents. This shift has largely been accomplished via a series of local-federal immigration enforcement collaboration programs, collectively referred to as the Criminal Alien Program,[35] which includes the now-defunct 287(g) program[36] and the Priority Enforcement Program, formally Secure Communities.[37] These programs pull the work of immigration enforcement into the interior of the county.[38] And as immigration enforcement is diffused at various geographic levels, creating a "multilayered jurisdictional patchwork,"[39] the vulnerability of undocumented people to deportation becomes proportionately more acute.[40]

Lucero senses this shift. He arrived from Mexico City in 1989. He recalls that even though he entered without authorization, his experience was not the clandestine desert crossing commonly represented in media. He simply came through a port of entry with his family. Because he and his siblings were so young, he says, no one bothered to check their papers. He's lived in South City ever since, where he works in construction. The ease of that initial crossing becomes the baseline for his assessment of the risk of deportation now.

> Because it's even more difficult [now]. Because before, about 10–15 years ago or so, immigration would come here, to the streets, and would take people. But now, for some minor offense they take you to county, they pick you up and it's much more difficult. It's a fear that makes you have to be more cautious about what you do. You don't want, for example, a cop to stop you for some reason.
> —Lucero, undocumented, 40–50 years old, construction

La migra certainly wasn't absent when he first arrived, but over the course of his time in South City, Lucero has witnessed the way local police have become more entangled with immigration enforcement. Whether as a consequence of Secure Communities or as a simple professional courtesy between law enforcement agencies, ICE agents maintain a presence in county jails. Prior to the big border enforcement buildup of the early 1990s, if undocumented immigrants successfully crossed the border without authorization, they were largely free from the scrutiny of federal officials. Today minor encounters with local police can ultimately result in deportation.

As Héctor's story at the opening of the chapter suggests, however, deportation programs are not the only way immigration law is enforced. A car impoundment is perhaps the most common risk in the daily lives of the Mexican immigrants in this study. An impoundment occurs when a police officer seizes a person's vehicle, often for a mandatory 30-day period, because the individual was driving drunk or without a valid license. These impoundments are executed during police DUI checkpoints, special police patrols targeting drunk drivers, and regular police stops. As I detail in the next chapter, however, these impoundments mainly ensnare unlicensed, undocumented drivers who experience these seemingly racially neutral public-safety programs as a form of immigration enforcement that foments anxiety and distrust within the immigrant community.

Coupled with the uptick in municipal-level immigration policy making, the local has reemerged as a critical battleground in the fight over immigrant inclusion and exclusion.[41] In the aftermath of the 2006 immigrant rights marches, for instance, 1,059 pieces of immigration-related legislation were introduced in state legislatures, of which 167 became law in 2007: more than double all the immigration-related laws enacted in 2006.[42]

The Consequences

The effects of these contemporary transformations in immigration enforcement are many. Most consequentially, the death rate at the border has increased steadily over time. According to the National Foundation for American Policy (NFAP), based on data provided by the US Border Patrol, the number of immigrant deaths on the border peaked in 2005 at 492 and was closely followed by the 2012 figure: 477. When this figure is measured as a proportion of Border Patrol apprehensions, however, we see that the immigrant death rate crossing the border has steadily increased from approximately 2 deaths per 10,000 apprehensions in 1998 to approximately 14 in 2012. Interestingly, the NFAP reports that this historically high death rate occurred in the same year that fewer undocumented immigrants were crossing than in prior years.[43] In total, 5,595 have died attempting to cross into the United States without authorization since 1998. This increased death rate is attributable in large part to ramped up immigration enforcement at key crossings on the US-Mexico border, shifting clandestine migratory routes into more rugged and dangerous terrain.[44]

In terms of deportations, since 1997 the United States has deported 4 million people: twice as many as the sum total of all individuals deported between 1892 and 1996.[45] In fiscal year 2013, deportations reached a record high of 434,015,[46] disproportionately targeting working-class

Latino immigrant men.[47] Since that time, these numbers have declined as undocumented immigration in general has declined and as growing numbers of states and municipalities have refused to cooperate with interior enforcement measures. Of course, the effects of deportation extend beyond deportees and challenge the myth of deportation as a "surgical" immigration enforcement tool. Many undocumented immigrants live in families with one or more citizen children. According to Pew Research, in 2008 over a third (37 percent) of all undocumented immigrants were parents of US citizen children.[48] The Applied Research Center estimates that as of 2011, 5,100 children were currently living in foster care due to the deportation of a parent. That study showed that family separation was more likely in jurisdictions that aggressively participated in local-federal immigration enforcement programs.[49]

Family separation occurs both as a consequence of deportation and as a result of parents' constrained choice to leave their children in the home country to provide for them *al norte*. The emotional toll of such a separation is high, especially for mothers and their children.[50] The dangers associated with crossing the border—treacherous terrain, unscrupulous coyotes, violent gangs, corrupt Border Patrol agents—are especially acute for women who are vulnerable to rape,[51] and for queer migrants who are likewise vulnerable to sexual violence and, until as recently as 1990, were excludable and deportable from the United States as "sexual deviants."

For those migrants who evade the dangers of both the border and deportation, they continue to be haunted by their status. Living "out of status" impedes educational mobility,[52] reduces the likelihood of reporting workplace violations like wage theft,[53] influences perceptions of health and disease,[54] and dramatically increases the likelihood of incarceration and the length of the sentence.[55]

Edgardo's experience as an undocumented immigrant highlights a more mundane, and so overlooked, indignity. Unable to procure a driver's license, he's restricted from more than just driving.

> I don't understand why the police, or why in so many places they won't let you go in. If you go somewhere with your girlfriend, and want to invite her out to, I don't know, have a drink or simply to chat with her, go out dancing or to where they play the music she likes and she wants to go in,

but you can't go in because you don't have the right identification. You
get me?
—Edgardo, Mexican, undocumented, South City, 40–50, owns
 small party supply business

As Lucero notes above, immigration status is an increasingly salient feature not only in relation to local police, but also in everyday life. The
simple inability to get into a bar to spend time with friends or to go on
a date serves as a small but powerful reminder of his undocumented
unfreedom. Status is far more than a legal designation. It is a social
marker that constrains one's mobility in ways big and small.

Immigration enforcement, generally, and deportation, specifically,
are "powerful tool[s] of discretionary social control" that affect both
one's presence in the nation-state, and one's place in society.[56] Deportability is the ghost that looms largest in the lives of immigrants.[57] The
undocumented immigrant problem—produced by a substantively unequal visa system and beset by historically unprecedented levels of immigrant enforcement—is an expression of this history of dependence
on, but distaste for, Mexican immigrants. This history haunts the daily
lives of immigrants who must cope with displacement, dispossession,
and indignity. Conceptually, the specter of deportation refers to more
than these risks, however. It links past historical episodes to the present
dilemma: a political and legal arrangement in which immigrants are at
once necessary and unwanted.

Race, gender, and sexuality are layered onto this dilemma. Race offers
an illusory but powerful justification for the subjugation of Latino immigrants; these racial others are purportedly unfit for inclusion into the
national polity because of either their language or their criminality, or
their welfare dependence, or their leeching off America's abundance, or
their living arrangements, or their political beliefs, or some combination
of these.[58] This arrangement sustains their marginal social and political
status, just as it functions to reproduce capitalism and the logics of subordination related to race, class, gender, and sexuality that justify their
marginalization in the first place.[59]

The Browning of America

This history shapes the social location of Mexican immigrants (and immigrants generally) in the present. And this social location can be outlined by current demographic trends, which indicate both novel transformations in the demographic composition of immigrants and important continuities. As I described in the introduction, immigration after 1965 initiates a major demographic shift in the United States that is driven by immigrants from Africa, Asia, and especially Latin America. According to a recent Pew analysis of the US Census Bureau's 2015 American Community Survey, the United States continues to be the world's leader as a destination for immigrants.[60] In 2015, the total number of immigrants was 43.2 million: a massive jump from the 1970 figure of 9.6 million. Measured as a percentage of the total US population, however, immigrants represent 13.4 percent of all those living in the United States: a number that approaches but does *not* exceed the all-time high. In the period from 1890 to 1920, immigrants made up just less than 15 percent of the total US population (14.8 percent in 1890).

At present, the total immigrant population has grown 44 percent from 31.1 million in 2000 to 40.4 million in 2011 and to 44.7 million in 2015. Mexico continues to be the largest sending country, accounting for 27 percent of all immigrants, or 11.5 million immigrants living in the United States in 2015. A substantial majority (72 percent) of younger immigrants, ages 5 to 17, speak only English at home or speak English very well, while a lower proportion (50 percent) of older immigrants age 18 and older are similarly proficient. The median household income is lower among the foreign-born than the native-born ($51,000 vs. $56,000), while the median income among the Mexican-born is significantly lower ($40,000). The rate of homeownership among the foreign-born (50 percent) lags behind that of their native-born counterparts (65 percent). Mexican-born immigrants' rate of homeownership is significantly lower than that of both groups (46 percent). The poverty rate of the foreign-born (17 percent) is higher than for the native-born (14 percent) and significantly higher for the Mexican-born (22 percent).[61]

Of 44.7 million foreign-born in 2015, 11 million, or approximately 25 percent, were unauthorized immigrants.[62] As Passel and Cohn note, the undocumented population in the United States has grown steadily since

1990 when it numbered 3.5 million, peaking at 12 million in 2007, and then declining, for the first time in two decades, to 11.1 million in 2009, where it has stabilized into the present.[63] Douglas Massey attributes the growth of the undocumented Mexican immigrant population in the United States to ramped up border enforcement efforts beginning in the late 1980s. "Given the rising costs and risks of unauthorized border crossing," he argues, "migrants quite logically minimized crossing—not by remaining in Mexico, but by settling more permanently in the United States."[64] The recent decline in the total undocumented population was due largely to the decline in the Mexican undocumented immigrant population. Mexican undocumented immigration fell from a height of 6.9 million in 2007 to 5.8 million in 2014 (though undocumented immigration from Central America, Asia, and sub-Saharan Africa rose over the same period).[65]

Interestingly, net undocumented Mexican immigration to the United States is now negative: more undocumented immigrants are leaving the United States than arriving. This downward trend is the result of the declining economic opportunities in the United States in the wake of the Great Recession of 2008, improved economic conditions in Mexico, a declining Mexican birth rate, and the deterrent effect of ramped up federal enforcement. For those millions of undocumented immigrants still living in the United States, and unlikely to leave because they are raising citizen children or have developed steady employment, the problem of deportability remains.

An additional unanticipated consequence of the constriction of avenues for legal migration and growing enforcement was defensive naturalization by which those with legal permanent status became naturalized citizens. Legal migration, in addition to unauthorized immigration from Mexico has also increased, growing from an average of 63,000 per year in the 1970s to 170,000 per year from 2000 to 2010. To safeguard their place in the United States and because naturalized citizens can sponsor visas for spouses, minor children, and parents outside of any numerical limits, legal migration from Mexico also surged over this period.[66] In this way both legal and undocumented immigration have contributed to the browning of America.

This demographic profile suggests several conclusions. The number of immigrants living in the United States, as a proportion of the total

US population, approaches but does not exceed the all-time high. This fact indicates that the size of the immigrant population is *not* historically unprecedented, as some alarmist mainstream voices have asserted. Furthermore, while the immigrant population is very diverse, Mexican immigrants clearly predominate. While most mainstream depictions of immigrants focus on Latinos generally and Mexicans specifically, this disproportionate focus on Latinos and Mexicans obfuscates the diversity of immigrants in the United States and the range of experiences that are grouped together under the broad umbrella term "Latino." For Latina migrants, for instance, the causes for migration,[67] and their experiences of home and labor, are shaped by gender,[68] but also education and occupation.[69]

In sum, Mexican and Central American immigrants tend to arrive with lower levels of education, earn lower levels of income, occupy positions in the lower rungs of the US labor market, encounter very long waits to enter the United States with authorization, and are disproportionately targeted by a highly repressive immigration enforcement regime relative to their European and Asian counterparts.[70] For the Mexican immigrants in this study, their overall profile indicates that they face serious obstacles to incorporation.

Immigrant Politics in the Deportation Nation

While immigrants have endured these inequalities, to be sure, they have also mounted resistance to them. They act individually to manage these everyday violations and mobilize collectively to contest the conditions of their exploitation. On the one hand, the unprecedented size of the Latino immigrant population, coupled with their growing electoral and movement-based political power, sets the stage for significant transformations of the American political scene. Beginning in the mid-1960s, major demographic shifts driven by global political economic developments, shifts in US immigration law privileging family reunification and employer preferences, and long-standing migratory patterns between US commercial interests and Mexican laborers have contributed to a swelling Latino constituency that breaks to the political left and is largely sympathetic to undocumented immigrants.[71] Subsequently, the breadth of immigrant collective action and electoral power has begun to reshape the American political scene in general. The Chicano/a and Brown Power movements of the 1960s, like the East LA Blowouts or schools walkouts in 1968, are evidence of this emergent political power.

More recently, both Democrats and Republicans have, with varying levels of success, made overtures to the Latino community, dramatized by Donald Trump's 2015 announcement of his presidential candidacy in which he called Latino immigrants "rapists" and "criminals" and the subsequent fallout among Latino business and media. This episode evidences an emerging political reality in which Latinos must be contended with as a group. Though this group contains tremendous internal diversity, it is constituted as a group in media, in government, and among both the Latino working class and the elite. An American history of displacement, immigration, and dispossession has produced this bona fide political constituency. While much of the forgoing history may be captured with the expression "We want your labor, but we don't want you," we are now facing a political moment in which Latinos' contributions to the economy and society have become the basis for a renewed democratic practice waged from both inside and outside of formal membership.

Simultaneously, and as I hope the subsequent chapters bear out, the political aspirations of this movement are moored to their material and quotidian origins. Claims to the rights that attend citizenship—to drive, obtain credit, afford education, and so on—largely comport with neoliberal standards of work, family, and deservingness. Given the centrality of labor both to the history of migration and to the self-conceptions of Mexican immigrants, it is perhaps no surprise that work resides at the heart of political claims to deservingness. Their claims seek not to de-link the willingness to labor and fitness for citizenship established in the wake of industrial capitalism and the subsequent crisis in the meaning of liberal citizenship,[72] but to assert their worthiness for membership on those same terms. To make this claim from outside formal citizenship, as many undocumented immigrants have done, offers a powerful challenge to the limits of liberal democracy. And yet, the experiences of dispossession and deportability, responded to most often via atomized strategies of individual avoidance and insulation, produce a desire to inhabit norms of citizenship.

As Sandro Mezzadra has argued in his "autonomy of migration" approach to the current crisis: while "new *dispositifs* of domination and exploitation are forged within migration . . . , new practices of liberty and equality" simultaneously emerge from within these relations of subordination.[73] It is to this question—the way resistance is enabled and constrained by these conditions of vulnerability—that I turn in the chapters that follow. As I illustrate in the subsequent chapters, to narrate the Latino immigrant experience requires attention not only to the causes and contours of illegality, but also to the immigrant politics that push through the cracks of the deportation regime. But first, the next chapter examines car impoundment as an everyday example of the risks facing undocumented immigrants. The ways they manage these risks create both an opportunity for and a challenge to organizing immigrant communities.

2

"The Sense of Law Is Lost"

Car Impoundments and the Racial Naturalization of Mexican Immigrants

"The Latino Is Being Treated Like a Child"

> E: Because in reality, the Latino is being treated like a child right now: intimidated and punished. If you do something, we will arrest you. And the Latino believes what the police say: they are all going to be taken to jail and ICE will be at the jail. It is like telling them, "If you eat that candy, not only will I punish you, I will hit you." That is how the have us right now. They say, "If you drive I will arrest you and take you and deliver you to ICE." Okay? If you don't cooperate with the police you become a criminal and will be taken and delivered to ICE. "You want that?" "No, we don't want that." "Then stay put and behave." You get me?
>
> G: Like a child.
>
> E: Yes. I mean they don't let us do anything.
>
> —Edgardo, Mexican, undocumented, South City, 40–50, owns small party supply business

Edgardo came to the United States in 2000 from Guerrero, Mexico. He crossed the southern border where he was detained, deported, and treated by the border patrol, as he says, like "an animal." Entering successfully on his second attempt, he came to California where his brother received him. He's lived in South City for 12 years and in that time has had no fewer than four cars impounded. We sit across from each other in a narrow living room, perhaps a newer addition to an older home. I sit at one end of a futon and Edgardo sits in a chair. The space forces a physical intimacy. He recounts a time that he was giving his brother a ride from one side of town to the other. His brother, who had had run-ins with the police before, was on probation when they were stopped.

He addressed my brother. He asked, "Are you Francisco?"

"Yes."

"Okay, get out." And the officer started to search him. Then another police officer arrived and they began to search him thoroughly. After he told me, "Okay, now you get out." I got out and asked him, "Why did you stop me?"

"Because we have to search him," he said.

"But why?" I asked, "As far as I know you're not a probation officer or anything of the sort."

"No, but the probation officer will be here shortly," he said. "As a matter of fact, the only thing I want to ask you is that you show me your documentation. Give me your license and proof of insurance."

I told him, "But I don't understand why you are stopping me."

"It's because you're with him," he replied.

"So what? Can't a person have someone else in the car with them?" I asked.

He said, "No. Give me your license and proof of insurance."

Those are the type of bad experiences I have had with the police, and because of that I have no trust in the police.

Edgardo, undocumented and without a driver's license, subsequently had his car impounded. The infantilization that Edgardo describes is about more than the risk of deportation and the humiliation arising from interactions with police officers themselves. If, for instance, the message that law enforcement communicates to Mexican immigrants is to "stay put and behave," then we are certainly talking about more than compliance with the letter of the law. At issue is "racial naturalization": a kind of naturalization not to formal citizenship, but to US racial hierarchy and the street-level processes of subordination required to maintain it.[1] The consequence of immigrants' recognition of the many excesses of enforcement is that the "sense of law is lost." Immigrants mistrust the police and, consequently, lose faith in potential for justice that law contains. This mistrust, however, is not unequivocal, but ambivalent. Their reliance on police in emergencies or to ward off crime chafes against their rejection of police tactics.

In 2009 police in California seized 24,000 cars at sobriety or DUI checkpoints, up from 17,900 in 2008 and 15,700 in 2007.[2] Costs associated with these impoundments—fees paid to the city, to the police, and to the tow yard—typically range from $1,500 to $2,000, though Gabrielson reports these numbers can climb as high as $4,000.[3] In all, towing fees and police fines came to $40 million in 2009, while an additional $30 million in California Office of Traffic Safety grants funded the checkpoints themselves, including overtime pay, checkpoint equipment (e.g., lights, signs, etc.), and administration.[4] These cumulative figures do not include money paid to private tow companies. And because a car impoundment can also be executed in the course of a regular police stop, not solely at a DUI checkpoint, the total number of impoundments reported above is likely an underestimate since those figures are derived only from DUI checkpoints. Indeed, in many of the stories recounted below, immigrants were stopped outside of a DUI checkpoint under what they say were dubious pretenses, often involving a broken taillight.

Car impoundments of unlicensed drivers will certainly include those nonimmigrant California drivers who, for a range of reasons, never obtained a driver's license or had their license suspended. Tellingly, however, cities with majority Latino populations are seizing cars at three times the rate of those cities with small numbers of Latinos. While officers impound, on average, seven cars for each drunk driving arrest that they make, in cities with large Latino populations, the disparity is much greater. San Rafael saw 15 impoundments for each drunk driving arrest, while Montebello saw a staggering 60.[5] These disparities evidence mission creep among law enforcement. More importantly, they signal the pervasive quality of these informal immigration enforcement mechanisms in the daily lives of immigrants. While much attention from scholars and advocates has been rightfully paid to Secure Communities and deportation in general, car impoundments have received relatively less consideration due to their *informal* quality as a technology of immigration enforcement.

Consequently, police stand out as one of the greatest threats to Mexican immigrants in their daily lives. They readily understand the growing overlap between criminal law and immigration enforcement: a legal and social transformation that scholars refer to as "crimmigration."[6] This chapter is about mistrust between immigrants and police who operate as both peace officers and proxies for a growing deportation regime. It is also about the way police work is about more than strictly enforcing law.

Officers participate in the racial naturalization of Mexican immigrants to American hierarchy.

As Edgardo demonstrates, Mexican immigrants recognize this eminently social process that is enacted in these routine interactions. Police are inextricably involved in the political work of undermining or reinscribing the social hierarchies of race, class, gender, and sexuality that are both reflected and reproduced in the laws that police are charged with upholding. Such an expansive view of the role of police in the racialization of Mexican immigrants takes us beyond a narrow consideration of devolution or deportation per se, though, as I outline in the previous chapter, these developments distinguish the contemporary immigration enforcement regime from previous iterations. While deportation is the most consequential tool states use to enforce immigration law, deportations represent the tip of the iceberg when it comes to the many forms of risk that immigrants daily confront. The car impoundment deserves closer inspection because it is an informal, and so understudied, feature of the immigration enforcement regime; it creates a serious financial burden for immigrant families; and it constitutes a ritual of humiliation and subordination, of racial naturalization. This chapter carries forward the previous chapter's history of inclusion through exclusion by presenting the car impoundment as a key exclusionary campaign that does not banish immigrants, but reinforces their racial subordination. The car impoundment is the main risk that undocumented immigrants run in their everyday lives and shapes the social location out of which their politics emerge.

And while the car impoundment is perceived as unfair, immigrants' assessments of police in general are not unequivocal. Like Edgardo, many immigrants describe their encounters with police in negative terms. Some, though, are resoundingly positive, including in the case of domestic violence. Interestingly, even among those immigrants who are most intensely critical of police, they still demonstrate ambivalence about whether police can be trusted. Mistrust is widespread, but they rely on police to respond to crime and in emergency situations.

This ambivalence can be read in two ways. On the one hand, mistrust signals the deteriorating relationship between racialized, working-class immigrant communities and police: a pattern that resonates with historical and contemporary relations between African Americans and police. On the other hand, this ambivalence suggests immigrants still rely on police as a bulwark against the chaos they fear might reign in their absence. Their abiding faith in police as an *institution* chafes against their first- and secondhand experiences with actual police in their daily lives.[7] While relations between Mexican immigrants and police are imperiled by the "institutionalized practice"[8] of the car impoundment and the broader crimmigration trend, this ambivalence may also be understood as a generative opening—an invitation—to develop effective community-police relations premised on police prioritizing in their work serious social harms, not immigration violations.

Racial Naturalization

Devon Carbado defines racial naturalization not as the way race and racism come to bear on who is permitted to naturalize to formal US citizenship but as the "social process that produces American racial identities."[9] He elaborates this concept in three ways: (1) racism is a social process that inaugurates individuals to American racial hierarchy, (2) law informs but does not exhaust the racial terms of this naturalization, and (3) racial naturalization is a process of both inclusion and exclusion.

For Carbado, Americanness is related but not reducible to formal citizenship. To be American is the "capacity, as a racial subject, to be a representative body—figuratively and materially—for the nation."[10] Take, for instance, the case of Japanese internment during World War II. While most of those interned were formally citizens, they were regarded, by the state and by many white Americans, as "forever foreigners." They could not be American, not really, because their race was conflated with disloyalty. Racism undermined the legal protections guaranteed by citizenship.

Take the converse case, the *Dred Scott* (1857) decision, which affirmed that black slaves could never become US citizens. And yet their status as the property of white slaveholders and as the key source of labor that sustained the plantation economy meant "they were intelligible as Americans—more particularly, as inferior beings that belonged to America."[11] Leti Volpp makes a similar point: "Citizenship as a form of legal status does not guarantee that they will be constitutive of the

American body politic. In fact, quite the opposite: the consolidation of American identity takes place against them."[12] In this case, she is talking about the social figure of the terrorist, but the lesson is portable. Cultural belonging does not flow automatically from legal membership. And neither does full legal membership flow from cultural belonging, especially when "belonging" means incorporation into American hierarchy or inclusion through exclusion. The sociocultural category "American" is constituted against some "other" (Japanese citizens, black slaves, and Islamic terrorists in the above examples), whether or not they are legally citizens. Membership, inclusion, subordination: these processes are related but not reducible to law, evidencing the central role of race in constituting the cultural figure of the American.

I expand upon this line of argumentation by taking a more granular view of the interactions with police that sustain the subordination of Mexican immigrants by inaugurating them to American racial hierarchy. Ethnie Luibheid and Sylvanna Falcón cogently argue that border patrol agents police not only the territorial boundaries of the United States, but also the social boundaries of normative gender and "compulsory heterosexuality" through exclusionary border policy and sexual violence.[13] Police work, too, is intimately bound to the social and political work of reinscribing hierarchy.

In the case of Mexican immigrants, particularly the undocumented who are vulnerable to car impoundments, they are obviously not citizens and yet their Americanness, the degree to which they are included in the body politic, is being fiercely contested in the present. Their belonging can be assessed in at least two ways: (1) from their own bids at inclusion and (2) their inclusion through exclusion as economically necessary, but socially undesirable.

Mexican immigrants' contemporary social movement efforts for expanded legal citizenship are built upon their demonstration of key features of American identity. In my conversations with Mexican immigrants, documented and undocumented, they themselves regularly use "American" and "güero," or the more pejorative "gabacho," interchangeably, revealing their own conflation of Americanness with whiteness: a qualification they know they do not meet. But they also stress another key qualification of both US citizenship and American identity: labor. The very common political slogan "we are not criminals, we are workers" evidences this claim. In the wake of the industrial revolution, the advent of wage labor, and the partial democratization of US citizenship, being a member of the landed gentry, that is, owning productive property, was no longer the sole qualification for citizenship. To labor, specifically to "freely" sell one's labor power in the capitalist marketplace, qualified one for membership in the legal and cultural category of American.[14] While the Americanness of Mexican immigrant identity is contested, Mexican immigrants make bids to inclusion often, though not only, by highlighting their contributions in sweat to the US economy. Their labor justifies their eligibility for citizenship, both legal and social.

As I argue in the previous chapter, immigrants are not excluded exactly. Instead deportation serves as the key mechanism by which their labor is subordinated.[15] Immigrants *are* incorporated into the nation just at the lowest rungs of the US labor market. Simultaneously, Mexican immigrants, disproportionately targeted as a group,[16] are uniquely vulnerable to police as undocumented and as Mexican. Their subordination is legal; consequently, law becomes the medium through which their racialization unfolds. Their subordination is racial precisely because of the historical and contemporary efforts to criminalize their migration variously justified by the mythical linkages between immigration and crime, job loss, fiscal waste, and the erosion of an American culture defined by whiteness and against bilingual education and ethnic studies curricula, for instance. As the below narratives illustrate, their everyday encounters with police, perceived as racial profiling, contribute to the perception that they are targeted on the basis of their race. Hierarchies of race and class together contribute to the subordination of immigrant labor and racialize immigrants as undeserving interlopers whose technical illegality, presumed cultural incompatibility, and racial otherness mark them as unfit for citizenship. This dual process of criminalization and racialization unfolds in interactions with city police.

To return to the excerpt that opens this chapter, Edgardo does not simply regard police negatively. Instead he makes a distinction between being "intimidated and punished," "punished and hit." The function of police is not simply to address crime but to make sure that immigrants "stay put and behave." Beyond strictly enforcing law, police inculcate docility in Mexican immigrants in order to sustain their utility as low-wage laborers, to use Foucault's language.[17] This racializing process, the unique vulnerability of undocumented immigrants to law enforcement, is a form of naturalization. Racial naturalization for Mexican immigrants, especially those without documentation, is to be put in one's place: immigrants' tentative incorporation into a segmented American labor market where their social location as mobile laborers and socioeconomically immobile denizens is sustained through street-level processes of humiliation and control that mark them as undocumented and as Mexican.

Car Impoundments and Crimmigration

For quite some time, immigrants could, in fact, obtain a driver's license. Santa and Perfecto, undocumented and longtime North City residents, recount this legal shift and its material and symbolic consequences:

> S: In 1997, I had a driver license from California and then they didn't
>   want to give me back my driver license. I'm afraid of driving because
>   there are racist police officers; if they see someone Mexican, they stop
>   you even if you don't make a traffic violation, that's why I'm afraid.
>   When I go to the store with my children, I'm always thinking about
>   the police. I drive with fear, I don't feel free driving.
> G: So you drive less frequently because of this fear?
> S: Mhm.
> G: Are there any ways of avoiding these risks?
> S: We go out during the day but not at night. Even we need food
>   or milk for our children, we don't want to go out. . . . Just for
>   necessities. . . .
> P: If our child asks for milk or food and we don't have it; and it's at 7:00 PM
>   we can't go for it because we're afraid of the police and we don't have a
>   driver license. We go out at 4:00 PM or 5:00 PM but not later, we're afraid.
> —Santa and Perfecto, undocumented, North City, 40–50,
>   field-workers

The risk of driving was not always present. Santa and Perfecto's recounting of their sudden inability to renew their driver's licenses evidences the political nature of law and the social processes at the heart of criminalization.

I met Santa and Perfecto down the street from their home at a neighbor's house a week or so prior to our interview. The neighbor was a local school teacher and administrator who agreed to host a house meeting with La Unión to discuss car impoundments and an upcoming city election. Santa and Perfecto's children attended the same school and knew the host. As I describe in the appendix, Santa was especially reluctant to grant this interview, but the quick intervention of primary informant Leticia smoothed things over. When I returned to their street to conduct the interview, they greeted me at the door of their suburban tract home. All stucco and beige, the boxy home leads with its garage and pushes against the boundaries of the lot on which it's built. I enter through a tall entryway that extends up through the second story. A couple of children play in a plastic play place that stands in the corner of an otherwise sparsely furnished living room. The children's grandmother shuffles in and out of the kitchen, preparing food, looking after the children, and tending to the house. Santa and Perfecto, both dark-skinned and short in stature, sit side by side on a loveseat, while I sit at the end of another couch that's closest to them. They came to North City 20 years ago from Oaxaca. At various points in the interview, Santa translates my Spanish into indigenous Mixtec for her husband Perfecto. They both work in the fields. They used to pick strawberries, now grapes. Their work is hard. Bosses demand unwavering speed and the heat is intense. Though they used to migrate with the seasons, they report it has been too difficult to cross in the past 10 years given the expense and the danger,[18] so they've settled in North City where their children attend the same local school as the teacher who initially brought us together.

It's not just work that's hard. Police have become "too hard." The pervasiveness of impoundments constrains their physical mobility in the city. Knowing that *reténes* (roadblocks) or DUI checkpoints are typically set up in the evenings, Santa and Perfecto minimize their risk by refusing to drive at those times, even to conduct those spontaneous errands that children often demand of their parents. The threat of the impoundment serves as an embodied reminder of their undocumented status and their subordinated place in their community.

The risks associated with a car impoundment are not only material, but also symbolic. Driving has long been figured as a distinctly American expression of freedom.[19] Obtaining a driver's license at 16 for some native-born youth continues to be an important coming-of-age ritual in which freedom is achieved through increased physical mobility. The car marks a transition to tentative adulthood and independence. The denial of this mobility to immigrants and the disincentives that arise from the risks associated with driving without a license produce more than inconvenience. They represent embodied reminders of their place outside political membership, of their diminished independence as a consequence of their physical immobility.

Car impoundments predate formal federal-local immigration enforcement programs of which Secure Communities is the flagship program. To understand the criminalization of undocumented drivers, we must look back into California's recent history. Here we find Gordon's ghost that haunts immigrants in the present. The infamous Proposition 187, passed in 1994 with 59 percent of California voters in support, attempted to bar immigrants from accessing public education and public health care, and required evidence of citizenship or residency for all public services, including the issuance of driver's licenses. Proposition 187 was the policy expression of growing and widespread anti-immigrant sentiment, spurred by the economic recession of 1994 and capitalized upon by various politicians, in particular Republican Governor Pete Wilson. As in other historical periods, the mid-1990s were marked by the renewed scapegoating of immigrants for a variety of social ills from unemployment to crime. Federal District Judge Mariana Pfaelzer struck down most of the so-called Save Our State initiative as unconstitutional in November 1997. Enjoined from its first days, most of the law's provisions never took effect. The new requirement that a social security number be provided to obtain a license, however, survived these legal challenges, producing this conflict in the present.[20]

Criminalization refers not simply to laws we find objectionable, but to the process by which formally legal or unregulated behaviors are transformed into criminal ones. Car impoundments have resulted in tens of thousands of vehicle seizures, primarily those of immigrants. They are the ghost that Gordon theorizes.[21] They are the lingering evidence of a social process of immiseration that occurs through formal immigration enforcement initiatives like Secure Communities and informal immigration enforcement practices like car impoundments. This informal strategy of mass dispossession has substantially enriched local cities to the tune of $40 million statewide in one year.[22] The criminalization of undocumented drivers reinforces to immigrants their place outside citizenship and their racially subordinate status.

Car Impoundments as Racial Naturalization

Many respondents had had their vehicles seized. During house meetings with La Unión in both South City and North City, Mexican immigrants most frequently identified the car impoundment as their primary grievance. For immigrant respondents, the unfairness of the practice stems from the pretexts that officers would use to justify a stop, as well as officers' focus on "old, beat-up cars" and the timing and location of the checkpoints. Lucero, introduced in the previous chapter, finds impoundments unfair because their occasion is marked by a technical infraction, not a serious crime like drunk driving.

> G: Have they taken a car away from you?
> L: Oh yes.
> G: How many?
> L: It has happened about two times.
> G: Twice?
> L: Yes, twice.
> G: And what happened?
> L: Well, the other time he was following me, got right behind me and stopped me. Gave me the excuse that my taillight was not working. No, that it was broken. It did work, but it was broken.
> G: The light.
> L: No, just the taillight cover. The light was working and everything, it was just the cover that was broken. So he stopped me, asked for my license and well, they took away my car.
> —Lucero, undocumented, South City, 40–50, construction

Respondents readily understood the pretextual nature of officer stops. Broken taillights, or in this case a broken taillight cover, as well as the rosary *colgada* (hung) from the rear-view mirror were common justifications that officers gave to respondents.[23] The pretexts that officers offered up, many respondents reported, underlined the unfairness of the practice, and they saw neither their status nor their cars' faulty taillight as a serious crime. The car impoundments inspired negative assessments of police officers, who were perceived as capricious as a result.

In the below excerpt, Itzel and Armando, both North City high school students and legal residents who came to the United States when they were about three years old, report that if a car marks its occupants as poor and brown, then they are subjected to heightened scrutiny.

> I: Like, I just saw . . . the car you have, that it really matters, it really matters.
> G: What happened if you are driving a . . . broke down?
> I: They are going to pull you over.
> A: They are going to pull you over.
> I: And they are not going to pull over a white girl who is driving a Beamer, they are not even going to question it, they don't care if her face looks drunk, they are going to let her go right on. And if you just have an average job as a Mexican, working, and you have a very little car with all your family inside, they will pull you over and they will ask for everything, they will find every single reason to take that car.
> —Itzel and Armando, legal resident, North City, 20–30, student

Recognizing that police have a role to play in securing public safety, Itzel laments the lasting effects of racial profiling:

> I mean, if you see someone drunk on the street whatever they are carrying, a twelve pack of beer, go ahead, arrest them, but if you just see somebody that to you looks suspicious, there is no point in questioning them because those kind of experiences really can stay with the person.

Race has long served as grounds for suspicion among police. And while the role of race in policing has been hotly debated among criminal procedure scholars and social scientists studying racial profiling, court doctrine justifies the use of race in immigration enforcement specifically.[24] The markers of race, however—the way race is "read" from person to person—extends beyond skin color and phenotype. The various trappings of class together with color and phenotype are fodder for the racialization of Mexican immigrants as Mexican. These markers of class and poverty themselves constitute the racial identity of the Mexican immigrant because of the prevalent assumption that "all poverty is Mexican."[25] The small, run-down car filled with family marks its occupants as Mexican immigrants deserving of greater scrutiny. A double standard comes into view: Mexican immigrants perceive policing as capricious because it ignores what they see as a real danger (drunk driving) in favor of targeting them for what they see as a minor infraction (driving without a license). As Epp and his coauthors argue, it is the "institutionalized practice" of the car impoundment and not simply officers' behavior, varying as it does from the polite to the punitive, to which immigrants object.[26]

This double standard came up again as I continued my conversation with Lucero. He recalls a case in which a local politician was arrested for drunk driving, something of a local scandal. Lucero considers this politician's arrest in light of the seizure of undocumented immigrants' vehicles:

> L: It is like in Mexico, they fry all the small fish and sometimes they have to throw in a big one to appease the people so they don't think they are the only ones being attacked. But that's the only difference, because there are a lot of people who drive drunk in [a nearby neighborhood predominated by wealthy whites] and out there they don't set up any checkpoints. They don't set up checkpoints [there]. And here, they mostly place the checkpoints where the Latino people pass through. Most Anglos don't pass through [a street running through a predominantly Latino neighborhood]. They don't go down [there] much, and these are places where they. . . .
> G: And it's because of racism?
> L: That's what I see. Something fair for me would be that they set up a checkpoint in [nearby neighborhoods dominated by wealthy whites].
> —Lucero, undocumented, South City, 40–50, construction

The location of DUI checkpoints evidences to Lucero that Latinos are specifically targeted since these checkpoints rarely occur in wealthy white neighborhoods where residents also drive drunk. The timing of these checkpoints offered further evidence to respondents of the unfairness of car impoundments. In North City, this was a very common objection. Only a few roads led from the city to the agricultural fields where many Mexican immigrants picked everything from strawberries to sugar beets. Police would often set up DUI checkpoints in the early evenings on these roads: at about the same time as immigrant workers would return from work. Many respondents argued that officers took advantage of the limited vehicular access between the fields and the town to produce a natural trap for undocumented drivers. Santa, introduced above, argues that the DUI checkpoints begin too early:

> I think farmers leave at 5:00 PM or 6:00 PM and police have checkpoints at that time. And they have to go to the store to buy food or something for their families. In think the checkpoints should be at 9:00 PM and it would be good for drinkers or gangs but for working people that law at 5:00 PM or 6:00 PM isn't good. But at 9:00 PM or 10:00 PM there are drunk drivers or criminals.
> —Santa, undocumented, North City, 40–50, field-worker

Indeed, early in my fieldwork, La Unión had addressed the issue of car impoundments by attempting to convince local police to delay the start time of these checkpoints, since vehicle traffic at 5:00 and 6:00 PM is dominated by residents traveling home from work.

As Carbado's notion of racial naturalization makes plain, legal standing is no safeguard from racial profiling. Indeed, Carbado opens his article by recounting two incidents in which he was racially profiled, though he enjoyed legal status. Carbado's point is twofold: citizenship is no guarantee of protection from the excesses of racist policing. And, much like Genova's inclusion through exclusion, the experience of profiling represents an indoctrination into racial hierarchy.

Take the experience of Ricardo, marked by an utter devotion to work and avoidance of "trouble." His experience fits almost perfectly the profile of the ideal citizen subject. Ricardo came to South City from Aguascalientes on the auspicious date of July 4, 1986, 25 years prior to the date of our interview. As with many respondents, we met at a house meeting hosted by La Unión where I solicited this interview. He crossed without authorization. Initially detected by Border Patrol, he and those he was crossing with evaded the agents and escaped northward in a van arranged by their coyote. All but Ricardo piled into the back. He rode in the front seat because he had the lightest skin. Soon after his arrival, he adjusted his status under the 1986 Immigration Reform and Control Act amnesty, first becoming a resident, then a naturalized citizen, and has lived in South City ever since. When I met Ricardo for our interview, I immediately noticed how orderly and quiet things were in his home. A young son worked diligently on his homework in the living room, while another older son passed quietly from his room into the kitchen where his wife was tidying up after dinner. The home was spotless and appointed with custom cabinets and tilework, a home gilded with the fruits of his sacrifice. He owns a small landscaping business with five employees, some of whom are undocumented.

Hardworking and, as he reports, never drinking or doing drugs, Ricardo would seem to be a model citizen subject. Though, as people of color and scholars of race have long pointed out, shielding oneself in the armor of respectability is but a thin layer of protection from racial profiling.

R: Yes, I have seen it. I say I am 50–50, I don't trust [police] 100 percent. I think that they may have something against us Latinos. Yeah, that's it. But 100 percent I don't trust them. They have never given me a ticket for no reason. One time I was on my way to work and I was stopped by a highway patrol officer and he told me that my back tire was wiggling. I didn't want to say anything to him, but the tires were new. I had just put the tires on the day before, so I did not believe him. I think he stopped me because I am a Latino to see if he could take away my truck or something. Since I am a gardener my hair is always unkempt and I'm always wearing a hat, so I think that's why he stopped me, because a tire would not move like that.

G: How did you feel at that moment?

R: Not bad. He was doing his job, but I am doing things right. I have my license, my ID, insurance so it was okay. Do your job, I said, there is no problem, but I know he was lying when he stopped me and said that the tire was moving that way. There was no problem, do your work, I said.

—Ricardo, naturalized citizen, South City, 40–50, owns small landscaping business

Protected by his documented status, Ricardo recognizes that he was stopped under false pretenses and because his appearance signaled that he was Mexican and perhaps undocumented. The interaction does not provoke a rejection or demonization of the police, but it begins to undermine his trust in them ("50–50"). Even with documents ("doing things right"), a racial and class-based politics of respectability (unkempt hair under a hat) mark him as suspect regardless of his formal legal status. These are the everyday, street-level experiences of police that naturalize Mexican immigrants into American racial hierarchy in which race continues to be used as leverage in everyday police work.

From these experiences of dispossession, we can cull a racial common sense among Mexican immigrants. Police cannot be trusted, or only tenuously so, because they target Latinos unfairly. This targeting is evident in the mission creep in DUI checkpoints, which detain far more undocumented, unlicensed drivers than drunk drivers. It is evident in the pretextual quality of officers' stops of immigrants for minor infractions, which rest on the widespread understanding that poverty marks Mexican immigrants as Mexican and that this elision forms the basis of the heightened racial scrutiny to which Mexican immigrants are subjected. The timing and location of DUI checkpoints, early in the evening and rarely in isolated enclaves of white wealth, further evidence the way police practice requires race for the formulation of suspicion.

Racial subordination is accomplished through immigrants' impoverishment at the hands of local police. Car impounds are both an informal technology of immigration enforcement and an instance of racial naturalization. Officers' reliance on racial cues in the formulation of suspicion, as well as the timing and location of DUI checkpoints, reaffirm to Mexican immigrants their unique vulnerability to police scrutiny and their subordinated position in US racial hierarchy. Physical and social immobility are bound together in this practice of mass dispossession and constitute a central part of the experience of being Mexican and undocumented on the road. Deteriorating trust between immigrants and police officers has consequences for officers' ability to maintain public safety. Interestingly, many immigrants are deeply ambivalent about their willingness to call on police in times of need. I argue this ambivalence reflects an ongoing normative investment in police as an institution that wards off chaos. This ongoing reliance on police chafes against immigrants' actual experiences with them.

Police (Mis)trust

To mistrust police, to view them as a source of threat and not protection, is another way to apprehend racial naturalization. Scholars have long made the claim that police function as front-line enforcers of the color line in America. W. E. B. Du Bois most prominently made this argument in his *The Souls of Black Folk*, where he coined the notion of double consciousness, or the way American blacks must see themselves through the eyes of a simultaneously pitying and contemptuous white gaze.[27] His notion of the veil suggests that a gulf exists between whites and blacks in their experience and perception of America: an America whose heritage of prosperity and opportunity is always undermined by racism and capitalist exploitation. The veil persists in important ways. Polling data, for instance, regularly demonstrate whites place higher levels of trust in police than other nonwhite groups, especially blacks, while Latinos fall somewhere between these racial poles and are more evenly divided in their perceptions.[28]

Police themselves recognize the importance of trust to crime reduction. Initiatives like former Attorney General Eric Holder's National Initiative for Building Community Trust and Justice, launched September 18, 2014, suggest as much. Consequently, one's relationship to police, trusting or not, can be used as a measure of racial naturalization. In the case of Mexican immigrants, their ambivalence reveals that they are often and unfairly the targets of police, even while many are broadly invested in the institution of police whose purpose is to protect all residents from the chaos that would otherwise reign in their absence. To trust police is a powerful indicator that someone is a part of the group deserving of protection: those who are not criminals. Of course, the trouble is that even while undocumented immigrants see their undocumented status as largely a matter of necessity and not crime, the state does not. And the ongoing use of race as a basis for suspicion in policing belies the claim that police are fair and so deserving of trust. Mexican immigrants' ambivalence represents not only the recognition that police treat them unfairly and that this unfair treatment marks them as racially "other," but also their own understanding of themselves as largely law-abiding in a world filled with actual, non-immigration-related crime that must be intervened upon by agents of the state. Their objection then is not to police, per se, but to policing that relies on race to sort out their status and unfairly lumps them in with the group of criminals whom they think the police ought to target.

Consider Magda, who came to the United States from Acapulco in 2003. She crossed without authorization to rejoin her husband from whom she had separated several years before. But on the very night she was to cross, her husband told her that he did not want to be with her any longer and was not interested in rekindling their relationship. Devastated, she decided to cross anyway; she had already come so far. Her journey was harrowing. Her party was assaulted by bandits (she thanks God that her male cousin was with her and protected her). She joined her sister in the United States. She has since remarried, had two more sons, and reunited with her eldest son from her first marriage. They all live together in a suburban home in a middle-class neighborhood in South City. I asked Magda whether she has ever had a run-in with police.

> M: I have never had an encounter with the police, but I don't know.
>   I think I can't trust them, because the first time they took our car
>   away, according to the police officer we couldn't turn left, but he only
>   stopped us. We were in the car with my husband and two of my kids.
>   But the rest of the cars were turning there and he only stopped us,
>   why didn't he stop all the other cars too. That was the only time they
>   took away our car.
> G: How did you feel when they took the car away from you?
> M: Very sad, because I was pregnant, and because the car was a gift. It
>   was our first car. It was old but [my husband] used it to go to work.
>   It was quite expensive to get the car back. He paid the ticket for not
>   having a license. He also paid the ticket for the traffic violation. We
>   did have insurance, but he didn't have a license.
> —Magda, undocumented, South City, 40–50, stay-at-home mom

Interestingly Magda reports never having had an encounter with police, but in the very next sentence reveals her car was impounded: indeed, an encounter with police. Our exchange reveals an interesting distinction made by many Mexican immigrants in the course of my fieldwork. To be stopped by the police implies wrongdoing on the part of the person stopped. To be interpellated by police as an undocumented immigrant who is violating the law by driving challenges their perception of themselves as law-abiding and hardworking.[29] They perceive their illegality as illegitimate: the result of an unfair arrangement in which their labor is desired, but they are not. Consequently, the question "have you ever had an encounter with the police?" is met with an automatic "no" because that time that they did, in fact, encounter the police was not because they were doing anything that they see as wrong. It reflects both a normative evaluation of law and a sense of sadness or shame at having been identified as undocumented. If what it means to "encounter" police is to be guilty of wrongdoing, then Mexican immigrants, even when their cars have been impounded, have not, from their perspective, "encountered" police since they are guilty of nothing more than being subjected to an unfair and historically recent restriction on their ability to drive. Car impoundments mark them as undocumented and Mexican, but they resist this interpellation by rejecting the notion that they really have had a run-in with police in the first place. Car impoundments are not good law. They are instead the local extension of unfair national practices of dispossession and criminalization. This sense of unfairness underpins Magda's mistrust.

Roberto and Maritza, long-term residents of South City who came to the United States in 1996, participated in a community forum with the police chief and several officers, a largely productive and positive conversation, hosted by La Unión. They came away trusting police somewhat. Still their conviction that police racially profile Latinos undercuts that trust, giving rise to their ambivalence.

> I think that I can trust them, according to what I've seen in the last meetings. I don't know if the police officers are racists but despite that I can trust them for our safety, in the first place. I understand that the police have to do their job but sometimes they exaggerate. They focus . . . if ten Americans go in front of me, the police most surely will confront me, no matter if they had the cars torn to pieces, they will focus on me. That is for sure, and I'm not the only to say this, all the Latinos say the same.
> —Roberto, undocumented, South City, 40–50

Positioning Americans opposite Latinos, the disproportionate targets of police, Roberto avoids the label "racist" but remains skeptical of police because of their exaggeration, as he says, or the racial profiling of Latinos.

This qualified trust suggests their ambivalence, and points to the limits of "procedural justice"[30] for mitigating the worst effects of racial profiling by enhancing police legitimacy by stressing respect and courtesy in interaction. Epp, Maynard-Moody, and Haider-Markel, in a highly original survey project, argue that even when officers are polite and courteous, drivers are still left feeling resentful of police.[31] They conclude that this abiding resentment reflects an objection by drivers not to the tone of the interaction, but to the practice that guides it. The problem is not impolite officers (though, clearly overtly racist officers have no place on a police force), but "institutionalized practices," or policies, training, and tactics that incentivize the disproportionate targeting of black and brown drivers. While Epp and his coauthors focus on the investigatory stop, executed with the intent of investigating the driver under the guise of intervening upon some minor violation, the concept of the institutionalized practice illuminates a critical part of the problem between police and Mexican immigrants: even when brought into collaborative settings, like community forums, where relationship building between both groups can occur, these strategies leave intact the underlying practices to which Mexican immigrants object. Certainly respondents deplore poor treatment at the hands of police, but that is an objection not only to tone, but to car impoundments *as a practice*. These community forums encourage Roberto's faith in police, but his ongoing trepidation about police "exaggeration" cannot be assuaged by potlucks and face time. Car impoundments, and the broader perception of police as capricious in their use of race to do their daily police work chafe against his tentative trust, inspiring ambivalence and uncertainty.

This trust is, of course, undermined when law enforcement act directly as immigration enforcement. Magda continues:

M: I don't feel safe in the street during night and more with that of . . . safe communities [Secure Communities], no.

G: No?

M: Because somebody told me that once she was walking on the street I don't if it was on [street name] and she was walking on the sidewalk and suddenly she saw a gang with five or six guys, she was walking and suddenly they grabbed her purse . . . so she called 911 to make the report and the police officers took her away and she was the victim in this case. And the police officer said, "okay, who called 911?" and she said, "I did" and they asked her "do you have documents?" and she said, "no," so they took her away in their patrol car. So, they took her to the police station and then a friend of this person said, "can you imagine that? If the gangs want to kill us we can't even call the police because these gangsters have documents and we don't have legal documents" so, she told me that, this was seven months ago.

G: Wow!

M: They stole her purse and she tried to defend herself because she had her money there and she called the police and she was the one taken away.

G: And because of this story you don't trust. . . .

M: Exactly, that's why I don't feel safe because if you are walking in the street and I don't know, a gang sees you and they do something bad to you and then you will be in the police station instead of these gangsters, they don't take them away. That's what she told me, she was working in a hotel and she was walking to her home. Yes, those are a lot of things that happen but that's the way it is so for that reason I feel safe in my home, I close my bedroom and that's where I feel safe.

The circulation of tales of police abuse also undermines trust because "informal contacts influence immigrants' views of the police and of crime."[32] When police abuse occurs, that abuse is not limited to those directly affected. Immigrants' personal networks amplify the consequences of abuse by proliferating the tale. A single incident can broadly reinforce the perception that police produce more risk than they mitigate. Widely trafficked stories like this one remind immigrants that visibility is dangerous because police might use an encounter as an opportunity to police immigration violations, too. This fear of authority in general is reinforced in these stories and contributes to what I describe in the next chapter as "the shell": immigrant strategies to insulate and avoid, that is, to remain invisible as their primary strategy of risk management.

Detaining the victim in the course of reporting her victimization, moreover, reveals a two-tiered criminal justice system ("we can't even call the police because these gangsters have documents and we don't"). It is precisely this ability to see police as trustworthy that indicates full membership—legal and social—in the polity. While they may depend on the police in an emergency, when they have no other choice, the widespread conviction that calling the police is itself a risk positions immigrants outside the political group of people whom police are bound to protect. To be unable to rely upon those state agents charged with public safety, to be targeted by them instead, marks Mexican immigrants as threatening, criminal, and racially "other."

But their perception of police is not uniformly negative. They are scared, but also dependent on the police to ward off greater danger. Mauricio, a 14-year undocumented resident, sits on the couch next to his wife Maritza, who rejoined her husband in South City four years ago. Both came from Michoacán. Mauricio exemplifies this ambivalence:

> Well, I am scared of the police just because of the driver's license and because of everything you hear on TV, that they are arresting those that don't have a driver's license. It's okay to me to have police. If we didn't have them, the city would be a mess. It already is and if there's no police, it will be even more. It's like when you go here to Los Angeles and it's real chaos because there's almost no police there. There are police but since the city is so big, there are not enough.
> —Mauricio, undocumented, South City, 30–40, landscaping

Mauricio objects to a specific police practice and not to the institution of police. Pointing to the "chaos" of nearby Los Angeles, he perceives a real need for police to prevent crime, even while the threat of an impoundment and arrest makes him fearful. This double bind characterizes the experience of immigrants in this study in general: they fear police even as they rely on them in emergencies.

Of course, not all experiences with police are bad. Xiomara exemplifies the difference positive interactions with police can make in the minds of those immigrants who call on them for help. Xiomara, whom we first encountered in the introduction, called the police in 2007, six years after her arrival to South City, for the same reason she fled her home state of Zacatecas: domestic violence.

X: Another time that I had police in my house was a few years back, but it was for domestic violence. That was also terrible for me. It was a very bad time. It was approximately . . . in 2007, about four years ago for domestic violence in my house, terrible. But that's it.

G: How did the police treat you?

X: Beautifully.

G: Oh yes?

X: Yes, they were very kind to me. Also when they took my son's car I got to speak with a police officer that spoke Spanish, very nice. The police officers have been very kind to me. I am not afraid of them. To the contrary, when I see a police car I feel safe and protected.

G: Wow.

X: It is true.

G: So then it is possible for the police to make you feel comfortable while interacting with them?

X: Yes. Those two occasions that I have had the chance to speak with them, with the police officers, for me have gone very well. For my domestic violence case they sent me some help, like therapy. Very nice. I know and understand that I am without a license and breaking the law, but it is purely out of necessity. Purely out of necessity. Because in Mexico it was the same, domestic violence every day with the father of my children and I came fleeing from the father of my children. So I'm not here because I want to, I came because I had no other choice. When I see the police, I know the risk I am running, but at the same time I feel protected. I feel safe because I know what I am risking, but I know that I have everything okay, I don't have any problems with anyone, I try to do my best in everything and if one day they stop me, which hopefully they don't, I know that I don't have a license. I know it. So when I see them, it does not scare me.

—Xiomara, undocumented, South City, 40–50, housekeeper

Xiomara, an undocumented single mother of three, recalls that police spoke with her in Spanish and connected her with local service providers. Considering the academic literature that has stressed the unique vulnerability of immigrant women to domestic abuse as a consequence of their dependence on resident spouses for their visas, language barriers, and general fear of police that prevents reporting, Xiomara's experience is a powerful example of the way police can counter the presumption that they cannot be relied upon for protection.[33] The significance of that support from police officers, approximately four years prior to the date of the interview, lingers in her memory. Even when they later impounded her eldest undocumented son's car, she continued to regard the police positively: they make her feel protected. Her example is startling evidence of the power of a positive interaction with police. Acutely aware of the risk she runs by continuing to drive without a license, she avoids trouble at all costs, attempting to limit her exposure to police. And yet, her prior experience of the police as protectors militates against a negative appraisal in general. Police stand out as figures of both threat and safety, threatening because they may one day take her car and a source of safety because they helped her extricate herself from an abusive relationship and safeguard her children. This seemingly contradictory stance is emblematic of the way police can either cultivate trust by enforcing criminal law without regard to immigration status or foment mistrust by acting as de facto immigration enforcement agents. In Xiomara's case, both are true, but the power of that positive interaction sustains her faith in police even while she recognizes they may one day be the source of her impoverishment.

Undocumented immigrants see themselves as responsible community members whose technical illegality should not be criminalized by local police who impound their cars. Coupled with the widespread, though not uniform, perception that police target them on the basis of their race gives rise to this fear, which impedes reporting crime and cooperating with police investigations. This fear wrapped in ambivalence is another facet of Mexican immigrants' racial naturalization. To stand outside the protection of law, to be its target for reasons that many Mexican immigrants believe are illegitimate, is to reinscribe hierarchies of citizenship and race in everyday encounters with police. Seeking meaningful forms of belonging and fearing crime, immigrants come to rely on police even while they may not trust them.

The Sense of Law Is Lost

The car impoundment is a de facto, if not de jure, form of immigration enforcement. Mission creep in anti-drunk-driving programs has meant that the vast majority of vehicles impounded at DUI checkpoints are not those of drunk drivers but those of undocumented, unlicensed drivers. Car impoundments executed during regular police patrols are often justified with thin pretexts. Mexican immigrant drivers are stopped on the basis of a minor infraction only to have their vehicles taken from them because they are unlicensed. The widespread perception that officers rely on race to formulate their suspicion, stopping old, run-down cars filled with brown-skinned people contribute to the perception that police target Mexican immigrants as Mexicans whose poverty marks them as racially other. The timing and location of checkpoints at hours when drunk drivers are likely not on the road and on streets trafficked by immigrant workers also evidence the capriciousness of these informal mechanisms of immigration enforcement.

The consequences of this targeting are visible in the material impoverishment that attends a car impoundment, but also in the racial subordination of immigrants, that is their racial naturalization. These encounters affirm to Mexican immigrants their outsider status, despite their earnest attempts to demonstrate their law-abiding and hardworking behavior that is central to Americanness. The implicit and de facto racial effects of the car impoundment indicate its legal and political impacts. Racially neutral on its face, this informal technology of immigration enforcement is also a street-level process of racial subordination, an interactional inauguration to American racial hierarchy in which police cannot be trusted to ensure the safety of immigrants precisely because undocumented Mexican immigrants do not belong to that group of noncriminal citizens whom the police are oath-bound to protect. Direct and indirect experiences with police put Mexican immigrants in their place: outside the law's protection and naturalized exclusively to the US racial hierarchy.

Subordination breeds mistrust. This mistrust, however, is not unequivocal, but rather ambivalent. Dolores captures this sentiment when in response to my question about whether she would call the police in an emergency, she says:

> I would call but I wouldn't give them my name because I'm afraid to be involved, because you have seen such crazy things that you don't know what to expect. The sense of law is lost.
> —Dolores, naturalized citizen, North City, 50–60

At stake in the wake of crimmigration and devolution are, of course, the material interests of immigrants, especially undocumented immigrants, whose illegality impedes their physical and socioeconomic mobility. Also salient are the political consequences of an enforcement regime that operates not only in through widely publicized raids and deportations, but through informal and nominally race neutral practices like the car impoundment. Police work conducted in this way imperils the potential for justice immanent to law.

The car impoundment, as a street-level form of racial naturalization, is but one example of the everyday precarity that defines the social location out of which Mexican immigrants' agency emerges. These quotidian risks give rise to and constrain the scope of their resistance. The car impoundment is but one manifestation of a long history of the inclusion through exclusion of immigrants that haunts their daily lives in the present. The car impoundment as a problem for immigrants emerged in the wake of Proposition 187 and is sustained by the presumptively race-neutral police practice of punishing unlicensed drivers. Dealing with the pitfalls of driving while undocumented is a top priority for Mexican immigrants. Dealing with the broader mistrust that the practice inspires is an issue not just for undocumented immigrants, of course, but also for the broader Latino immigrant community of which they are a part. As I argue in the next chapter, having to contend with these quotidian forms of risk is itself a form of immigrant agency that both inspires immigrants' critical consciousness and constrains the forms of collective mobilization for which they are motivated and available. As I describe, the shell, or the practice of avoiding and insulating oneself from these kinds of risks, becomes a form of protection from these immediate-term risks, as well as an encumbrance to their broader civic and political engagement.

3

The Shell

The Inward Turn in the Everyday Lives of Mexican Immigrants

De mi trabajo a mi casa,	From work to my house
no se lo que me pasa,	I don't know what's going on with me
que aunque soy hombre de hogar,	Although I'm the head of the household
casi no salgo a la calle,	I almost never go out
pues tengo miedo que me hallen,	Because I'm afraid that they'll catch me
y me pueden deportar,	And deport me
De que me sirve el dinero,	What's money good for
si estoy como prisionero,	If I live like a prisoner
dentro de esta gran nación,	In this great nation
cuando me acuerdo hasta lloro,	When I'm reminded of this, I cry
aunque la jaula sea de oro,	Although this cage is made of gold
no deja de ser prisión	It's still a prison

—"La Jaula de Oro," Los Tigres del Norte, 1984

Teresa

I met Teresa through her father Alfonzo, whom I had met at a house meeting in the apartment complex where they both lived. I interviewed several respondents like Teresa at this same low-income housing complex tucked against a bend in the freeway that ran through the westside of South City. The apartments across the street were home to students who attended the city college just on the other side of the freeway. Immigrant residents often complained about the noise that spilled onto the street late at night from their complex. Teresa came to South City with her husband seven years prior to our interview in 2005. Initially, she left her children in her seaside hometown of Lázaro Cárdenas, Michoacán, telling them that she was going to the store and that she'd be back soon. Her children knew something was wrong and cried when she left, just as she did for many months after she arrived in the United States separated from her children. During that first year, she and her husband stayed with her father in a town 20 minutes to the south of South City. At the end of that year, she returned for her two sons, ages 17 and 11, and her daughter, 13, and settled in South City. Her children speak English, though Teresa does not, insisting they speak Spanish at home. She's backed off this demand in recent years since, as the kids say, "Why did you bring us? We have to learn." Though she appreciates South City's beauty, the ample work opportunities, and the sense of inclusion and community she derives from participating in school activities,[1] she fears deportation.

T: No. When I saw them in the apartments I locked myself in here. This happened twice.

G: Twice?

T: Uh-huh, on one occasion they told me not to go out but I had to take my kid to school, so I asked a neighbor if she could take him to school and she did. She said, "They won't do anything to me; I'll let you know when I'm there so that you can open the door for me." And I stayed in here; she had to pick him up from school too. I was getting ready to go to work and I heard that two cars came in but they had no inscription, they got out of the car and that's when I saw the inscription on their backs. So, I called the manager and she told me, "Why didn't you call me? This is private property; they can't just walk in like that. They have to let you know." "I didn't know." They came in through the driveway. At that moment, all kinds of thoughts come to your mind, that they might be coming for you, although you haven't done anything bad, the kids . . . I don't want to separate from my kids.

G: And what happened?

T: No, the person they were looking for no longer lives here. There was a deportation order for him.

Many respondents recounted experiences like this. They hid when they learned ICE was nearby. They relied on documented friends and family to transport kids to school when the risk of doing so yourself was too great. Many had heard stories of neighbors who did not have a deportation order, but when confronted by ICE were detained anyway. In this post-border moment, marked by increasing collaboration between local police and federal immigration enforcement, immigrant communities have responded, out of necessity, with strategies of insulation and avoidance that mitigate the daily risks of apprehension and deportation. While immigrants run these risks to attain greater opportunities for educational, occupational, and economic mobility for themselves and their families, they sometimes feel as though they are imprisoned, as the title of the famous Los Tigres del Norte song allegorizes, in "La Jaula de Oro," a cage of gold. Though their hard work and sacrifice have produced material success, a sense of freedom does not flow from the fruits of their labor. They still experience the United States as a prison.

Car impoundments and ICE raids, informal and formal features of the immigration enforcement regime, are not the only social forces that spur their insulation. The everyday racism and xenophobia of other residents reinforce their racial naturalization.

> T: Sometimes people look at you in a bad way, but I don't mind.
> G: How do you feel when you notice that? What is your reaction?
> T: I simply turn around, but you feel bad, at least at work on one occasion someone said, "Oh, she's Latina, we should shoot her." And I didn't understand [at first] and my son told me what she had said and he asked me, "Mom, why doesn't she like us?" "I don't know. We're not stealing anything from her. Let's go." That was the only occasion, and if my son wasn't there I wouldn't have understood what she was telling me.
> G: How did you feel? Because all that happened in front of your child?
> T: I just told him not to pay attention, we're all the same and we all come here to work, we're not doing anything wrong. And he said, "But she shouldn't have said that." "No, she didn't have to say that." And then he went into his room.
> —Teresa, Mexican, undocumented, 40–50

This woman's casual xenophobia, repeated by her son as he translates from English to Spanish, forms part of the everyday racism that hangs over the Mexican immigrant experience in the United States. While Teresa hides in her room to avoid deportation, her son hides in his to cope with the pain and confusion caused by the woman's racist remark. These are the legal and cultural forces that inspire the shell: those habits of avoidance and insulation that both protect and encumber.

Stories of the Latino immigrant experience in the United States are often rendered in terms of the inequality that many immigrants, especially undocumented immigrants, confront daily. Risk, fear, and uncertainty form central features of the Latino immigrant experience, especially for undocumented immigrants, vulnerable to dispossession and deportation and subject to economic exploitation. And yet, no empirical portrait of this experience is complete without an accounting of the various forms of agency that immigrants manifest in their management of those risks. A consideration of the relationship between everyday risk management and collective mobilization broadens our focus beyond one or the other and raises a new question about how the former is related to the latter.

While social movement organizing was optional—presented by organizers to Mexican immigrants and potential activists—atomized strategies of avoidance and insulation were not. This simple reality forms the quotidian foundation of Mexican immigrant activism. Everyday strategies of risk management form the submerged portion of the iceberg, while the tip represents the marches, rallies, and acts of civil disobedience. These latter forms of immigrant agency are most visible, sensationalized in media, and debated at length by pundits. Avoidance and isolation represent the material moorings of their activism. The contentious activity of Mexican immigrants emerges out of this everyday and embodied negotiation of their economic and legal precarity, the dual risks of dispossession and deportation. Paradoxically, these same strategies that offer cover from the reach of state agents function as barriers to involvement in the wider community, including social movement organizing. I use the metaphor of the shell to capture this duality: immigrants' necessary strategies of avoidance and insulation are both a form of protection and an encumbrance upon social movement emergence.

The Strategies of the Shell

Immigrant respondents employed a variety of strategies for coping with the risks of living and working as undocumented in the city.

Encountering police, generally, and the threat of car impoundments, specifically, constituted the primary risks for many respondents. I ask Lucero, who came to the United States in 1989, what he does to protect himself.

> L: Yes, simply not go out more.
> G: Oh yeah?
> L: Yes, not go out when we don't need to.
> G: Stay at home?
> L: Yes, better to stay in the house. Be more cautious and not go out just to be in the streets, especially in the car.
> —Lucero, Mexican, undocumented, South City, construction worker

Similarly, Xiomara avoids going out, especially driving:

> Yes, I avoid going out a lot, driving. If I do not need to go out, I don't go out. On Sundays I make my kids' food here instead. It is what I try to avoid, driving. If I don't need to, I don't drive. I don't drive and the kids know it. I hear a lot families saying that they went to [a nearby city] and I know that they do not have a license, and I think to myself, "How could they risk it with all their kids, you know?" And that's what I do, I feel safe at home when I am not driving and I try to avoid crowded areas, or driving in places like that.
> —Xiomara, Mexican, undocumented, South City, 40–50, housekeeper

Both respondents make specific reference to avoiding driving because they are undocumented and cannot obtain a driver's license. Driving a car was a necessary risk undertaken by undocumented immigrants, living in California and often working multiple jobs in different parts of the city (especially true for house cleaners and landscapers).

Even when faced with police abuse, Lucero describes avoiding further problems by deciding not to file a complaint:

> L: On one occasion we were going to try to do something but we decided not to in order to avoid further problems.

G: What did you try to do?

L: What happened was that one day we went to [a town just south of the county] and we went to a dance, to a nightclub. When we came out of the nightclub, we were heading to the car and we were smoking a cigarette before getting into the car while we were on our way to where the car was parked. A police officer arrived and yelled at us that we had to leave already, to get in the car and leave. To which we replied, yes. We didn't get offended or anything, we just said yes, that we were going to finish the cigarette and then we would get in the car. But no, he said we had to "beat it" and he got out of the car. Then he told my brother, "I'm going to arrest you and take you in since you don't want to leave," but we still had not gotten to the car. In fact, he was about to get into the car when the police officer told him he was going to arrest him. So they arrested him, but they threw him on the ground and about four or five police officers had him on the ground. Then another police car arrived and the police officer had a baton and he was provoking me. He kept asking me if I wanted trouble with them, too. I don't know what happened at that moment, I tried to look over to see what they were doing to my brother and he grabbed me and threw me on the ground as well. My sister-in-law was going to record it with her camera but the police grabbed her by the throat, threw her, and told her she could not do that. They arrested us both, my brother and me. They held me for almost nine hours. My brother got charged for resisting arrest. And for me they put that, this was what I didn't understand, they got me for being intoxicated. But what was the reason for him having to throw me on the ground and almost dislocating my arm. . . . There is no security with the police. We tried to see about what action to take, to ask a lawyer about what we could do, but my brother didn't want to after all. Because since he wants to get his papers he didn't want to have any problems with the authorities, so he decided to just leave it alone. But yes, it was something that for me was much worse because they nearly scraped most of my face and arm, I can say that they almost broke my arm.

—Lucero, Mexican, undocumented, South City, construction worker

Even after the police nearly broke his arm, he and his brother's undocumented status led them to "just leave it alone" for fear of jeopardizing future efforts at legalization. These protection strategies, avoiding trouble and insulating oneself from risk, become internalized as a mode of being in and moving through the city. Even in the face of violence and clearly perceived injustice, the impulse to protect the gains that they and their families have made by arriving and working in the United States trumps using institutional mechanisms to redress a grievance.[2] Keeping one's head down becomes a habit whose central lesson—lump it and move on—becomes internalized as the default response to the unfamiliar, the risky, and the unjust.

Héctor describes one way undocumented immigrants look out for one another in the face of the threat that police represent to the Latino immigrant community. Some have formed a phone network to avoid DUI checkpoints where many car impoundments occur:

> H: I know some drivers and I know many taxi drivers and also pizza
> men and. . . .
> G: So, people who are working in the city?
> H: Yes, people moving all over the city and if they can't tell me, then [my
> daughter] lets me know or any other friend, they let me know and
> in 5 minutes I call 10 people that I know, I mean, for those without
> driver licenses. And they call another 10 people and after 20 minutes
> most of those in the community without driver licenses will know
> about the inspection and they don't go outside. They don't go to that
> area. And when they change the place of inspection, I have some
> friends who are taxi drivers and pizza men or many other people and
> we start all over again, we keep communication with each other. Very
> quickly and after a while the street is empty but the police [still] stop
> many people because some people are not in touch, they just don't
> know, but we can. . . .
> —Héctor, Mexican, undocumented, 40–50, handyman and
> restaurant employee

A savvy and strategic collective response to the threat of car impoundments: this mobile network still figures as an avoidance and isolation tactic insofar as it does not intend to oppose police or challenge the legal and political structures that render them vulnerable to police apprehension. Using mobile phones to share information helps undocumented

Mexican immigrants insulate themselves from risk and collectively avoid police. And though sharing information across a large group is collective, the activity it informs—avoidance and insulation—is undertaken individually. Primary informant Esmeralda, along with her husband and whatever friends she could gather, would often warn drivers of an upcoming checkpoint by holding signs several blocks ahead the checkpoint, giving undocumented drivers an opportunity to alter their route.

Bayat's quiet encroachment of the ordinary offers a useful conceptualization of this activity because it seizes on the way that largely atomized and individualistic survival strategies are engaged in by whole groups who sometimes act in knowing concert with one another and sometimes do not.[3] In this case, there is a clearly networked quality to these survival tactics: whole groups of immigrants can avoid these risks with this information. And yet, this collective information sharing is leveraged, not to promote coordinated resistance, but to augment individualized strategies of survival and protection.

Avoidance and insulation—remaining home, avoiding crowded places, avoiding driving, and information sharing that facilitates this avoidance—are decidedly forms of agency. And yet, these actions are not undertaken in order to oppose or transform the existing relations of power that render them vulnerable to immigration enforcement. Instead, these are strategies of survival and risk minimization. Individuals seeking to protect themselves and their families from apprehension and property seizure employ these strategies. Sometimes coordinated and sometimes not, avoidance and insulation make a group-level impact when significant segments of this community adopt these tactics. As Héctor mentions, eventually the street is empty, as more and more people learn what part of the city they should avoid. These everyday strategies of risk minimization limit the reach of the immigration enforcement regime: strategies born not of defiance, but of necessity.

Barriers to Participation: El Miedo

My primary informants often described the difficulty of recruiting and retaining members to the regular La Unión immigration committee meetings, in addition to the difficulty in "turning out" people for community events and other key meetings. In the course of my

interviews and observations in both North City and South City, organizers and immigrant residents offered three primary explanations for
this difficulty: fear (*el miedo*), work obligations, and laziness (*la flojera*).
Respondents regularly cited fear of interaction with authorities and
unnecessarily drawing attention to themselves in public as impediments
to greater participation. Roberto, whom we met in the previous chapter
with his wife Maritza, explains:

> R: The changes in immigration made it very difficult to organize a
> movement.
> G: Can you give me an example of the changes in the legislation?
> R: When there was the law SB. . . .
> G: Oh, SB 1070 in Arizona.
> R: Even [here] we can suffer those types of problems, so we thought it
> was better to stop there and leave things the way they were.
> —Roberto, Mexican, undocumented, 40–50

Roberto, Maritza, and their two girls came to South City in January 1996
from Mexico City. They have had four cars impounded, the most recent
after leaving a summer festival. The officer assumed Roberto was driving drunk since, as he says, "he has the face of the drunkard," though
he isn't one. Roberto's medium-brown skin has a rosy glow, especially
around his cheeks. They live in the same mostly immigrant apartment
complex near the city college as Alfonzo and Teresa (from above). They
often notice a patrol car parked outside the 7-Eleven that stands at the
end of the single street that connects the main road to the residential
street where their apartment is located. They have to drive past this
7-Eleven every time they come in and out of their neighborhood. When
they see the officer, they feel nervous, not safe. They recognize that
while no law comparable to SB 1070 has been passed in California, the
potential importation of the aggressive and racist enforcement practices
of Maricopa County's infamous Sheriff Arpaio represents a shot across
the bow for many immigrants. Coupled with the everyday threat that
police represent, it takes little more than the suggestion of apprehension
to deter political mobilization. Fear is both diffuse and potent, reinforcing the reflex to keep one's head down and avoid additional conflict.

THE SHELL | 91

In a group discussion with several women from North City who are more consistently involved with the work of La Unión, I asked why it is difficult to stimulate participation in political activity. Patricia and then Erica explain:

> P: Because they don't want to get involved in these things.
> E: I think it is fear.
> P: I think it's a matter of growing in that respect. Because the majority of Latinos are always saying, "Don't go over there because of that . . . or don't do that because of this. . . ." We're always being brought down so we can never really develop the way we need to. Simply put, we let time pass and expect others to do something. When do we want to get involved? When the issue hits directly in our family or in our own life.
> —Patricia and Erica, 50–60

By "being brought down," Patricia describes a feature of everyday immigrant life, a broadly shared culture of caution that helps immigrants manage risk and protect the gains they have earned through their migration and their labor. This unwillingness to participate can change, however, when immigrant residents have a personal experience with the police or with ICE. In these cases participation arises out of a sense of necessity or desperation. Patricia and Erica articulate exactly the double bind that I call the material moorings of immigrant activism. The experience of "being brought down," of not finding the social mobility promised by the American Dream, can constrain involvement, assuming others will pick up the fight (the free rider problem). But they refine this notion by arguing that if this quotidian struggle is disrupted,[4] if dispossession or displacement are experienced directly, then potential activists may be moved to participation. As I elaborate in the next chapter, disruption can be a powerful motivation to action.

Barriers to Participation: Work

Beyond fear lies a more quotidian barrier. Respondents often cited the pressures of work as a deterrent to participation. For immigrant residents who work long hours for little pay, their scarce free time is often dedicated to family and rest. In a conversation with Mixtec field-workers Santa and Perfecto, he explains:

> S: And you? Is it difficult to get involved in these kind of activities? [interpreting the question in Mixtec for her husband.]
>
> P: [RESPONDING IN SPANISH]: I want to participate in the meetings. I want [the city] to be better, but as my wife said I don't speak English and because we work in the field we get very tired at home. Sometimes my daughter wants me to take her to the park and I feel very tired from working in the field. I also want to go to the school to learn English, but I get very tired and I can't participate, but I'd like to do it. I want to support my children. And I want my children to support the community and to work.
>
> —Santa and Perfecto, indigenous Mexican (Mixtec), undocumented, field-workers

Santa and Perfecto's story evidences the embodied toll of exploitative labor relations. Whereas work may serve as a barrier in a general way, in which it figures as the top priority in the economics of the family, there is another more visceral way in which work serves as a barrier to social movement participation. The physicality of exploitative labor relations renders undocumented immigrants unavailable for protest. Work is an economic lifeline that sustains the family at the same time that it saps the energy that resistance to those very labor relations requires. Santa and Perfecto have worked in the fields in North City for 20 years. Perfecto's fatigue at the end of the day makes it difficult to spend time with his daughter, let alone participate in social movement organizing or other community activities, such as English-language courses. Their social location toiling in the bottom rungs of a segmented labor market is the source of their grievance, a potential inspiration to action, and an impediment to involvement.

The deterrent effect of work ebbs and flows in response to broad-scale economic shifts, suggesting a temporal dimension in immigrants' availability for protest. Teresa's father, Alfonzo, introduced at the beginning of the chapter, describes the difference the Great Recession of 2008 made to his involvement in community work.

A: Before I knew some guys who were [at a local social service organization serving Latinos and Latino immigrants], and I cooperated with
   them with my contribution, because people didn't want to cooperate.
   So, I told [an organizer], "You know what? I'm going to help you with
   my contribution. That's the only way I can help you. Nobody wants
   to come and sometimes I can't come either." But then he stepped out
   too, the crisis came and it ended, we started thinking about ourselves, we could no longer provide money for that, so I lost contact
   with them.

G: What changed after the crisis?

A: The fact that I could work a little bit more. That's why I could attend
   the meetings before, because I had enough time, and now on the day
   I should attend the meeting, I have work to do. And because I'm the
   only employee I can't tell my boss that I'm not going to work late that
   day.

Limited work opportunities in the wake of the economic crisis opened
up time for his participation with this social service organization. But
as the recession gave way to renewed employment opportunities, his
availability for community work shrinks in inverse relation to the time
he dedicates to paid work. The temporal quality of the recession and its
aftermath evidence both their prioritization of work over community
service and the relationship between the economic precarity of working-
class immigrants and their availability for political engagement. Those
immigrants who experience most acutely the precarity imposed by the
exploitation of their labor under neoliberal capitalism are also least
available to combat it.

Barriers to Participation: La Flojera

Participants also cited la flojera or laziness as a reason that immigrant
residents did not become more involved. In observations and interviews, respondents sometimes reported that other immigrants needed
to turn off the *novela*, get off the couch, and participate. A more complicated relationship exists, however, between laziness and the pressures of
work as explanations for nonparticipation. As the following interaction
makes clear, laziness may be an oft-cited reason for nonparticipation

in movement work, but this explanation also eclipses the wider structural disadvantages discussed above. During a North City community summit attended by approximately 100 people designed to address the Latino achievement gap in local schools, I noted the following exchange between two Latina participants, both of whom had children attending local schools:

> A woman raised her hand and she talked about the declining levels of participation among Latinos and she highlighted the march in 2006 as a clear example of when that happened: the potential for Latino activism. But she went on to say that at other marches and in other opportunities for participation locally, she didn't see nearly as much participation. She said that this is a symptom of laziness among people and that they need to get off the couch and participate, take an active interest in their students' education and in the community. As she was saying this, another woman who was working in a small group at the front of the room stepped out from the group at the front of the room and approached the woman who was speaking from her chair in the center of the room. She took 10 steps forward and was now approximately 10 steps away from this woman. She says, "excuse me but some of us have jobs, some of us work in the fields, and we don't have time to participate in these things." She explained that it was not the case that they don't care, but they don't have the same opportunities to participate as other people.

This exchange between two community members was a clear instance in which laziness as an explanation for nonparticipation chafed against the socioeconomic barriers to participation that many immigrant families face. This tension was common in respondents' answers to the question about what barriers exist to broaden immigrant participation in the work of La Unión. Though organizers themselves never blamed laziness for nonparticipation when I was present, they readily understood that organizing immigrant communities requires asking potential activists to sacrifice what little free time they had available to them. What some community members perceive as laziness may be just as readily understood as the enjoyment of the stability they have carved out for themselves through work. This stability is precious because it is hard-won and also fragile, especially so for undocumented immigrants who are subject to deportation. As I described in the introduction, Flacks makes the argument that for most people, grievance is typically confronted not through collective action in public, but through the expansion of the "time, space, and resources available in the personal sphere for personal expression and fulfillment."[5] As we have seen, Mexican immigrants feel most secure in the privacy of their homes where their sense of control and safety is highest. To enjoy what little leisure time is available to them might be better described as coping with the rigors of economic precarity and, for undocumented immigrants, legal vulnerability, in the personal sphere where this heightened sense of control and security allows for personal rejuvenation and fortification. Though leisure in private may do little to alter the broader structures of exploitation that produce immigrants' economic and legal vulnerabilities, to revel in the fragile stability of home is nevertheless a form of agency that prioritizes the enjoyment of the present given the risks of the future. This shell may be an encumbrance to participation in collective action, but its inward focus allows immigrant people a moment of replenishment and escape, though they will soon have to confront again the harshness of labor and public life in the deportation nation.

More commonly laziness and work were woven together in explanations for nonparticipation. Héctor illustrates this tension:

A lot of people have two jobs, most of the people I know have two jobs, five days in the morning and five days during the afternoon and they don't have time and also they have to do their own things and I think they don't earn much money and they don't have the opportunity to have just one job. That is one of the reasons . . . that is the main reason for this situation, people can't go to the meetings or get involved in this organization. And the other reason is that we belong to a culture that is like that, we don't feel interest, we see that we are going through a difficult time but we don't do anything to get information, we don't provide something to the cause and we don't go the meetings.

I think if we have the interest of going to these meetings I think that would have an impact in the police actions or before any other authority, a voice to express our feelings and, if they see the group is strong, if they see there is a lot of people interested in the situation, I think they would feel the impact of all that. But if they see that we are just a few people, just a small group of people they will say "they don't make any noise." So, it is very important to keep looking for plans, for example in the radio or spread the information in the community or programs like these and we could have more people, one by one. Don't expect to receive something, if you don't speak out.

Héctor leads with work as the primary explanation for nonparticipation. This explanation, echoed by nearly all respondents and organizers, is followed immediately by another, though perhaps secondary, issue: culture. Respondents also cited a culture of noninvolvement, of keeping one's head down, whether as a response to poverty and status or as a causal factor in itself, as the other obstacle to the emergence of a sustained movement. As with individual laziness, the problem of cultural explanations lies in its easy comportment with essentialist explanations for complex social and political problems. And as with laziness, for some respondents, this line of reasoning was sufficient in itself. Héctor's comments, as with Patricia and Erica's above, can also be read as a habituated response to risk, which teaches that unless a threat is immediately proximate, it's best to avoid conflict and confrontation. This avoidance may be a feature of Latino culture only to the extent that Mexican immigrants are uniquely targeted by a deportation regime that inspires broader norms of risk aversion and lumping it in order to cope with the pressures of detention, deportation, and dispossession.[6]

Active participants in various community organizing efforts could be especially critical of some immigrants' dedication to work that crowded out time to engage with the broader community. In a group interview with three immigrant women in North City, they explain the limitations of this focus on work. Each of the women in this interview worked in some community leadership capacity: two are caseworkers, one is a school nutritionist. Each had participated in an eight-week training program, facilitated in part by La Unión, that developed community-organizing skills. Ana and then Irene critically discuss the work ethic among immigrant families:

A: Yeah, because the people here dedicate themselves to work and work and work. Neglecting the family and social aspects [of life] a great deal.

I: And personal.

A: Yes. I used to go to the meetings for my daughter, I have always gone since she was in kindergarten, and it was sad because they would always offer classes for parents, etc., and they had very low attendance. These are schools with a large school population [of Latino immigrants] but it was truly very few of us there. And these were trainings that were worthwhile because they would give you important information, and more. So, why wouldn't more people come? Because they are tired, they worked all day, but I think we need to create awareness for families and parents that it is more important to dedicate time for their children than to buy them the latest cell phone in style, or iPod, all those things. They make sure . . . a lot of parents, you can see it, it's very easy to identify, the parents are not present but the children are entirely equipped with the latest technology, and they are working to give their children all the best things, that's what they say. But all the best is not material, I think the best thing is . . .

I: . . . your time. . . .

A: Unfortunately, all of that is not valued here because they dedicate themselves to work. If you ask any immigrant, "What did you come to this country for?"

"To work."

"For what? What did you come to work for?

"To make a better life."

But what is a better life? Material things? A house, a car, and technology for your children? The latest shoes and fashion? That is not what is important. I tell my daughter every day, if you have a BMW and you didn't go to school that does not make you a better person. What makes you a better person is what you know, what you learn and no one can ever take that away from you. You take it with you until the day you die.

—Ana and Irene, 40–50

Ana and Irene question whether an intense dedication to work, when oriented to materialistic goals, results in the genuine betterment of the lives of immigrants, especially their children. This perspective may well be sustained by their elevated role in the community as social service workers to whom others in the immigrant community turn for advice. They argue that this inward focus on work in order to attain material goods prevents some immigrant families from engaging more fully in their children's education and other aspects of their lives. They are implicitly identifying the shell in their critique composed as it is of an extreme work ethic and vulnerability to apprehension and deportation. They highlight its limit by suggesting that a work ethic born of deprivation is perhaps understandable, but contains as much promise as pitfall. It expands opportunities of a certain kind, even while it fosters a myopia focused on the material at the expense of deeper, personal engagement with family and community. The shell is an outgrowth of both fear and focus, the result of two forms of precarity: legal and economic. Its facets reflect a necessary coping with the vulnerability that attends low-wage labor sustained by the deportation regime.

Barriers to Participation: Status

While status was less frequently cited than the above explanations for nonparticipation, some respondents raised doubts about the genuine benefits of passing pro-immigrant legislation and whether the effort to achieve it would be a worthwhile use of time and energy. Ricardo describes why he decided to become more involved with the work of La Unión:

G: Have you ever participated in a community organization?

R: No.

G: No? Okay. Aside from the meeting the other day?

R: No.

G: So then, why did you participate in the meeting? Because that is something new for you, right?

R: Yeah, the first time we participated over there with [José]. I don't know if you remember.

G: Yes, I remember.

R: He called me and told me that the meeting was going to happen. I did not even know what it was about and then once I heard, it seemed important because well I have brothers that are undocumented. I would hope that if something happened that people would get involved, that's also why I held the meeting here so more people would come. It does matter to me and interest me, plus if in the future they decide to give licenses it would benefit me because I have my workers who drive without a license. Only one of them has a license, but I have two others who do not. So it is significant for me, to protect myself from an accident or from my guys getting the cars taken away for not having a license. It's my business and they are driving around in trucks. I would like to get more involved in this.

G: Did something change for you to make you decide to participate more?

R: No, not really. Basically, if it passes then good, if not well . . . but it was not some drastic change in me. No. If it goes forward then I can continue, if not. . . .

G: So it was an opportunity?

R: Exactly. An opportunity came up and if it moves forward, that is great.

—Ricardo, Mexican, naturalized citizen, 40–50, owns landscaping company

When I conducted this interview, I was surprised at the time by the apparent nonchalance of Ricardo's response to the value of greater legal rights for immigrants (a sentiment he echoes in another excerpt below). Working with a social movement organization whose primary mission was obtaining greater legal rights for undocumented immigrants, I noted his relative lack of interest in those goals, as well as my own expectation that he would share them. He recognizes the significance of legalization and driver's licenses for undocumented immigrants, some of whom are his family and employees. And yet, his response suggests that his work and his life would continue with or without increased legal recognition for undocumented immigrants ("No, not really. Basically, if it passes then good, if not well . . . but it was not some drastic change in me. No. If it goes forward then I can continue, if not . . ."). This nonchalance may stem from his own documented status: he is a naturalized citizen, and so legalization is not his problem any longer. Still, he is cognizant of and empathetic toward the situation of other undocumented immigrants in his life. Part of this nonchalance may emerge from the recognition that he, his family, and his coworkers will continue to work and live with or without recognition at law.[7] Ricardo's tepid response is born of his already secure status. It also reflects the primacy of work in the lives of documented and undocumented immigrants alike. The gap that exists between the potential benefits of collective mobilization and the immediate benefits of work is sufficiently wide to make social movement organizing seem beneficial, but not necessary.

For undocumented immigrants, as well, a lack of interest in social movement participation can stem from the perception that the prospect of legalization is highly unlikely. Héctor explains:

H: Or sometimes we know we have a big problem but we don't want to do something to improve the situation.
G: Why not?
H: I think sometimes the lack of time but sometimes it's like . . . our Latino culture is like, "they won't help me anyway," we are like that. And have you noticed that there are a lot of people who say: "why bother? The law will not change."
G: Uh-huh.
H: And that's precisely why the law is the same.
G: It is not worthwhile because nothing is going to be changed.
H: I will lose my time, our society is like that and I know people who are like that, not everybody, but a lot of people are like that.
—Héctor, Mexican, undocumented, 40–50, handyman and restaurant employee

Héctor argues that many people feel as though the additional effort to participate in political action is simply not worth the trouble since "'they won't help me anyway.'"[8] Importantly, Héctor notes that the perception that the law is immutable ensures that it remains unchanged. As I discuss in greater detail in the next chapter, potential immigrant activists had to perceive that an opportunity existed for efficacious political action in order to be moved to action. Participants must reasonably believe that their action will produce results.

The Shell

The shell represents the relationship between immigrants' "inward turn," the adoption of avoidance and insulation tactics, and the obstacles that stand in the way of greater community involvement and political participation among Mexican immigrants.

Structurally vulnerable to police apprehension and deportation and nearly singularly focused on work and family, the social location of the Mexican immigrants in this study is usefully characterized using the Weberian metaphor of the shell. In Weber's *The Protestant Ethic*, he describes the "iron cage": a metaphor for the way rationalization makes social institutions and daily life more predictable and controllable, but also more inflexible, impersonal, and less autonomous.[9] In the context of early capitalism and the advent of modern bureaucracy, Weber described both the structural permanence of rational bureaucracy and the growing individual dependency on rationalization at all levels of daily life. Derek Sayer argues that the "iron cage" is an "unfortunate translation."[10] He explains that the "shell" is a better analogy:

> If we are to translate metaphorically, a better choice of analogy than Bunyan's man in the iron cage . . . might be the shell (also Gehäuse) on a snail's back: a burden perhaps, but something impossible to live without, in either sense of the word. A cage remains an external restraint: unlock the door, and one walks out free. This Gehäuse is a prison altogether stronger, the armour of modern subjectivity itself. Dependency on "mechanized petrification" has become an integral part of who we are.[11]

Individuals have become increasingly dependent on rational organization, even as it constrains them. In this way, rationalization is both a structural characteristic of early capitalism and a feature of modern subjectivity. Extending this metaphor to the experiences of Mexican immigrants, the shell captures the simultaneity of protection and encumbrance. It represents the dilemma faced by many undocumented immigrants: their protective strategies of insulation and avoidance not only minimize the risk of apprehension and deportation, but also form a barrier to participation in social movement activity. The barriers to participation described above, coupled with the everyday work of avoidance and insulation, evidence an inward turn that stems both from immigrants' focus on betterment of self and family (often inspiring migration in the first place) and from their strategic management of the daily risks of deportation and dispossession.

My conversation with Francisco, a young Mexican immigrant working in the marketing department for a local Spanish-language radio station in North City, inspired the metaphor of the shell, which he describes thusly:

F: They are in a box. The people are in a box.

G: In what sense?

F: In the sense that they don't have anyone to take us out of there and show them the path. Especially here in [the city], we're 70 percent of the community, the Latino community, and there aren't people to represent us and take us out of our comfort zone. There isn't anyone to take them out of this box and show us other things in the community. It's also difficult because the people drive the city, but there is no help. They need someone to grab them by the hand and show them the community because the people here in the city, Latinos, don't do it for themselves. They don't go out and try to get out of their comfort zone, so they need someone from the city or a leader from the community to grab them by the hand and show them what's out there and how to get involved.

—Francisco, Mexican, naturalized citizen, North City, 20–30, marketing

I met Francisco through his then-fiancée and primary informant Leticia. Francisco was often at Leticia's side during La Unión events and himself coordinated a Latino business group that promoted Latino enterprise, facilitated networking, and assisted new business owners. He shared with Leticia a dedication to their hometown of North City, particularly to the Latino immigrant community. Francisco notes that even while Latinos make up 70 percent of the population of the North City, they have very little representation in city government and in local business. He explains this state of affairs with the metaphor of a box in which Latinos are stuck. This box or shell reflects a widely shared practice of avoidance and insulation that mitigate the risks that attend living and working as an immigrant, especially an undocumented immigrant, in the city. This aversion to risk bleeds into a more general aversion to the unfamiliar as the shell is folded into the identities of immigrants who are living and working at the edges of US economic and social life. Leadership from the city or from the community, Francisco argues, is critical if Latinos are to overcome these barriers.

Returning to my conversation with Ricardo, he describes an extreme work ethic, which functions to improve the financial security and educational and occupational mobility of the family—priorities for Ricardo—but also deters participation in politics and community activities. Ricardo, while a naturalized citizen who enjoys protection from deportation, still evidences the shell:

> R: I don't involve myself too much in the whole solving issues business, but yes a little bit only not much. I prefer to be separate from that and focus on my business and my family and that's it. I would rather not involve myself with political problems and such. I do vote during elections here for mayor and the sort, but nothing further. I don't really involve myself in issues of whether the city is good or not. I feel that it is okay that's why I don't. . . .
> G: But why?
> R: I don't know. I am very reserved. I don't like to go out much except on the weekends with my family to [the main] street. We walk around and see the city, but that's it.
> —Ricardo, Mexican, naturalized citizen, 40–50, owns landscaping company

Several moments later in the same interview, Ricardo says:

> Maybe because I got that fixed as soon as I arrived. I got my papers right away. I never went back to Mexico illegally. When I came, it took three years and I got my papers. And no, I never felt . . . at that time I was working for someone else and that is all we did. I worked seven days a week. I worked in landscaping seven days of the week, including Sundays. And that's why I never really felt . . . well in other words, my life has been nothing but work. All my life I have worked since I was young. I have no vices, I never drank, nothing, so I just work and work. So no, I never felt neither

better nor worse; I always felt good just working. I got my papers and kept doing the same thing, just working. Nothing really changed.

An extreme work ethic forms a central part of the identities of many immigrant workers and underpins a desire to focus on bettering self and family through work and in lieu of participation in social movement organizing.[12] Even after adjusting his status and exercising his right to vote, Ricardo continues to "keep his head down" and focus on work in order to stay out of trouble.[13] Despite his secure legal standing, his approach to work is embedded in his sense of self and everyday practice. The barriers to political participation are not only external to immigrants, but also internalized responses to the economic precarity of immigrant life in the United States. These ways of being—keeping one's head down—persist even after legal status is achieved, alleviating some of their legal precarity, suggesting that the barriers to wider civic engagement are embedded in the subjectivities of immigrants.

The shell becomes a way of living and moving through the city. These habituated strategies of risk avoidance and minimization become sedimented at the level of identity. The shell is not the expression of ongoing rational cost-benefit analyses. Instead, it is a way of life, a reflex, developed in response to the economic and legal vulnerability with which immigrants reckon daily.

Engaged in out of necessity, this inward turn stands, nonetheless, as a barrier to participation in social movement organizing and community engagement more generally. The very same tactics that allow undocumented Mexican immigrants to manage the risks of everyday life also deter participation in contentious activity. While scholars have unequivocally demonstrated the possibility and power of immigrant political activity,[14] this political action is not an automatic outgrowth of the threat of structural violence that so many immigrant communities confront daily. Instead, these manifestations of political action are cultivated over time and through community organizing: questions that I attend to in the following chapters.

Conclusion

Collective mobilization among undocumented immigrants faces a particular set of obstacles that emerge from the specific social location of undocumented Mexican immigrants in the United States: they are economically necessary, but socially unwanted and politically marginalized. The consequent uncertainty and risk that they face inspire strategies for avoidance and insulation that also come to constrain collective mobilization. The specific social location of Mexican immigrants—characterized by an extreme work ethic and the daily management of risk that attends their and their loved ones' deportability—mitigates their vulnerability at the same time it obstructs participation in collective action designed to alter the broader conditions that give rise to that vulnerability in the first place. The barriers to participation in social movement organizing range from fear to work to purported laziness.

This inward turn is a response to precarity of two kinds: economic and legal. An extreme work ethic is central to the identities of the Mexican immigrants in this study; it serves to ward off economic deprivation (often their motivation for migration in the first place), and, at the same time, it can foster a myopic focus on work at the expense of other personal and political pursuits. Deportation and dispossession are rather different kinds of precarity; their violence more pointed and immediate. Avoidance and isolation are the default remedies. These become folded into the subjectivities of Mexican immigrants whose primary response to the unfamiliar is avoidance and to injustice, lumping it. These are the material moorings of immigrant activism.

I capture these responses to precarity in the metaphor of the shell: strategies that offer cover from the reach of the state and the threat of impoverishment also function as barriers to social movement participation aimed at transforming the structures of inequality that give rise to Mexican immigrants' grievances in the first place. By considering multiple forms of agency at once—namely, everyday forms of agency outside social movement organizing—the quotidian origins of Mexican immigrant organizing come into focus. The May Day marches of 2006 offered a dramatic example of the power and scope of immigrant political action. But as immigrant agency goes, spectacular outpourings of political outrage of this sort are only the tip of the iceberg. While social movement organizing may be optional for many Mexican immigrants, everyday strategies of risk minimization are not. They are irrevocably related to broad-scale contentious action because these avoidance and insulation tactics are necessary and, at the same time, moor their collective action to the exigencies of deportability.

To be clear, I am not arguing that immigrant subjects passively accept or simply learn to tolerate the conditions of labor exploitation, racial subordination, and gender violence that so often attend the immigrant experience. My claim is that while immigrants engage in collective political action, this resistance does not exhaust the many forms of agency in evidence within immigrant communities, nor does it spring automatically from their grievances. Nor am I arguing that undocumented immigrants are "self-segregating," and so their marginalization is basically their fault. I argue that the practices of avoidance and isolation that I characterize as everyday forms of agency are strategic and savvy responses to the daily risks of exploitation, property seizure, apprehension, and deportation that immigrants face. I do not claim that the barriers between strategic avoidance and insulation and social movement organizing that compose the shell render social movement organizing impossible or even unlikely. As the historical record bears out, these barriers are regularly overcome and the pathway for political participation cleared. I offer here a reflection on the relationship between contemporary relations of racial subordination and the complex forms of agency inspired and constrained therein.

Indeed, the next chapter follows the emergence of immigrant activists as they come out of the shell and participate in social movement organizing. As immigrants mobilize collectively, however, the shell is not entirely left behind. Elements of the shell—its focus on pragmatic, material results—abide in the instrumental quality of their organizing. These individual and collective forms of immigrant agency are not walled off, one from the other. They bleed across these categorical boundaries, inspiring a politics that are at once pragmatic and potentially liberatory.

4

Instrumental Activists

A Pragmatic Immigrant Politics of Making History to Make Life

Pragmatic Participation

When we last encountered Edgardo in Chapter 2, he described his utter lack of faith in police. Late in that same interview, I asked him what his ideal community would look like.

> Well, in reality, to be very honest, I don't believe that a perfect community exists. However, there can be more flexibility. Flexibility, because I believe that we too have the right to have a car, that my friend can come over from the [next] street and not be stopped because he does not have a license, or that I can go to the store and not have to come home pushing a shopping cart because I don't have a vehicle to drive, you know what I mean?
> —Edgardo, Mexican, undocumented, South City, 40–50, owns
>   small party supply business

To be able to drive is to secure a basic sense of dignity: not pushing the shopping cart home. Edgardo had participated in organizing activities with La Unión, though only sporadically since he often had other work or family responsibilities to attend to. The desires that underpin his political action suggest a more grounded and quotidian set of commitments. Working with a social movement organization, I was struck again and again by the pragmatic scope of immigrants' demands. Even among those who participated regularly in La Unión's movement work, they sought not to transcend but to burrow into the normative conventions of work and family that attend legal status.

Though immigrant activism faces a series of unique barriers, the historic marches of 2006 and the wave of organizing in cities and states that followed remind us that immigrant social movements are possible and probable in an era of mass deportation and failed reform. And yet, when they occur, the shell is not entirely abandoned. The material moorings of immigrant activism are visible in their motivations for participation: instrumentally, to protect what concrete gains they had secured for themselves and their families in their time in the United States. Their politics were motivated by the promise of stability that might be realized by acting collectively.

The collective mobilization of the immigrants in this study, while it exceeds the confines of the shell, is also moored to it: their activism remains concrete and pragmatic in its scope. Immigrants, especially undocumented immigrants, *must* engage in avoidance and isolation to secure their person, property, and mobility, both physical and socio-economic. This everyday risk minimization moored the activism of the Mexican immigrants in this study to the betterment of their quotidian circumstances. Even the most far-reaching expression of immigrant agency—social movement organizing—is both enabled and constrained by its material roots. The same thing that makes collective action worth-while is also what limits its scope: namely, the desire to *adelantarse* or *superarse*, to get ahead and better oneself and one's family. The prag-matic scope of their political action suggests that agency should not be uncritically conflated with progressive or radical activism.[1] These immi-grant activists engage in social movement organizing instrumentally, to the extent that it can aid in securing greater stability and stasis in pursuit of their primary goal: making life. The political activity motivated by these desires reflects not simply a progressive politics oriented to social justice, but a desire for the stability and stasis that political action may be able to secure.

They report wanting stable employment, the opportunity to take out a loan to start a business or buy a home, and educational opportunities for their children: often the very same goals that motivated their migration in the first place. La Unión organizers played a key role in shaping im-migrant politics, identifying the targets, and shaping the tactics for their campaigns. Some immigrant activists incorporated these organizing mod-els into their own evolving political consciousness, especially "core lead-ers" upon whom La Unión organizers regularly relied and who were most familiar with the tactical strategies and activist philosophies of La Unión (for more, see the appendix). In this way, La Unión organizers were not working to organize apolitical immigrant subjects. Instead, their efforts were always in dialogue with immigrants' own sophisticated understanding of their relationship to the structural features of nation and neighborhood that constrained their life chances. While full-time, paid organizers may be motivated to participate in politics for politics' sake, immigrant participants were more often motivated by the prospect of achieving concrete and material improvements in their daily lives.

Coming out of the Shell: Organizing Resistance among Mexican Immigrants

In South City, the idea for a house meeting campaign emerged to address the barriers to participation I outlined in the previous chapter. As I described in the introduction, the house meeting campaign was a central organizing strategy among César Chávez, Dolores Huerta, and the United Farm Workers. The idea is simple: organizers reached out to community leaders and core organizational constituents and asked them to host a house meeting to which they invite their family, friends, and neighbors. Gathered together in living rooms, in garages, and on patios, organizers made presentations to the assembled community members, solicited their grievances, and attempted to recruit them to future social movement work, such as rallies, marches, lobbying, and so on.

South City primary informant Esmeralda, naturalized citizen and longtime La Unión volunteer, drew on this house meeting tradition to expand La Unión's reach by going out to the community instead of asking the community to come to La Unión's offices. In the period from mid-December 2011 to the beginning of April 2012, or approximately three and one-half months, we hosted approximately 50 house meetings and contacted several hundred local residents.[2] In addition to offering information and discussing legal rights, Esmeralda used these meetings as opportunities to stress the importance of participating and showing up to movement activities, such as hosting the next house meeting or public forum.

Inviting Activists

Some respondents needed only to be invited to activism. Xiomara, for instance, contends that she did not need to be convinced to participate, only asked.

> G: How did Esmeralda convince you to have a meeting at your house?
> X: How did she convince me? Well, the thing is that she didn't need to convince me. I heard in one of the meetings all the good things and great information that you have for us that we don't know about. I am sure I am not the only one; there are other people here in this neighborhood that don't know about everything that is happening. And thanks to you all, I want to have the meeting here at my house and I have the hope of doing another one with even more people.
> I want to ask people to come because it is something that is very important and that everyone needs to be aware of. Emeralda did not have to convince me, I did it out of the kindness of my heart and I will do it again!
> —Xiomara, Mexican, undocumented, South City, 40–50, housekeeper

Countering my presumption that she needed to be convinced, Xiomara asserts that she needed only to be invited. Even though Xiomara did not need convincing to participate in the house meeting campaign, her relationship with South City organizer Esmeralda likely formed an important part of her calculus to participate. When Xiomara moved to South City, Emeralda was one of the first people she met. Esmeralda, who works as a "family advocate" at a local elementary school, helped enroll her son in school and assisted Xiomara in finding a job. Over the years, Esmeralda was one of the first people whom Xiomara turned to when the police impounded her car and then when she survived domestic violence. Her acceptance of this invitation hinged on her relationship with Esmeralda. The trust between them critically motivated Xiomara's willingness to participate.

The invitation was not so simple after all. Xiomara needed not only to be asked, but to be asked by the right person. Xiomara's subsequent participation grew both out of her commitment to her community and out of her commitment to Esmeralda, to whom she felt connected and perhaps indebted. Importantly, trusted leaders needed to extend the invitation. As community organizing goes, I don't think this point can be overstated. Esmeralda's deep roots in South City and her place of leadership as the go-to person for the many immigrant parents whose children attended the school where she worked earned her a certain respect and authority in the broader Latino community. Her effectiveness as a community organizer, specifically getting people to participate, springs from an organic trust that she had cultivated with the local community over many years. The social movement literature has long pointed to the critical role of social movement organizations (SMOs) in sustaining protest. Organizations work best when their staff and volunteers are organically connected to the communities that they represent.[3]

Cultivating Activists

But more often, participants expressed reluctance in committing to future movement work, including hosting a house meeting. They stressed work and family commitments, as well as fear of exposure to the authorities by participating in these activities. In order to overcome these objections, Esmeralda used a number of rhetorical strategies designed to stress immigrants' shared destiny and the power they have when they act collectively. She also drew on immigrant community members' own experience of their daily travails in order to transform those grievances into collective action.

In one such house meeting in January 2012, we meet in Regina's small second-story apartment. When Esmeralda and I first arrive, Regina and her husband invite us to eat. Most of the group that they had invited to this house meeting live in the downstairs apartment directly below Regina. She serves *albondigas* (meatball) soup with tortillas. We sit down to eat around a small, round table whose tablecloth is covered with a thick protective layer of plastic. While light food and drink were nearly always offered at house meetings, it was rarer to sit down to a full meal together. The effect is at once relaxing and unifying as we make small talk about our days, getting to know one another a bit before the six neighbors from downstairs join us. When we finish eating, we soak our dishes in the sink and join the neighbors who are arriving in Regina's small living room. As Esmeralda introduces herself and La Unión, participants pepper her with questions. She answers them quickly, but reminds the assembled group that it would be better to pose these questions to the police chief himself, with whom she had scheduled an upcoming public forum regarding car impounds (a meeting recounted in more detail in the next chapter). As we talk, one of the participants recounts to

Esmeralda and to the small, assembled group the story of *el pajarito,* or the little bird. A middle-aged man with dark weathered skin says that a little bird lived in the forest with its family. One day the forest caught fire, threatening the bird's family and all the other animals that lived in the forest. As the fire grew, the little bird left its nest and flew to the nearby lake. There, the little bird dove and dipped under the surface of the lake for but a moment, just long enough to wet its wings. It reemerged from the lake and flew over the fire, flapping its wings and raining water droplets down on the fire. The man pauses here and then continues. By itself, the little bird cannot put out the fire. But if all the birds in the forest join together, the water they drop on the fire will not amount to mere droplets, but to a rain that will put the fire out. Esmeralda excitedly seizes on this near-perfect encapsulation of the very mind-set that she hopes to inculcate in her small audience. She stresses that acting together the birds can put out the fire, but acting alone the water droplets from the wings of a single bird cannot put out the fire.

The story demonstrates the power of collective action. It contains a negative and positive lesson. First, the smallest actions, when performed in concert, can produce significant changes for one's community. Though we may feel as though we cannot have a significant impact on broad-scale social issues, together our small actions can produce significant change. Second, the story emphasizes the shared destiny of the immigrant community. Esmeralda seeks to cultivate a sense of shared fate by drawing attention to a generally shared socioeconomic location and experience of inequality related to race, labor exploitation, gender, and immigration status that are at once positively and negatively valenced. The story allegorizes a common refrain in the labor movement: *La unión hace la fuerza,* there is strength in numbers. When we act collectively, we are positioned to win concrete improvements for our community: an imperative she regularly refers to as a "responsibility." But the story also contains the warning that if we fail to act together the lives of these Latino immigrants could worsen. The forest will burn. The dual quality of this allegory offers both positive and negative incentives for collective action, to convince listeners that the additional effort and sacrifice that collective action entails are worthwhile and necessary.

In another house meeting on South City's westside in mid-January 2011, we sit in Lourdes's living room, sipping *atole.* Three couches against three walls form a U shape around a television and entertainment unit. As neighbors file inside, some of whom were sitting on the front porch prior to the meeting, loud music spills out of a back bedroom where someone has opened a door. Esmeralda, half-jokingly, asks whether whomever is at the back of the house will be joining us. Lourdes gets up and walks down the hallway adjacent to the living room. Soon, the music quiets, but the man, whom we later learn is a family friend staying with Lourdes temporarily, does not join the group. One participant has brought her teenage son to the house meeting. His presence stands out since house meeting participants are typically adults in their middle years.

As we begin, Esmeralda impresses upon the approximately 15 people gathered the importance of telling their story. We are preparing for a community forum with the local police chief, during which we will ask for an end to car impoundments for unlicensed drivers, which have disproportionately affected the undocumented immigrant community. She asks if anyone in this house meeting would be willing to share their story during the community forum. She cautions that if only the community advocates like her and I attend, but directly affected community members do not, the police chief will wonder *quien le importa*, who cares about this issue?

Esmeralda presses Lourdes, our host, to tell her story. She seems reluctant. She speaks a sentence or two before Esmeralda has to press her for additional details. She does so three times as Lourdes recounts her story. She says that she was backing out of her driveway one morning when she struck a fence post in her front yard, knocking it over. Her neighbor, a nosy woman who works for the police department as an administrator, saw this and called the police, even though the "accident" took place on Lourdes's own property. When the police arrived, they discovered that the car was registered to someone else and that she didn't have a driver's license, so they impounded the car.

Esmeralda punctuates the subsequent silence, as she often does, with *ahora* and a dramatic pause. She says that it's precisely these kinds of stories that we need to have for our meeting with the chief so that he understands just how serious this issue is and how it has affected so many in our community. She flips open a binder she is holding (indicating a stack of written testimonials that she has collected) and reiterates that Lourdes is not the only person in this position. In fact, she has collected many testimonies about people who have unfairly had their cars impounded. She says that if you're not comfortable, it's okay not to tell your story, just be present and raise your hand when Esmeralda asks who has had one car impounded. Two? Three? She encourages the people in the room to raise their hands all the way up. She raises her hand only partway, level with her shoulder and in a timid, quaking voice says "no así, pero así!" raising her hand as high as she can reach. She is encouraging people to work past their fear of authority and to assert themselves. Esmeralda goes on to say that she understands that there is a lot of fear in the community, but this is "nuestra lucha, nuestra comunidad, y nuestra responsibilidad." Even though we are afraid, we must fight in order to make change happen.

In both voice and comportment, she encourages the group to be assertive and confident, anticipating their reluctance to speak out in the face of authority. In her exhortation to raise their hands all the way up, she is working to shake her audience free from the embodied constraints of the shell, to speak boldly in the presence of authority. She also repeatedly refers to "our" community and "our" fight and "our" responsibility in order to impress upon the group the shared destiny of the immigrant community and the responsibility incumbent upon each member to stand with one another in the stewardship of that community. She offers a visual aid, a stack of testimonials, each recording a story much like the one our host shared with the group. Esmeralda works to lessen any shame or isolation that crops up when the police impound undocumented immigrants' vehicles by stressing how many other immigrants have found themselves in a similar situation. She exhorts them to action by stressing the commonalities in their experiences and the responsibilities they have to one another as immigrants who are vulnerable to the many risks of living out of status. As she issues these pleas, her voice and energy oscillate from assertive and energetic to subdued and solemn, communicating both the urgency and the gravity of these demands.

The previous executive director for La Unión, Ana, had a common retort when met with immigrants who were fearful of participation. She would say "you already took the biggest risk when you crossed the border. If you can risk that, then you can do this, too." The simple fact of their unauthorized migration became evidence that they were not in fact as risk-averse as they might think.

Esmeralda had another strategy for shaking immigrants of this fear. Recognizing the shell as the preferred mode of coping with risk and vulnerability, she would undermine the risk-management strategies of isolation and avoidance favored by immigrants, especially the undocumented. She might say, for instance, that it is not enough to drive well and keep your head down because the police will always find some excuse to stop you and impound your car. She gives the example of a rosary *colgada* (hung) from the rear-view mirror. While this basic display of religious devotion may not seem in the least bit risky, Esmeralda explains that the police can and will use it to stop you, since it is technically an infraction to hang anything in your car that could distract the driver or impair the driver's vision.[4] Good behavior does not put one beyond the reach of the police. Esmeralda's intent is not to spread fear, but to undermine undocumented immigrants' reliance on individual risk management to spur their participation in collective action. The strategies of the shell will not deliver immigrants from dispossession, detention, and deportation. Only social movements can do that.

In North City, I attended these house meetings with North City organizer and primary informant Lucero in late August 2012. In one such meeting, we gather in Lupe's garage. The garage is situated at the back of a long lot. It appears she may use the space for entertainment or storage. Round tables are stacked against one wall and a wet bar sits toward the rear of the garage. Hip-hop music spills down from a room above. The meeting is set for 6:00 PM, but most arrive closer to 6:30. Lupe has arranged metal folding chairs in a circle around an easel that Lucero has set up. Once the approximately 10 participants arrive, Lucero explains the origins and mission of La Unión, solicits their concerns about the local community and writes them on an easel, and finally attempts to secure their commitment to attend a *junta grande*, a large meeting where they will plan their fall 2012 electoral organizing campaign. Lucero outlines quantitative goals for the campaign: the number of precinct captains, *ayudantes* or helpers, and precinct walkers that they will need to win.

As this conversation continues, I note that Lupe gets up frequently to arrange food on the table or check the coffee or move things around. As she's doing this, Lucero is asking people to fill out "commitment cards," which are quarter sheets of paper requesting their contact information with check boxes next to the activities that they will commit to, including attendance at the junta grande and volunteering to be a precinct walker. One woman says she'll go to the junta grande but won't commit on the card because it's too far in the future. She doesn't want to say she'll do something and then not be able to attend in the end and make someone upset as a result. Others start to offer reasons people may not show up.

Lucero responds, this time at a slightly higher volume, that we have to *quitar los pretextos*, stop making excuses, and convince people to show up. It is our job to make them see how important it is to do this work as a community. Only a few people fill out the commitment cards. Lucero sits next to some attendees and fills the cards out for them. Lucero suggests that Lupe host another house meeting. She responds, "What do I say to them?" The others suggest that she ask the other neighbors whom she didn't invite today. The one male who is present at the meeting, a man in his 50s with dark, weathered skin and a cap, stands to leave and says that if he is here, he'll come to the meeting.

In a subsequent meeting in another North City neighborhood, we encountered the same man again. Lucero asks him again if he plans to attend the junta grande. The man responds, "If I don't have to work, I'll be there." Clearly exasperated, Lucero retorts briskly, stuttering a bit, "If none of us had to work, we'd all be there." Lucero goes on to say that we will always have other responsibilities, but we must make this work a priority because the safety and betterment of our community depend on it.

I found this waffling from the house meeting participants interesting because in the course of lamenting the barriers to participation for other members of the community, they are themselves reluctant to commit to the upcoming events that Lucero wants them to attend. Their initial reactions speak to the obstinacy of the shell. Even as they recognize the barriers and attitudes that exist about participation in social movement organizing, they find those same barriers difficult to surmount themselves.

Lucero, like Esmeralda, often escalated the urgency of his requests by using more assertive language and addressing each person individually in front of the group, asking for their specific commitment. He would occasionally tell attendees to stop making excuses and stress their responsibility to commit to this work. In other meetings, Lucero offered an oft-cited refrain he learned from César Chávez when he used to organize alongside him with the United Farm Workers: "Ochenta por ciento de organizar es recordar," 80 percent of organizing is reminding. Persistence is an organizer's central ethic.

These interactions illuminate the challenges organizers faced when recruiting Mexican immigrants to social movement work, as well as the strategies they employed to overcome them. Forming and stewarding trusting relationships with community members, offering multiple forms of higher risk and lower risk participation, and using more assertive language to cajole commitment from otherwise reluctant participants, Esmeralda and Lucero stressed the responsibility, born of their linked fate, that each participant had to their community.

Close Calls

A close call with immigration enforcement motivated some immigrant respondents to participate in La Unión organizing efforts. A number of the immigrant community members whom we recruited to offer testimonies at key meetings, for instance, had either experienced or witnessed a close call with immigration enforcement and had turned to La Unión organizers with whom they had a relationship for help.

In one such instance in April 2011, I ride with another South City organizer Michelle to a legislative visit where we will lobby our state representative for his support of an anti-deportation bill. Michelle is young, recently graduated from the local university, and very soft-spoken. Still, she had taken to the role of community organizer with verve, working long hours and earnestly seeking out relationships with La Unión volunteers. During this meeting, she had arranged for a community member to tell the story of his brother who had nearly been deported a few weeks earlier. As we make our way across town in her car, she previews the story that this young man will share with the politician.

This young man had been pulled over to the side of the road with his key in the ignition and the engine on so that he could send a text message. A police officer noted this as he drove by and stopped the young man. He was undocumented and so he didn't have a driver's license to produce when the officer asked for one. The officer arrested the young man, whose fingerprints were shared with ICE through Secure Communities and a detainer was issued. Sometime later, ICE arrived to take him into custody. The young man never signed a voluntary departure order and eventually was brought before an immigration judge, who set bail. That same day, his mother, who had offered her son's testimony in an earlier legislative visit, was in Los Angeles posting bond for her son: a process that had taken her most of the day. They expected that her son would be released this same evening at 5:00. In recounting how this young man's mother came to contact La Unión in the first place, Michelle says that they had a mutual friend who had encouraged her to do so and that, without this mutual friend's support, she was fearful of reaching out, even to La Unión.

Struck by this, I remarked how surprised I was to hear that the fear in the community ran so deep that some Mexican immigrants regarded even immigrant advocacy organizations like ours with suspicion. Michelle responded that such a fear was common. I asked her whether it was typically a personal experience with immigration enforcement that caused people to become more involved with La Unión, sharing their stories during a legislative visit, for instance. She responded that it was. Though many undocumented immigrants have a generalized fear of immigration enforcement, they don't think that they or another loved one will be caught. People often become more involved with La Unión's work after a harrowing experience with immigration enforcement. It was interesting that immigrants experience a palpable fear of enforcement but do not think they will be directly affected. People seem to become "activated" after an immediate experience with immigration enforcement. Michelle agreed that this was often true.

The shell, as I described it in the previous chapter, insulates immigrants from risk at the same time as it forms a barrier to social movement participation. This shell also produces a limited and normalized sense of invisibility that, in turn, contributes to the perception that the actual likelihood of their apprehension is low. This fragile sense of relative safety is shattered when a family member or loved one encounters immigration enforcement. In this instance, this invisibility functions in two ways. It produces the perception that participation in civic organizations and social movement organizing (even contacting an SMO for help) is a risk: the risk of being made visible and potentially drawing the unwanted attention of authorities. On the other hand, this invisibility, produced by the shadows of illegality under which undocumented people live, produces a sense of insulation that makes distant the threat of immigration enforcement. It is something to be feared, but ultimately unlikely to affect one directly. A close call with local police and immigration enforcement moved some undocumented immigrants to participate in social movement organizing.

Prior to devolution or the widespread embrace by local authorities of immigration enforcement, many migrants understood that if they could make it across the US-Mexico border, then they would be able to pursue work and family life in relative peace, free from the threat of apprehension. We are now witnessing a shift in which enforcement is no longer relegated to the border. A clandestine crossing is only the first of many potential encounters with the state. The broadened scope of immigration enforcement has consequently extended risk beyond the moment of crossing and into everyday life.

Status and Responsibility

Documented immigrants, a minority in my sample, sometimes evidenced an elevated sense of responsibility to their community that stemmed from their legal status. Lupita, who works as a hospice care nurse, came to the United States 23 years prior to our interview. She flew from her home state of Guerrero, Mexico, to the city of Tijuana, where she used her sister's resident ID card to cross at the Tijuana–San Diego border without authorization. South City was her first and only destination. There she met her husband, whom she married after one year. She gave birth to their first daughter a year later and a second daughter four years after that. She remembers those early years, when her daughters were young, as filled with long days of cooking, cleaning, and child care. Later a shift in her eldest daughter's school policy meant the curriculum would change from bilingual to English-only. This spurred Lupita to learn English so that she could more readily communicate with teachers and administrators. She began taking English as a second language (ESL) classes at the local community college, leaving her children with the school day care. As her English improved, she began to seek out work outside the home, eventually landing a job as a certified nursing assistant with a hospice care service. I asked her if she feels as though she is a part of the community.

> When do I feel like that? Well, like for example when they called me [to remind me] to vote. Yes, my husband got my documentation in order. He was already a resident when I married him so he fixed my immigration status. Then later I got my visa and I went to Mexico, I got my passport. After that I started studying for my citizenship. And so now when they call me to vote, or I get calls from the school to ask for my opinion, or even when I'm working because I am serving others, I feel happy.
> —Lupita, Mexican, naturalized citizen, 40–50, hospice care nurse

Lupita takes pride in her community involvement ("I feel happy"): a form of integration facilitated by her legal status, but especially her language acquisition.[5] Her civic participation and involvement at her children's school reinforce a sense of felt belonging. Though participation of this sort falls short of the social movement organizing that was the top priority for La Unión, legal status spurred a transformation in Lupita that she says was not only legal, but also "emotional." She described her fear of driving, especially on the freeway, a fear that she eventually had to face when she adjusted her status and secured work as a mobile hospice nurse traveling from one client's home to the next. She described her fear of police when she was undocumented, of being pulled over and taken from her children. She feared calling police for help when arguments between she and her husband became too intense. After she adjusted her status and felt more independent, she became more involved with her children's school and dedicated herself to studying English at the community college, which she says were problems for her husband. "You spend all your day out in the streets," he would say. Though his objections kept her from getting involved in community work with her church, they did not halt her studies. "Oh well," Lupita would say.

Over time her fear of police abated: "More than anything it is fear. I did not know a lot of things that I know now. As time passed I learned that I also have rights even if I am undocumented."[6] As her anxiety subsided and she built up the language skills that facilitated her integration in the community, room opened up in her life to pursue interests outside the home, which in turn prompted an enduring commitment to serving others whether in her job, her children's school, or in the local community.[7]

In an interview with wife and husband Evelinda and Ignacio, they describe the responsibility they feel to their community and to their hometown of Salamanca in the state of Guanajuato. Ignacio arrived in 1987 when he was 17 years old and immediately adjusted his status under the provisions of the 1986 Immigration Reform and Control Act (IRCA), allowing him to work and travel. He visited Mexico about once per year, and during these visits he met Evelinda, whom he later married. She joined him in South City in 1994. Subsequently, he adjusted her status, as well. In this excerpt, I ask what responsibility they feel, as citizens, to support their family and community.

I: Since I'm a citizen I feel I have rights and power too. Because I can do a lot of things, I can go out and cross the border any time I want and also I can help my parents to have their documents and now I'm trying to help my brothers and I feel I have rights and power regarding immigration. . . .

E: I feel that way, we want to help our people and we feel good supporting our people who really need it because we had the opportunity to leave that country to have better chances, better opportunities and unfortunately there are so many families there and we don't want them to suffer the bad circumstances there. So, if we have the possibility to help, why not?

I: Yes, as she mentioned, I think we have to be involved, I feel that way, we need to help others, if she has the time to do that and, for example, I have a lot of work to do but I can take one hour or two hours to help in the school. Then I can help with that and if I'm available, I don't watch TV, I decide to do something more useful and also I try to enjoy life with my family, helping people and I think God gave me a lot, more than I ever imagined I'd have. We don't have anything material, but I think we have a lot and now I feel responsible to help other people. And there is a phrase, "those who cannot provide for others, cannot provide for themselves" (*El que no sirve para servir, no sirve para vivir*)[8] and I feel that way, too.

G: That's good.

I: We need to help the community, it is our responsibility; we need to get involved with the community.

—Evelinda and Ignacio, naturalized citizens, South City, 40–50, stay-at-home mom/landscaping

For Evelinda and Ignacio, their legal status confers upon them a responsibility to support "our people" in their journeys as migrants. This responsibility is not a superficial obligation to support those who arrived too late to avail themselves of a pathway to citizenship, but a felt sense of community and solidarity that has become a principle by which they live their lives. This ethos of solidarity informs their participation in La Unión and in transnational hometown associations in which Mexican municipalities work with Mexican expatriates living in the United States to fund public works projects in Mexico.[9]

Notably, their politics are linked to the shared experience of material deprivation and legal vulnerability. When Evelinda first came to the United States in the winter of 1994, she crossed without authorization. Pregnant with their first child at the time, she waited for three days at the US-Mexico border before the coyote indicated the time was right to cross. She went an entire day without any food, though she feels lucky that most of the journey involved traveling by car, sparing her the grueling crossing on foot while pregnant. Early years were tough. Because the cost of rent in South City was very high when Ignacio first arrived, he stayed in apartments packed with friends and extended family. Later, when Evelinda joined Ignacio, she feared going outside their home at first because she did not have any form of identification. Their commitment to their community arises from their ability to directly relate to those who are experiencing the material insecurity of being a new immigrant in the United States.

Organizations Shaping Immigrant Activism

As organizers recruited immigrant community members to social movement organizing, they inevitably influenced the form that immigrant activism took. As a combination 501(c)(3) and 501(c)(4) nonprofit organization,[10] La Unión was able to engage in educational, nonprofit activity, as well as full-time electoral organizing and governmental lobbying. During electoral season, or the four to five months prior to an election, organizers would channel their members into electoral work, including precinct walking and phone banking. Prior to the presidential elections of 2012, organizers in North City conducted their summer house meeting campaign with an eye toward building a base for the junta grande to mobilize their election volunteers. At this large meeting, community members would gather together to learn more about pressing propositions for the state and concretize strategies for turning out the Latino vote.

So in August 2012, approximately 100 to 120 people gathered in a large community center. The space was cavernous and propped up by pillars thick and thin. The floor was made of worn wooden slats, not unlike what you would find in a high school gymnasium. Around the room we taped up ten long sheets of paper listing the various issues and problems community members had identified: lists culled from the grievances discussed during the preceding house meetings. Each sheet was titled at the top with a category, such as public safety, or immigrant rights, and so on, under which people listed specific concerns. The longest sheets were for education and public safety. They trailed down the columns to which they had been posted and spilled onto the floor.

After individually acknowledging each precinct captain who had recruited neighbors to attend today's junta grande, North City lead organizer Leticia reviews the grievances listed on the sheets. She explains the importance of political, and specifically electoral, power. She notes the long list of issues that the people in the room have identified. She says that we care about these issues and to get something done to address them, we need to have people in power who understand these concerns and the needs of the community. That is why we all need to be involved in electoral work, so that we can elect people who will address our concerns. After she draws this connection between community grievances and electoral work, she goes table to table asking individuals from each precinct to introduce themselves, give their precinct number, and say generally where their neighborhood is located. As she moves from table to table, people stand and introduce themselves, state their precinct, and are applauded.

The grievances listed on the sheets emerged from the housing meetings. The strategies for addressing them, however, are shaped by the tactical preferences of organizers who are committed to social change through electoral reform. As Zlolinski has described, SMOs play a key role in setting agendas, choosing tactics, and identifying targets.[11] While they share the same broad political commitments, the organizers, not community members, largely set strategy, timelines, and tactics.[12] With La Unión at the helm, the immigrant activists driving these campaigns bear the mark of La Unión's own tactical preferences and organizing philosophy.[13] The shape of immigrant activism is not simply a spontaneous expression of immigrants' grievances. Instead, it emerges from within established repertoires of contention that are reproduced by La Unión organizers.[14]

Organizations also play a key role in shaping immigrants' own political orientations. Core leaders, upon whom La Unión regularly relied, came to incorporate these organizing principles and priorities into their own evolving political consciousness (see the appendix for an extended discussion of the role of "core leaders" in La Unión's work and in this study). Maria, for instance, came to the United States in 1988 and eventually became a naturalized citizen. She earns money through a state program that funds domestic caregivers. Maria cares for her mother who lives with her in a working-class neighborhood in North City. During our interview at her home, she would take periodic breaks in order to check on her mom in a back bedroom. We sat on two couches that were positioned in an L shape. I asked Maria how she first became involved with La Unión. La Unión initially contacted her as a potential voter during a local political campaign supporting a progressive, pro-immigrant candidate. Unwilling to support anyone without first learning more about them, she arranged with La Unión to have the candidate make a presentation in her home. Reflecting on her initial involvement, she says:

> So, I have some leadership certificates, and I think I have a potential for [leadership], and they noticed that and they told me they wanted me there. I would like to be more useful but because of my job, sometimes I can't. It's good to tell people who are going to vote what they are going to vote for, who to vote for, what is the candidate proposing and to vote the candidate who is going to be more beneficial for the nation and the community and individuals. We are not going to vote for our enemy who is going to strangle us because that would be ridiculous, right? We have to

vote for someone who is going to represent us as a community. What are the candidates proposing? We want healthy and affordable housing and we want this service and that. The owners are this or that. . . . Okay, but the owners also have their rights. There are some tenants who are very dirty, who destroy their homes, you have to see that too. We must help them have affordable homes but they must also learn that they have the responsibility of looking after those homes.

—Maria, Mexican, naturalized citizen, 50–60, in-home care
    provider (for her mother)

Maria's own cautious skepticism, willingness to learn, and prior leadership experience led to an opportunity for her to work with La Unión on its electoral campaigns. Subsequently, she came to see the relationship between electoral organizing and the betterment of the immigrant community. Her experience with La Unión amounts to the introjection of the importance of electoral organizing into her own evolving political consciousness.[15] Throughout our interview, she referenced the importance of electing city leaders who understand the grievances of the immigrant community whose support they enjoy. While Maria had prior leadership experience, her own political consciousness is marked by La Unión's approach. She folds this key linkage between community organizing and electoral organization into her own political philosophy. Her commitments and values as a political subject, like all of our own, are mutable and inflected by her time organizing with La Unión. Organizations, especially when staffed by organizers who are organically connected to their communities, play a critical role in coalescing atomized immigrant residents into a political constituency, inevitably shaping the strategy and tactics used to address those grievances.

Over the course of my observations, organizers played a key role in inviting and cultivating activists whose personal relationships with organizers, close calls with immigration enforcement, or documented status motivated their participation in social movement organizing. Stressing the shared destiny of the immigrant community, as well as the responsibility to participate in movement activities, organizers tapped the authentic grievances of this community, while also coaching them to adopt and value the goals and tactics valued by the organizers themselves.[16] And yet, immigrant participants in this social movement activity come to this work not as tabulae rasae, but with knowledge, savvy, and goals of their own. Specifically, the immigrants in this study articulated sophisticated analyses of their own marginalization as Latino immigrants upon which organizers drew to inspire them to act in concert with others. In this way, the political mobilization of immigrant communities reflects not a manipulation of otherwise inert subjects, but a negotiation of immigrants' preexisting experience and wisdom that they brought to social movement work and from which organizers drew to demonstrate the gravity and urgency of their claims.

Instrumental Activists

Though the obstacles to immigrants' involvement in activism are many, contentious action is possible and the routes to participation in social movement organizing are diverse. In the previous chapter, I introduced the metaphor of the shell to describe immigrants' social location as low-wage laborers toiling in the lowest rungs of a segmented labor market while simultaneously managing the threats of dispossession and deportation. The shell is not an immovable obstacle, however. As the above narratives suggest, activism emerges, even though the shell is not entirely shrugged off. As a habituated mode of being in the city, the shell continues to orient immigrant activism to addressing the material exigencies of their everyday lives. These material motivations are evident in their accounts of what they want for themselves and their children in the future. These are the material moorings of immigrant activism.

In the below interview excerpts, I ask several La Unión participants, some of whom I identify as community members and others as "core leaders," or regular and longtime volunteers, about their hopes for the future. Their politics do not often stretch out beyond the normative conventions of work and family, but instead seek to burrow into them.

In a North City house meeting in June 2012, a group of core La Unión volunteers open the meeting by listing their grievances. These include an end to vagrancy and vandalism, the lack of street lights, the dearth of police who speak Spanish, and the need for a stop light or a stop sign and/or speed bumps at a nearby intersection that they say is often used by local schoolchildren.

In my conversation with Tomás and Petra, both of whom were only occasionally involved with La Unión, I ask what they want for their children in 10 or 20 years.

> They are beginning their studies; we are supporting them in everything. And in the future, I think that they have the right to decide to do what they want to do, because you can't force them, "you know what, I want you to study this, I want you to study that." So when they're grown up, they are going to decide for themselves what they want to study or what they want they want to be when they grow up: the option to choose their future, their profession.
> —Tomás, Mexican, undocumented, 30–40, landscaping

Notably, the goals they have for their children are oriented to concrete forms of social mobility: good education for their children and the freedom to choose their profession. Broadly representative of the respondents in this study, their activism was not about broad-based social transformation or social justice. Instead, they shared similar desires for themselves, their children, and their community: for clean and safe neighborhoods, the opportunity for steady work in a good job, and their children's professional success.

Esteban and his wife Marta, whom I identify as a "core leader," call for more employment opportunities.

Xiomara, whom we encountered in previous chapters, says:

> To have a driver's license here in South City, that would be for me. . . . I would not need anything else. I would feel safe and with a lot of freedom if they gave me a license only to drive to my work and my children's school. That would be ideal for me.
> —Xiomara, Mexican, undocumented, South City, 40–50,
>   housekeeper

In a group interview in North City, I ask what the group makes of the growing prospects for legalization for young students (e.g., the California Dream Act or Deferred Action for Childhood Arrivals), but the lack of opportunity for older immigrants. Erica responds:

It is not fair because if people are working and everything it is important that they give documentation to those that have been working. They are not depending on the government. We are paying our taxes.
—Erica, Mexican, 40–50

The undocumented immigrants in this study desire change in order to create spaces of stability and stasis, to participate in normative visions of family life, to own property, to work without the threat of deportation, and to enjoy leisure time with family and friends free of the fear that police will arrest their mobility and assault their dignity. Their participation is *instrumental* and focused on achieving a set of concrete, mundane goals. Unlike community organizers, by comparison, they engage in this work not out of a broader commitment to social justice work, but to secure the makings of a dignified life incubated by the relative security of a middle-class existence. Which is to say, immigrant activists engage in contention in order to achieve stasis.

Conclusion

This instrumental orientation to activism "highlight[s] the polarization between history and the everyday. [Movements] require members to risk their lives in order to make it possible to live. It therefore should not be surprising that movement mobilizations have a periodicity—an ebb and flow—as individual participants oscillate between participation and privatization as a means to fulfill their commitments to their lives."[17] To participate in social movements or not is not the difference between apathy and activism. It reflects, instead, the choice to deal with the precarity of everyday life in the private sphere versus the public. Indeed, Mexican immigrants oscillate between the private and public spheres to manage life in the deportation nation. The call to make history is most convincing when it stands to directly address the way immigrant people make life. To move into the public sphere and contest the deportation regime and the racialized economic relations it sustains entails a disruption of the everyday: lost time at work or with family, the risks of exposure to authority, and the potential for failure. These costs in part explain the ebb and flow of immigrant social movements.[18] Immigrants most often respond to the precarity of everyday life with private strategies to minimize risk (the shell). And still, when threats and political opportunities (as I explore in depth in the next chapter) shift and when organizers tap into existing local networks to cultivate an immigrant collectivity born of shared grievances, common language, and widely shared aspirations for self and family, immigrant collective action crystallizes.

The material moorings of immigrant activism shed light not only on the periodicity of immigrant social movements, but also on the tenor and substance of their claims. That immigrants can be moved to "make history" in order to "make life" under conditions that will allow them to meet their material needs suggests that their agency should not be uncritically conflated with progressive or radical action. In this sense, and as Saba Mahmood has argued in her study of the women's mosque movement in Cairo, Egypt, "agentival capacity is entailed not only in those acts that result in (progressive) change but also those that aim toward continuity, stasis, and stability."[19] Agency is not the opposite of power. Agency, in its many forms, emerges from within networked relations of power that both produce grievances and shape immigrants' responses to their subordination.[20] While paid organizers enjoy considerable overlap between realms of making life and making history—they can satisfy their material needs as they pursue politics—potential or sporadic immigrant participants do not. They must make choices between these two spheres. Most often the bulk of their energy must be dedicated to making life in the shadow of the deportation regime. When activism emerges, when they oscillate from private resistance to public contention, the individual work of the shell continues to influence the collective work of social movement organizing. Their politics seek freedom from legal violence and political representation not for its own sake but instrumentally, for the material benefits that such freedom can secure.

5

Opportunity and Threat

*Comparing Collaborative and Confrontational Tactics
in Local Immigrant Rights Struggles*

Devolution, the Failure of Reform, and Local Immigrant Organizing

In the immigrant rights movement, the local has reemerged as a key field of struggle. The vacuum left by multiple failed attempts at national immigration reform, the growing involvement of states and local municipalities in federal immigration enforcement (i.e., devolution), and the proliferation of state and local immigration legislation have led immigrant rights social movement organizations to respond by targeting local authorities.[1] Consequently, the form and content of immigrants' social movement tactics vary in response to the very different political climates in which these battles unfold. In some places immigrants are welcomed, as in San Francisco County, and in other places repressed, as in Maricopa County, where the infamous, and recently deposed (then convicted and later pardoned), Sheriff Joe Arpaio has zealously targeted immigrants living in his jurisdiction.[2] At every turn, however, highly organized immigrant protesters have met Arpaio's repressive policies with vocal protest and civil disobedience, even at the risk of deportation. In this way, devolution has proliferated sites not only of repression, but also of *contestation*.

The two cities under comparison here, North City and South City, are no exception and are distinguished by their contrasting political climates: the former more conservative and the latter more progressive. This chapter builds on the micro-interactional focus of the previous chapter by taking a meso-level and comparative view of the way local politics shape immigrant social movements.

Take, for instance, the dispute over a "mobile consulate" in conservative North City. The Mexican consul had regularly dispatched a mobile consulate unit to North City, located two hours north of the consul's home offices. This mobile consulate provided a range of consular services, including the issuance of the "matrícula consular," the identification card issued by the Mexican government to its expatriates, thereby making their services more accessible to the low-income Mexican immigrant population living there. In early April 2011, the North City mayor signed and sent the following letter to the consul of Mexico. It read in full:

> This is to inform you of the actions [the city] is prepared to implement should you continue to issue matricular identification cards within the jurisdiction of [the city]:
>
> 1. Upon learning of the time, date and location of an event, [the city] will formally request I.C.E. to respond to such event.
> 2. [The city] Police Department will respond to said event, and cite with probable cause, those drivers of vehicles who are unlicensed.
>
> These events must cease within the jurisdiction of [the city]. I ask for your cooperation.

These events, hosted in the parking lots of local businesses and community organizations and drawing hundreds of residents, generated a variety of public nuisance complaints related to traffic, noise, and trash. The mayor leveraged these complaints as a thin pretext for expelling the consul from the city.[3] By contrast, the mayor of South City had, at about the same time, publicly supported state legislation calling for the limitation of the federal-local deportation program, Secure Communities.

These episodes are emblematic of the battles over local immigrant inclusion taking place across the nation. The responses from immigrant activists and their allies are as varied as the substance of the conflicts themselves, ranging from city ordinances barring undocumented immigrants from rental housing to local police collaboration with federal immigration officers. In both places, the primary source of threat to Mexican immigrants was the police. This threat was more severe and more broadly experienced in North City, where it appeared as police killings of Latino residents, while in South city, it took the form of the car impoundments of undocumented, unlicensed drivers.

This relationship between the wider political climate and collective mobilization is a central consideration for social movement scholars. These different political climates, progressive in South City and repressive in North City, are referred to as political opportunity structures. Simply, political opportunity and its counterpart, threat, capture the influence that the wider sociopolitical environment exerts on mobilization. Doug McAdam popularly defined political opportunity with reference to four interrelated features.[4] First, elite allies refer to the presence of movement allies in places of institutional power and might include government officials, influential political leaders, celebrities, and so on. Division among elites refers to conflict among elite members of society, like those mentioned above, that activists can exploit in order to press their demands. State capacity for repression, especially when it is diminished, can lead to mobilization because the risks of engaging in protest are lower. Conversely, when repression grows, the likelihood of mobilization may also decline. Finally, increasing access to the political system refers to growing opportunity for the exercise of political power through protected institutional channels that obviates protest since grievances are being resolved by responsive and proactive government. While the relationship between political opportunity and social movements has been studied extensively, the specific effect of opportunity and threat on the tactics that activists adopt is less well understood. Consequently, the guiding question for this chapter is this: *How do these distinct local political climates—that is, differing political opportunity structures and differing levels of threat—influence mobilization tactics?*

The comparative quality of the data in this chapter allows me to evaluate the difference that these different political climates make, not for the likelihood that protest will emerge, but in the content and form that immigrant protest takes. The two campaigns profiled below both are emblematic of the uneven political terrain that immigrants encounter in the cities where they organize and serve as an example of the dynamic relationships among local political climate, social movement organizations (SMOs), and municipal government that influence the substance and tenor of immigrants' contention. As I have argued in this book, agency is not simply a response to grievances produced by wider structures of inequality, but is itself enabled and constrained by those very social conditions. As I widen the analytical lens in this chapter to encompass the local climate (though political shifts at the state and national levels will also prove important), we see that collective agency of immigrant social movement actors is expressed both through and against these wider political conditions.

Contestation in the City: Protest in Immigrant California

For the immigrant communities in this study, the most salient threat in their daily lives was the police. In both campaigns, the target was the police chief and the goal was improved relations between immigrant and Latino communities and police. In South City, car impoundments, as I described in Chapter 2, were nominally intended to halt drunk driving, but ensnared many more undocumented, unlicensed drivers than drunk drivers. Both documented and undocumented immigrants experienced this mission creep as unfair.

In North City, La Unión organizers had also identified car impoundments as a threat to the immigrant community, but an early, contentious meeting with the police chief made it abundantly clear that he had no intention of negotiating La Unión demands to either (1) offer a grace period to undocumented, unlicensed drivers to allow a licensed driver to arrive at a checkpoint and claim a vehicle or (2) delay the start of checkpoints beyond the end of the workday so that undocumented immigrants returning from work in outlying agricultural fields would not be stopped. The police chief's refusal to consider these demands followed soon thereafter by a spate of police killings pushed police violence to the top of La Unión's priorities.

In both cases, the distinction between police and immigration agent is blurred in the eyes of immigrants. While many craved better relations with police, many immigrant respondents felt police could not be called upon for help and were to be avoided. What enhanced the severity of threat in North City, the conservative case, is that police were lethally violent there. This threat resonated beyond the Mexican immigrant community to the broader Latino community and North City at large. As I explain below, part of what explains the positive effect of threat on mobilization in North City is the broad-based concern over about police violence. While the substance of the claims in North City (police killings) and South City (car impoundments) is different, the comparability of the cases stems from the fact that both campaigns have in common their target (police chief), the challenging organization (La Unión), and the threat (police), even while the intensity and scope of the threat vary between the two cases. This comparison reflects, moreover, the way that social movement organizations like La Unión, especially those that actively cultivate and communicate with the constituency that they purport to represent, organically respond to the sundry grievances of the immigrant community and the broader Latino community of which they are a part.

Because city politics are, as I argue, important for understanding the mobilization tactics adopted in each place, we must understand more about North City and South City before turning to the campaigns themselves. Part of the reason, for instance, that threats were elevated in North City to begin with is due to the more conservative composition of local government and the electorate there.[5] Which is to say, political climate has a direct effect on the threats immigrants might face in one or another locale and on the tactics immigrants adopt as they respond collectively to those threats.

A city of approximately 88,500, South City is about 38 percent Latino and 55 percent white, with very small numbers of other racial groups.[6] These 2010 figures represent a slight increase in the Latino population (35 percent) and a slight decrease in the number of whites (58 percent) over the past decade. Latinos often reside in largely segregated neighborhoods on the city's eastside and westside. Most of the respondents in South City were long-term residents, having lived in the community for a minimum of 10 years and as long as 20 years, often with citizen children attending local schools and playing in community sports leagues. They worked in construction and in the service industries that supported a booming local tourist economy. This city is also home to Mexican American families whose roots extend back generations. This small group of Mexican American elite are a minority in this community, but occupy prominent positions in the community as elected officials, business leaders, and medical and legal professionals.

North City, by contrast, is home to approximately 99,500 people, and the population is approximately 70 percent Latino and 22 percent white:[7] a racial distribution that many advocates critically noted was not reflected among city officials or business leaders. These 2010 demographics reflect a significant increase in the size of the Latino population up from approximately 60 percent in 2000, as well as waning numbers of whites, who made up 32 percent of the population a decade earlier.[8] Although most respondents were long-term residents, I also encountered more immigrant residents who had lived in North City for only as little as six months.

While employment fluctuated for some respondents, especially in North City, many respondents reported steady employment and some even developed their own small businesses in landscaping or party supply. North City is home to a variety of large agricultural growers. Strawberries, broccoli, and sugar beets are just some of the crops that are cultivated by the migrant farmworkers who predominate among the immigrant community there. Because North City is home to many more migrant farmworkers than South City, this group of immigrants was more mobile, following *la corrida* in search of work.[9] And while some farmworkers have settled permanently, the majority continue to migrate regularly (often to other parts of the state or region), presenting a challenge to local schools, city institutions, and social movement organizations that seek to build relationships with this community, albeit in different ways.

While some respondents reported wishing to return to Mexico at some undetermined point in the future, perhaps to retire, immigrants in both places understood themselves as more or less permanently settled in the county, even as they still yearned to return to extended family and community in Mexico. In short, this sample was rooted in this community through their work, their children, and their commitment to providing opportunities to *adelantarse* or *superarse*: to get ahead or better oneself and one's family. Notably, this sense of rootedness stemmed not from legal citizenship or formal membership in the space of the nation-state, since many respondents are undocumented, but from their physical presence in the community.

In South City, the police chief was Latino, as was a county supervisor and a city council member. Not just "brown faces in high places," they largely responded to the needs and grievances of the Latino community. The city council agreed to incorporate anti-deportation language into its legislative platform, and four of seven city council members issued personal letters in support of a state law called the TRUST Act (AB 4), which mandated noncooperation with Secure Communities. The police chief publicly stated that local police do not and will not cooperate with

ICE and had gone above and beyond the mandate of a recently passed state law by ending the 30-day impoundment of vehicles of undocumented, unlicensed drivers: a significant burden for low-income, immigrant families. Finally, a business association exists in the predominantly Latino eastside of the city that carries its own special political influence in a city largely dependent on tourism.

In North City, by contrast, there is little to no Latino presence in city government, in the executive administration of the police department, or among business leaders. The now-former police chief reportedly used anti-Latino racial slurs with some regularity, and the mayor, as demonstrated at the outset of this chapter, actively opposed service provision for Latino immigrants and had signaled his willingness to cooperate with ICE. An active and vocal chapter of the Minutemen makes its home in North City, and the city voluntarily opted into the E-Verify program for city employees (a largely symbolic and redundant move, since background checks for city employees already verify immigration status and since most undocumented Mexican immigrants do not migrate to the United States to take jobs in municipal government).[10] The letter from the mayor that opens this chapter is emblematic of the way the city actively worked to erode the resources available to its immigrant residents.

The prospects for political representation are made easier in South City since the Latino immigrant community is more permanently situated. Immigrant families in my sample have lived in the city for 15 to 20 years and worked in nonseasonal industries, such as service work, domestic care, and construction. In North City, by contrast, a greater proportion of the immigrant community is composed of seasonal fieldworkers, many of whom cycle through North City as they pursue different seasonal work opportunities. The more mobile character of the immigrant community in this largely agricultural region makes the cultivation of Latino political power more challenging.

In terms of electoral makeup, between the years 2000 to 2014, registered Democrats outnumbered Republicans in South City by an average of 25 percent. Though the numbers of Democratic voters were relatively stable over this period, there was a substantial decline in the number of registered Republicans. In North City, Democrats still outnumbered Republicans, but by a much thinner average margin of 5 percent.[11] As in South City, the number of Democratic voters has remained relatively stable while the number of Republican voters has declined, but at a slower rate, preserving only a marginal advantage for Democrats. In 2004, for instance, the North City electorate was almost evenly split between Democrats and Republicans. In other words, progressive electoral power is much more stable in South City, whereas conservative voters in North City continue to exercise considerable power in elected office even while the composition of the electorate may be slowly edging left.

From within these local political contexts, these two local immigrant mobilization efforts targeted their respective police chiefs. Growing opportunity in the progressive case, lower levels of relative threat, and an organizational commitment to maintaining good relations with state actors influenced the adoption of collaborative tactics: namely, the community forum. In North City, by contrast, reduced opportunity, lethal threat experienced by the broader Latino community, and coalitional work at a time of organizational rupture created the conditions to pursue a more confrontational set of tactics: a march and rally calling for the ouster of the police chief. The analysis is summarized in Table 5.1.[12]

TABLE 5.1. Opportunity and Threat in Comparative Perspective

	South City (progressive)	North City (conservative)
Elite allies	Opportunity = good relations with police chief	Threat = key elites (e.g., police chief, mayor) actively threaten immigrant community
Divisions among elites	No opportunity = police chief/department largely supported by city council	Opportunity = city manager unwilling to protect police chief, internal dissension among rank and file
Repression/enforcement climate	Mild threat = car impoundments, no lethal violence	Threat = series of police-involved killings, widespread fear and marginalization
Access/political representation	Opportunity = immigrants are minority but significant representation of their interests, growing electoral power, can leverage state-level victory in local conflict	Threat = interests not represented, no Latinos in power, city actively marginalizes immigrants, inchoate electoral power among otherwise conservative electorate
Organization/coalitions	Organizational culture of relationship building sustained by volunteer organizer, no coalition influence	Organizational culture of relationship building ruptured by economic hardship and coalition partner expands tactical repertoire
Protest tactics	The community forum, dialogue with police chief	March and rally calling for ouster of police chief

*"Con los Balazos:" North City March Calling for an End to Police
Killings, Police Chief's Ouster*

Three fatal shootings in the course of six months riled community
members in North City who went on to call for an end to police violence. In the six-month period between December 2011 and June
2012, police officers shot two local Latino residents, as well as one of
their fellow officers in a botched arrest attempt. The first shooting in
December 2011 occurred during a chase in which police pursued and
then opened fire on a Latino man, whom they identified as a gang
member who had reportedly brandished a gun. In the flurry of gunfire
that followed, two police officers sustained nonfatal wounds, which
were later revealed to be the result of friendly fire. The second shooting occurred when two supervising officers attempted to arrest a third
officer as he was ending his shift at a DUI checkpoint. When the supervising officers attempted to detain the suspect officer over his alleged
illicit sexual relationship with a 17-year-old female Police Explorer, the
suspect officer drew his weapon and opened fire. One of the supervising officers, and the suspect's best friend, returned fire and killed the
officer under investigation (residents at the time sometimes referred
to the incident as "suicide by cop"). In this instance, a Latino youth
was not shot, but the incident (1) contributed to the public perception
that the police were out of control since the gunfight erupted along a
heavily trafficked commercial corridor and (2) revealed internal divisions and conflict within the police themselves. In a third instance
in June 2012, another young Latino man, also identified by police as
a gang member, was shot and killed when he jumped from a car as
police were following him. The police reported that the young man
was armed. This third decedent was the cousin of a La Unión volunteer leader. In an interview with North City primary informant Leticia,
she recalled that the shooting "wasn't random, it was the family of our
leaders . . . it really hit close to home."

Immigrant community members cast doubt on these accounts and
faulted police for resorting too quickly to violence. In an interview
with Dolores, a La Unión volunteer, I asked her how the police have
responded to new problems in the city, like gangs, drugs, and poor housing conditions. She responded:

Well, lately the authorities have been answering with gunfire [*con los balazos*]. They persecute young people for any reason, and although they are unarmed the police say that the guys were going to shoot them or that they were carrying a gun, and they kill them. That's what we're worried about, because instead of helping the community the police are against it, and they are shooting our youth, there has to be another kind of solution.
—Dolores, naturalized citizen, 38 years in the United States,
  North City, 50–60

This spate of police violence and the clear perception that the police were violently opposed to the Latino community sparked a July march and rally outside City Hall where both news outlets and organizers reported approximately 300 community members, mostly Latino, wore white shirts and held candles in commemoration of those who had died. Organized by La Unión, a South City advocacy organization that works with gang-involved youth, and the family of the third decedent, the protesters called for an end to the police violence, reform of the local police department, and the firing of the police chief who had long been a controversial figure within and outside of the department. Following the march and rally, two more fatal police shootings occurred the following month, one involving an elderly Latino veteran who was reportedly armed when police confronted him, and another involving a Latino man who was gunned down after a chase that ended with him reportedly brandishing a replica gun. Shortly thereafter, the police chief was placed on administrative leave by the city manager, and resigned several days after that.

Prior to this spate of shootings, the police chief had inflamed tensions among rank-and-file police officers and was the subject of a formal complaint and a vote of no confidence by the Police Officers Association, which accused him of favoritism, using racist language on the job, and generally eroding officer morale, among other things. While the police chief had enjoyed the support of the former city manager in the face of earlier complaints, a new city manager could no longer deflect public pressure to remove the police chief. In addition, years of internal discord among rank-and-file officers contributed to the factious environment within the department. The march and rally expressed the deeply felt exasperation and anger on the part of the Latino community toward the police department and benefited from this confluence of events by capitalizing on the growing public dissatisfaction with the police chief.

The decision to organize a march and rally represented a higher than normal risk for the relatively small SMO given the time and resources required to organize several hundred people and the potential embarrassment of low turnout. The guiding philosophy of La Unión in both North City and South City was to build political power in two primary ways: (1) recruiting a base of support that can be called on during elections and various "issue" campaigns and (2) electing leaders sympathetic to the demands of the working-class Mexican immigrant community. The general idea is that if the organization has the ear of local elites or those elites fear an organized Latino constituency, La Unión's influence can be exerted with a phone call or strategic meeting, obviating the need to organize mass demonstrations each time the immigrant community is confronted with a threat.

In a follow-up interview with North City primary informant Leticia, she describes the events leading up to the march and rally as "random" (in the way that young people often use the term to mean strange, unusual, or surprising). First, in the wake of the 2008 financial crisis and mismanagement by a recently hired executive director, La Unión was in dire financial straits and on the cusp of being subsumed by a larger, regional SMO, which could offer greater financial stability and reliable leadership. Between the fall of 2011 and winter of 2013, the South City organizer and then the executive director had been let go and the South City office had been shuttered. Consequently, there was no clear leadership to whom North City organizers could turn nor a strategic plan to guide their work. In addition, two La Unión volunteer leaders were in close contact with a gang advocacy organization in South City, whose executive director was brought in to help develop a strategy for responding to the police killings in North City. Leticia reports that in the course of brainstorming how these two organizations should respond, youth participants in particular were very energized and committed to a public action.

And while the threat that police posed was clearly intense, it was also broadly experienced. Leticia, who happened to be in the area immediately following the fourth shooting, explains:

I remember just a really pivotal moment, because I was actually nearby when the fourth shooting happened; he was a guy who ran from the police and got shot. And I remember walking up, we actually saw the scene where it happened and people were showing up along with all the cop cars and, you know, here we were thinking this is more of a Latino issue, but there was even a white couple, and I heard this white woman go "Are they trigger happy? Are they ever gonna stop?" You could really feel the shift in public opinion. People were just tired of it.

—Leticia, US-born citizen, North City, 20–30, La Unión
    organizer

This threat, intense and resonating beyond the immigrant community, coupled with an episode of organizational rupture, the influence of coalition members who contributed a sense of urgency and outrage to their action planning, erosion of elite support for the police chief, and the police chief's own refusal to acknowledge or respond to the grievances of La Unión, created a political landscape in which contentious action—contentious in both form and content, a public march calling for the police chief to step down—was viable and ultimately effective.

Campaign to Halt Car Impoundments: A Community Forum with the South City Police Chief

In 1994, as a consequence of Proposition 187, California began requiring a social security number to qualify for a driver's license. As I described in Chapter 2, this new requirement forced many undocumented immigrants to begin driving without a license. Since this shift, most of the cars that have been confiscated by local police for driving without a license have been those of undocumented immigrants.[13]

Over several years and during the tenures of at least two executive directors, La Unión had been working at the state and local levels to find some relief for undocumented, unlicensed drivers. Efforts to lobby the police chief to change this policy had, up to this point, been unsuccessful. The police chief had maintained that this was simply a matter of state law and that his hands were tied.

Two things changed at the local and state levels that created opportunities for renewed social movement work on this issue. At the state level, political momentum was growing to halt the impoundment of vehicles driven by unlicensed drivers. In fall 2011, California Assembly Bill 353 was moving through the state assembly and senate. This bill required that officers offer unlicensed drivers detained at DUI checkpoints a grace period to locate an authorized, licensed driver to recover the vehicle from the checkpoint prior to impounding it. If the car was still impounded at the checkpoint, drivers would be exempt from the mandatory 30-day hold that would typically cost undocumented drivers between $1,500 and $2,000 to recover their vehicles. This bill passed and went into effect in January 2012, at around the same time La Unión had restarted its house meeting campaign under the leadership of long-time La Unión volunteer, new board member, and primary informant Esmeralda.

The second important change occurred at the local level. Given the staff cutbacks described in the North City case above, Esmeralda took the lead role in organizing the South City immigrant community. Importantly, Esmeralda had a particularly close relationship with the South City chief of police. Widely recognized in the community as a leader, Esmeralda had, for years, assisted the chief in organizing the Citizen's Academy and the Police Activities League: both programs designed to foster understanding between local residents and police officers. She recruited members of the Latino community to the Spanish-speaking meetings for these programs and helped graduate the largest classes in these programs' histories.[14] Over the course of their work together, Esmeralda and the police chief had developed a certain level of trust.

So, in the winter of 2012, Esmeralda suggested a community forum to address the most pressing issues for the Latino immigrant community that emerged during the house meeting campaigns. This idea for a public dialogue with the police chief seemed plausible and worthwhile, in part because these community programs, as well as the chief's relationship with Esmeralda, represented important lines of communication between the police and the Latino community.

But there was also an element of organizational culture at work, specifically an emphasis on the importance of relationships with state actors, which influenced the decision. In reviewing my field notes from these planning meetings with core La Unión volunteers, I noticed that Esmeralda had suggested the community forum format, which was readily accepted by the group as the appropriate tactic. That this tactical decision was something of a foregone conclusion in the group's planning led me to look further back in my field notes to see if a pattern might be identified, if this was part of La Unión's organizing style.

Earlier that year, La Unión hosted a similar community forum with the local South City sheriff regarding Secure Communities, a federal-local deportation program operating in local jails, which are typically the jurisdiction of sheriffs' departments. In October 2011, during a debriefing session following the forum, we discussed how we felt the forum had gone. Many were dissatisfied with the sheriff's responses to our questions about the dragnet quality of the program and whether the county could opt out of the program altogether. One of the participants said the sheriff "skated" over several other questions because of the way we tried to balance putting pressure on the sheriff and maintaining a dialogic tone.

For instance, Emma, an on-and-off volunteer but a well-known member of the community, suggests that in public it's difficult to put too much pressure on the sheriff because we want to keep the lines of communication open. Our executive director, Anthony, says that it is especially important to keep that dialogue open because he wants to be able to call the sheriff when we have particular emergency situations with community members. He says, for example, that community members call him when their son or daughter is in jail. The point is he wants to be able to call the sheriff and know the sheriff will take his call.

The premium placed on maintaining open lines of communication with this critical state actor was justified by referencing those occasional instances in which individual community members needed immediate help and the intervention of the sheriff. The prevalence of this tactic throughout my time at La Unión suggested to me that La Unión's tactics were an expression of an organizational culture of collaboration designed to preserve relations with state actors.

Returning to the forum with the police chief, he agreed first to an exploratory meeting with only the most active members of the South City immigration committee. Then, he indicated we could revisit the idea of a larger community forum.

At the first forum, held in the winter of 2012 at the elementary school where Esmeralda works, she told the chief that he could expect approximately 30 people in attendance. According to Esmeralda, approximately 90 community members attended: a response that she claimed was spontaneous and signaled the community's interest in these issues. She facilitated this meeting, in which we presented testimonies about the impact of car impoundments on the lives of Latino immigrants and discussed whether the chief would consider supporting a state anti-deportation bill and the issue of driver's licenses for undocumented immigrants. The police chief reiterated his longtime support of driver's licenses for undocumented immigrants and his opposition to local-federal immigration enforcement collaboration. His long-standing support for impounding vehicles of undocumented, unlicensed drivers, however, pushed this issue to the center of the discussion. But because AB 353 was already in effect, the police chief said that he had no choice but to follow this new law and offer a grace period to undocumented drivers at DUI checkpoints. As we pressed for the chief to go beyond the requirements of this law and to extend this grace period to all unlicensed drivers (including those stopped outside of DUI checkpoints), he rejected this demand, but said that he would end the mandatory 30-day impoundment period for all unlicensed drivers whether or not they were stopped at a DUI checkpoint: a small but significant victory.

At the second forum, held in the summer of 2012 at the same elementary school, between 200 and 250 people attended. The police chief, who had previously confirmed his attendance, was at the last minute not able to attend since one of his extended relatives had been hospitalized. He sent other executive staff in his place. At this meeting, the community applauded the changes to the impound laws and the end of the 30-day impoundment. In addition to discussing other statewide immigration campaigns, the police chief had also arranged for each of eight beat officers to be present.[15] The officers introduced themselves and the neighborhoods in which they worked and the various neighborhood programs they offered to the community. At the end of the meeting, Esmeralda had organized a potluck, which was arranged on five tables set end to end. Community members sat with different officers and shared food. As I circulated around the room, I noticed that while some conversations aired various grievances, most were more introductory in tone. Police officers and community members asked one another questions about how long they lived in the community and where they worked, and identified mutual friends and acquaintances.

Over the course of this campaign, there were clear grievances articulated by community members, specifically on the issue of car impoundments. Local relationships between community leaders and the chief of police, in addition to an organizational culture that privileged relationship building with elites, shaped a dialogic and collaborative mobilization strategy: the community forum. Importantly, changes in state policy forced the police chief's hand, but also provided momentum upon which local leaders seized. These changes in the local and state political field created an opening into which social movement organizing was channeled.

Threat, Opportunity, and Protest Tactics

Immigrants readily understood the threat that local police posed to their resources and safety in each place, though the intensity of that threat varied. La Unión organizers were perhaps less instrumental in shaping immigrants' interpretation of these threats than they were in shaping their collective responses: an approach inflected by La Unión's organizing philosophy, its relationships to police and various elected officials, shifting alliances within the local power structure of each city, and the enactment of new state law.

Threat and opportunity are present in nearly every political struggle.[16] Among social movement scholars, threat has received shorter shrift relative to opportunity.[17] More recent research has demonstrated that threat stimulates mobilization both in authoritarian settings and in Western democracies,[18] especially when threats are intense and broadly experienced, as in the North City case.[19] As in the two cases above and in the marches of 2006, immigrant mobilization is often a response to threat.[20] Dina Okamoto and Kim Ebert, in a first-of-its-kind study of pro-immigrant mobilization in 50 metropolitan cities, argue that political opportunities do not uniformly encourage pro-immigrant organizing. Echoing the general argument of this chapter, they find that "exclusionary contexts characterized by threats and segregation facilitate protest among immigrant groups, and inclusionary contexts characterized by higher degrees of and greater access to formal incorporation deter immigrant organizing."[21]

Though the concept of political opportunity continues to be the subject of much critique,[22] a second important development has resuscitated its utility. Activists and movement participants confront threats from within shifting political circumstances that are often not fixed features of structure, but the strategic negotiation of fluid relations of power. As with studies of "micromobilization," understanding the relationship between opportunity, threat, and mobilization tactics requires an interactional focus on the social process in which the meanings of threat and opportunity are coproduced by activists and immigrant participants in the context of a changing political climate. Indeed, in Okamoto and Ebert's study, the positive effect of threat on immigrant mobilization was visible 5 to 10 months after legislative activity threatening immigrants, indicating the temporal quality of immigrants' response to threat. Threat must be attributed, opportunities perceived, and solidarity cultivated.

The central focus of this chapter is to identify the influence of threat and opportunity on the tactics that immigrant challengers adopt.[23] In addition to threat and opportunity, at least two other factors influence activists' choice of tactics: the formal or informal character of the organization and the structural position of contenders.[24] While organizations are important for sustaining a social movement between waves of mobilization,[25] they can also exert a conservative influence on the way activists press their claims. In their seminal study of "poor people's movements," Piven and Cloward argue that the organizations that emerged out of mass movements tended to work against disruption because, "in their search for resources to maintain their organizations, they were driven inexorably to elites, and to the tangible and symbolic supports that elites could provide."[26] This perspective has been challenged by scholars who argue that decentralized and informal organizations can have the opposite effect and encourage disruptive tactics through horizontal processes of collective decision making.[27] Formality and informality may not be fixed characteristics of SMOs. As the cases above demonstrate, a single organization like La Unión can cycle through periods of formality and informality in response to a wide range of factors, like economic recession.

The structural location of challengers, that is their relative powerlessness, also influences tactical choice. Challengers with less to lose, like the unemployed or college students, are more likely to engage in disruption and other forms of "high-risk" activism.[28] The structural power of targets exerts its own influence. Walker, Martin, and McCarthy find that states, compared to educational institutions and corporations, are uniquely situated to repress, facilitate, and routinize contention, resulting in tactics that are more contained and less disruptive.[29]

In sum, when activists perceive opportunity, they often use institutionalized tactics to pursue their claims,[30] especially when the target is the state and even in the face of significant threat. Activists turn to disruptive tactics, by contrast, when little opportunity exists and institutionalized tactics seem ineffective,[31] especially when the target is a non-state actor and the challenger is not a formalized SMO.[32] Critically, "objective" measures of opportunity and threat do not explain mobilization or tactic choice by themselves. Micro- and meso-level factors, like organizational culture and activists' perceptions of threat and opportunity, are key to understanding why immigrant challengers choose certain tactics over others.

Collaboration and Contestation in the Immigrant Rights Movement

With these considerations in mind, I return to the four elements of political opportunity identified at the outset of the chapter: elite allies, divisions among elites, capacity for repression, and access to the political system.[33] By filtering the details of these two cases through these elements of political opportunity and threat, I argue that La Unión organizers in North City adopted confrontational tactics because threats there were intense and broadly experienced. During a period of organizational disruption, La Unión found itself uniquely available for high-risk tactics: a march and rally calling for the ouster of the police chief. In South City, by contrast, relatively milder threats and open lines of communication with the police chief himself, coupled with an organizational culture that privileged maintaining ties with elites, led to the adoption of a collaborative tactic: the community forum.

My primary informant in South City, Esmeralda, had an *elite ally* in the police chief, creating an opportunity. In North City, organizers did not have an ally in the police chief, nor did they have other elite allies in the city who could pressure the police chief on their behalf. Both the police chief and the mayor were openly hostile to La Unión and the Latino immigrant community generally.

In South City, few *divisions existed among elite members* of city government. While city leaders and the police chief sometimes differed on various issues, in the course of our lobbying work with the South City council, each city council member clearly valued the police chief's opinion about public safety issues, like car impoundments, and refused to take a public stance against him. While the North City police chief had previously enjoyed the support and protection of the prior city manager, the current city manager could no longer ignore the growing dissatisfaction with the police chief's performance both within the department and in the broader community.

While social movement scholars typically conceptualize *capacity for repression* as the state's ability to repress dissent,[34] I operationalize this element of political opportunity as enforcement climate. The target of state repression was not dissent, but the quotidian existence of Latino immigrant communities. While relations with police were deteriorating in both places due to their collaboration with federal immigration enforcement and the pervasiveness of car impoundments, this threat was particularly acute in North City, due largely to a string of officer-involved shootings in which nearly all the victims were Latino, as well as the positioning of DUI checkpoints in places that many community members felt were designed to snare undocumented, unlicensed drivers. This rash of police violence crystallized the perception among Latinos that the police were fundamentally opposed to the Mexican immigrant community and the Latino community in general.

Political representation and access to the political system were greater in South City where Latino immigrants enjoyed some representation in local government, the police administration, and the business community, even though they were a minority presence in the city. State legislation limiting the car impoundments of unlicensed, undocumented drivers augmented their political power on this issue and created an opportunity that allowed them to secure a small, but significant victory:

the end of the 30-day impoundment. In North City, Latinos generally had little political representation and little electoral power in the context of an otherwise conservative electorate hostile to a sizeable immigrant community.[35] Part of the reason that threat (in the form of E-Verify, car impoundments, police killings) was elevated in the North City case is because of the conservative political environment that incubated it.

Finally, and though La Unión meets the definition of a *formalized SMO*,[36] these campaigns were waged in a period of organizational transition in the wake of serious financial troubles that led to La Unión ultimately being subsumed by a larger regional organization. In South City, the absence of coalition partners and key organizer Esmeralda's adherence to an organizational culture of collaboration led to the adoption of the community forum as the preferred tactic for addressing car impoundments. In North City, this moment of organizational rupture coupled with the influence of a coalition partner led to the adoption of a more confrontational protest tactic.

Threat and opportunity do not only encourage or discourage protest. They also influence the shape that protest takes. Both the South City case and its North City counterpart affirm the general thrust of scholars who have examined threat: *both* increasing opportunity *and* threat can stimulate mobilization. Greater opportunity and mild threat in South City generated an opening for mobilization of a certain type: a collaborative community forum in which a small victory—the end of the 30-day impoundment—was won.[37] In North City threat stimulated a highly confrontational response to a state actor due to the breadth and intensity of the threat of police violence, the unique openness of La Unión to tactics that they typically avoided as a consequence of organizational transition, and the context of a mixed political environment in which one key element of opportunity presented itself: the erosion of elite and rank-and-file officer support for the police chief. Ultimately, the police chief resigned.

The selection of conventional tactics in South City is an effect of not only the state's unique ability to facilitate and channel contention,[38] but also La Unión's organizing philosophy that privileged relationship building with elites and elected officials: a philosophy manifested in their first preference for collaborative tactics. In North City, by contrast, the police chief made no effort to negotiate La Unión's demands. Police (and other elected officials including the mayor) were instead a source of direct threat. The facilitative potential of state actors was not realized, and La Unión turned to tactics that were more confrontational in both form and substance: a march and rally calling for the police chief's resignation.

Organizational "tactical repertoires" were the final key factor.[39] Formalized organizations avoid disruption precisely because of their organizational prioritization of relationship building with elites, as was the case in South City. The unique moment of rupture in which La Unión found itself in the wake of the Great Recession of 2008, however, destabilized the organization. The North City office's collaboration with a South City gang advocacy organization that was more informal in its structure and composed of a critical mass of energized young people pulled their tactics in the direction of disruption. This breach in the typically formal quality of La Unión operations led to a march and rally calling for the ouster of the North City police chief.

Conclusion

Local features of political opportunity and threat have taken on a renewed importance in the absence of federal reform and the proliferation of enforcement practices and legislation at the state and local levels that variously welcome or reject immigrants. Extending the key insights of the political opportunity and threat literature, this chapter honed in on the way both state and local opportunity/threat conditions, as well as micro-level processes of perception and attribution, influence protest tactics. La Unión's organizational culture generally privileged relationship building with elites. While organizers adhered to this orientation in South City, the North City case demonstrated that formalized organizations, in a moment of rupture following the Great Recession of 2008, pursued disruptive tactics when influenced to do so by coalition partners. In this way, internal organizational dynamics, situated in wider political contexts of opportunity and threat, led to the adoption of collaborative tactics in progressive South City and confrontational tactics in more conservative North City. Opportunity and threat both stimulate mobilization. They also play an important role in shaping the social form of that mobilization.

The social movement literature's concepts of political opportunity and threat offer immigration scholars a useful way to understand the critical role of political context that inspires and conditions the expression of agency from this marginalized community. The ongoing struggle of immigrant communities for recognition and safety commensurate with their contributions to the polity reminds observers of the abiding quality of agency, from the collaborative to the confrontational, in the face of threat. Just as threat varies from place to place, so does the form of its contestation.

Conclusion

American Dream, American Hypocrisy

Democratic citizens . . . have a choice: if they want to bring
in new workers, they must be prepared to enlarge their own
membership; if they are unwilling to accept new members,
they must find ways within the limits of the domestic labor
market to get socially necessary work done. And those are
their only choices."[1]
—Walzer, *Spheres of Justice*

America's Hypocrisy

Mexican immigration, as with much of immigration to the United
States, is primarily a labor migration. Spurred by regionally organized
economic precarity in Mexico and lured to the United States by cyclical
demands from industry for cheap and flexible labor, the social problem
of (undocumented) immigration reflects a socially organized hypocrisy. On the one hand, the American Dream for this so-called nation
of immigrants promises prosperity in exchange for hard work (and
its corollary: staying off welfare), perseverance, and avoiding criminal
activity. And it is indeed true that immigration leads to better outcomes
for (undocumented) Mexican immigrants. Evidenced by wage differ-
entials between the countries and the approximately $24.3 billion in
remittances sent from the United States to Mexico in 2015 (surpassing,
for the first time, oil revenue as the leading source of foreign income),[2]
this relative prosperity indicates the benefits of immigration to Mexican
immigrants.

And yet, this fragile economic mobility, leveraged by their central role
in various US industries from agriculture to hospitality, is undermined
by their legal and social subordination. Unable to fill the labor needs of
key sectors without immigrant labor, the United States has nevertheless

proven unwilling to expand the boundaries of membership. Not since 1965 has the US government substantially revised the way that it allots visas. This system—whose country cap functions as an artificial choke point for would-be legal immigrants—is a key structural mechanism by which immigrant illegality is sustained.[3] The other is, of course, a growing deportation regime that has fortified the barriers to entry and intensified the consequences of illegality. It has done so by extending enforcement to the interior of the United States through the collaborative effort of ICE, local police, and sheriff departments. Regional enforcement is carried out by Mexican police who, with US encouragement and material support, act as immigration enforcement inside Mexico. The Programa Frontera Sur attempts to stop Central American immigrants in Mexico before they can attempt an unauthorized crossing at the US-Mexico border. The border exists now as a radial extension both inward and outward from that place where the wall is.

Various other programs and practices by local authorities, like car impoundments of undocumented, unlicensed drivers, are neutral on their face, but, in effect, contribute to the subordinated standing of undocumented immigrants; that is, their racial naturalization. Combine this with the weakening of the protections that attend lawful permanent resident status and a broader "Latino threat narrative" that denigrates Latinos by marking them with the social stigma of illegality and unassimilability (even when their migration is authorized or they are native-born US citizens) and a certain hypocrisy comes into view.[4] This mode of cultural subordination has, moreover, been given renewed life in the wake of President Trump's victory among electors, if not among voters. The contradiction between Mexican immigrants' economic centrality and their broader social undesirability brings us to the hypocritical heart of the American Dream. We want labor without being prepared to offer membership: something for nothing, or for not much.

From the perspective of the transnational capitalist class, this situation is advantageous because it ensures a ready supply of exploitable, mobile labor whose subordination is sustained through these exclusionary campaigns. Though work site enforcement, like the highly publicized raids in Postville, Iowa, in 2008, has received greater emphasis in recent years, the great bulk of the immigration enforcement apparatus has been trained on the border and in collaborations with local law enforcement. Congress historically has been reluctant to come down too hard on industry. As Josiah Heyman has argued, this situation "creates and legitimates advantageous exploitability effects, but puts the risks (arrest, armed robbery, or death) and costs (smuggling fees) on the shoulders of immigrants."[5] Not conspiratorially organized by employers as was truer in the mid-1900s when a powerful agricultural bloc could directly influence enforcement practice, this condition of deportability is a relational one: an outcome of a structural chaffing between nativist exclusion and neoliberal transnationalism that accommodates American industry's appetite for cheap labor and Mexican immigrants' pursuit of social mobility.[6]

From the perspective of migrants themselves, this arrangement generates their economic and physical precarity. Their labor is the site of their exploitation, and so it comes as no surprise that their labor also forms the normative basis for their demands for rights and resources. This hypocrisy is not lost on the Mexican immigrants in this study. Roberto, sitting beside his wife Maritza in their living room, described their arrival to the United States in 1996. Maritza confided that although it was difficult to leave her family in Mexico, she wanted her daughters to be born in the United States to "give them a better life." Roberto described the city as a "paradise." Even though their "hearts were in Mexico" (*mi tierra de corazon*), they felt as though they "live in freedom" in South City as compared to their lives in Mexico. Probing to see whether they had any complaints about life in South City, I asked Roberto whether he thought daily life for Latinos is different than for white people. As he spoke, it immediately became clear that their experience was more complex than his initial response suggested:

> Because they live more comfortably than we do. They have more chances of buying a house; they can get a house while we can't. They are allowed to have a license and we can't. They can obtain loans from a bank and we can't. They have more chances to make money faster than we do. They can travel, they can move to a different place, with a passport, a visa, and we can't do that. We can't open a business. There are many of us who would like to have our own business, but we can't obtain neither the driver license, nor a work permit because we don't have a social secu-

rity number [*buen seguro social*]. If we, the Latinos, had a social security number, can you imagine what we could do? We would perform miracles. If we didn't have to put up with all this. For any job they request a social security number. That's a very important difference for Latinos.

Latinos suffer more, we provide hard work and we don't fly away and ask ourselves why, why us. We are here to do the hard work. The white people work behind their desks, and we have to work in the field. We receive education but we can't go to college, we don't have a social security number. We stay there and they continue studying. That's the big difference between a Latino and an American.

—Roberto and Maritza, Mexican, undocumented, 17 years in the United States, South City, 40–50

Roberto recounts the sacrifices he has made, working in the bottom stratum of a segmented labor market, providing necessary labor that "Americans" simply will not do. His suffering has gone unrecognized and unrewarded by an immigration regime that takes what it needs, but returns little in the way of opportunity. He does this without bemoaning his lot.

This is not merely an economic argument about the value of immigrant labor, but an ideological claim that relies on immigrants' economic utility, their work ethic, to mount a critique of an immigration system that stymies their development. It is an indictment of the present arrangement in which Americans rely on immigrant labor, but object to their substantive belonging. These are deeply felt, affective objections to their subordination. Immigrant people do not simply lump it; their experience illuminates the hypocritical terms of the American Dream: an aspiration for many, accessible to some, and built upon the labor of many Others. In this sense, the Dream, as Ta-Nehisi Coates has referred to it,[7] functions as aspiration and as nationalistic myth. Mythic both in the sense that hard work will yield middle-class prosperity (and not a more purgatorial state of perpetually making ends meet) and in the sense that the Dream obscures the reality of exploitation that does not just blemish but underpins American prosperity. Striving for material betterment in the context of exploitation illuminates the hypocrisy that Roberto describes. His experience, moreover, evidences the way the subordination of immigrant people purchases our surfeit.

The Dream, as both a normative aspiration and a source of immiseration, provides the essential context out of which immigrant agency and activism emerge. The material moorings of immigrant activism refer to the way that Mexican immigrants' economic precarity is sustained by this American hypocrisy and, in turn, shapes their agency. Mexican immigrants, the undocumented, as well as those in states of liminal legality,[8] default to the strategies of the shell—avoidance and insulation—in order to protect themselves from the threats of dispossession, detention, and deportation. The shell refers to a private strategy of turning inward in order to mitigate risk and to shore up the hard-won material gains they have secured for themselves and for their families through their migration. These habituated strategies of risk management are buttressed by an analysis of this American hypocrisy and inspire the grievances that Roberto articulates above. These broadly shared grievances are fertile ground for social movement organizing.

Of course, social movement organizing does not emerge automatically out of grievance, no matter how broadly shared or intense. The shell, an orientation that is fundamentally risk-averse, forms a counterweight against immigrants' participation in social movement organizing, throwing up barriers related to fear and work and a more general calculus that weighs collective mobilization against their first priority: the reproduction of family and enjoying what precious leisure time they have together.

These barriers can be overcome when community organizers who are organically connected to the communities they serve and supported by robust social movement organizations deploy compelling narrative frames that communicate the efficacy of collective action and immigrants' shared responsibility to take part. Wider local and national political conditions influence not whether collective action will occur, but the shape that their activism will take, ranging from the collaborative to the contentious. When immigrant collective action emerges, their orientation remains instrumental in its focus on the material gains that activism can secure: a conservative impulse to inhabit the normative institutions of law, family, and work that will allow them to secure the trappings of a middle-class existence, including homeownership, higher wages, education, a driver's license, and so on.

In their politics, their labor is central not only as the site of their exploitation, but also as the ethical ground of their political demands.[9]

They have toiled in the lowest rungs of the labor market and made investments in family, economy, and community. Consequently, they have earned their place in the United States and, in turn, demand legal and social inclusion commensurate with their contributions. As their imaginations stretch outward toward a future freedom, that aspirational vision remains moored to the material exigencies in the present that are their first priority.[10]

While radical, counterhegemonic blocs can be built out of efforts to address these material, bread-and-butter issues, these sorts of sustained radical movements are rare, I argue, because of the material moorings of immigrant activism. Cycles of immigrant social movement organizing are shaped by what political opportunities exist at the national level for reform, historically unprecedented levels of immigration enforcement, "grasstops" movement leaders' tacit acceptance of what Alfonso Gonzales calls "anti-migrant hegemony," and so on.[11] The account I offer here seeks not to trump these explanations but to add an account of the way that immigrant participation in social movement work is both animated and encumbered by the material conditions of Mexican immigrants' everyday lives and their necessarily short-term focus on protecting their fragile and hard-won mobility. It is as though to say, "It's right here in the present where the future will be made."

The material moorings of immigrant agency help to explain the periodicity of immigrant participation evident in social movement work generally. Though robust, local organizing continued after 2006 (e.g., the civil disobedience of the latter part of the DREAMers movement and the contentious anti–SB 1070 activism in Arizona), the demobilization of the immigrant rights movement after 2006, as well as my observations of immigrants' reluctance to participate in two California cities, suggest not the absence of agency but an oscillation between their instrumental activism and the defensive tactics of the shell.

While avoidance and insulation are necessary strategies of risk management, especially for undocumented immigrants, collective action is optional and subordinate to the quotidian struggle to make life in the deportation nation. And yet, the shell incubates a critique of the hypocrisy of the American Dream: a critical consciousness that can inspire participation in collective action. Even while barriers remain to the transformation of those grievances into social movement demands, the shell contains this potential for contention. And this potential is realized in the social process of community organizing where their grievances are remapped in historical terms and concrete strategies for action are laid out by organic leaders who guide the identification of opportunities for action. The material moorings of immigrant activism name this dilemma: everyday immigrant life is both a source of inspiration for collective action and an encumbrance upon the realization of this potential. The strategies of the shell and immigrants' instrumental activism bolt down this spectrum of agency in the material conditions of everyday life.

Immigrant Activism, Democratic Visions

The question of what animates immigrant politics seems especially important to me precisely because my orientation to the study of social movements reflects not only an interest in movement dynamics themselves, but also an effort to understand the alternative legal, economic, political, and social arrangements immanent to the immigrant rights struggle. That is, immigrant action in its individual and collective forms offers a window onto a more democratic social order that immigrant politics allow us to imagine. And yet, as I've argued throughout this text, Mexican immigrants often seek to inhabit, not challenge, those institutions that are responsible for their subordination. To what extent, then, do immigrant social movements provide this window onto a more radically democratic future?

Consider, for instance, Monisha Das Gupta's characterization of immigrant rights claims as a "transnational complex of rights" or a constellation of rights that is not grounded in a claim for nation-state-based citizenship.[12] Of its four components, I highlight the last: the desire on the part of the respondents in her study for "rights to mobility rather than to rootedness and citizenship."[13] Conducting ethnographic participant observation with seven different social movement organizations—feminist, queer, and labor in their orientations—in three states on the East Coast, Das Gupta offers an eloquent portrayal of South Asian immigrants engaged in space-making and not place-taking politics: "Place-taking politics will continue to conserve and consolidate its constituencies' privileges, while space-makers will seek to transform the conditions that exploit them."[14] Fernandez and Olsen advance a similar claim in their brief examination of Mexican immigrants in Arizona who are "pushing the freedom of locomotion beyond the boundaries of the nation-state, and thus of liberal citizenship itself."[15] In these portrayals, immigrant politics challenge not their exclusion, but the inherent exclusivity of citizenship itself. While the legal and social significance of terrestrial borders has not been washed away by the transnational scope of neoliberal economic policy, it certainly, according to these scholars, cannot encompass immigrant politics, which contain a transnational and transformative radicalism irreducible to belonging as citizenship.

And yet, other portrayals highlight a certain conformism in immigrant claims making. Take the work of Baker-Cristales, who compares the unprecedented marches of 2006 with the subsequent student walkouts, which were often dismissed as kids skipping class. She argues that the careful policing of Latin American flags and the showcasing of immigrants as model citizen subjects who are neither terrorists nor criminals reinscribe exclusionary citizenship by asking for inclusion in the category as opposed to the category's transformation. "The irony is," she argues, "that many protesters who clearly aimed to question the exclusion of Latin American immigrants from US citizenship came to use symbolic forms that emerge from an oppressive and exclusionary model of citizenship."[16] Barvosa, too, argues that immigrants are less like bigamists (with connections to two places) and more like divorcées who have remarried (they have important ties to the country of origin but are committed to life in the United States). She points to labor force participation, tax contributions, consumer activity, and especially having and raising US-born children as evidence.[17] This characterization of immigrant politics comes closer to Mahmood's portrayal of agency as inhabiting norms (see Chapter 4) in which the transnational remains central to immigrants' experience of mobility, but is not carried over into the center of their political aspirations.[18]

The notion of material moorings that I advance is presented not as an intermediary point between these distinct perspectives. The idea is not simply to be seduced by the gravity of the political middle, nor is it to propose a grand theory that should trump other conceptualizations. Instead, material moorings is the name for the dilemma inherent to immigrant claims making: the way material grievances enable and constrain the political imagination. Immigrants will, of course, negotiate this problem in various ways, as will scholars writing about them. While portrayals will differ, I argue that attention to this dilemma helps ground analysis in *both* the liberatory *and* the pragmatic facets of immigrant politics. When migrants engage in citizenship as a practice, their politics are potentially transformative in at least two ways: claims for inclusion may simply expand the category to encompass migrant citizens in waiting, or they may call for a more radical transformation of the terms of inclusion and the rights that attend that status.[19] As I argue below, the everyday immigrant politics that I observed embody elements of both. To delineate these facets, I return a final time to narratives of immigrants themselves.

Mooring the Material to Politics

First, recall Roberto's comments from above. His deservingness is justified by his labor. This link between labor and deservingness has been long established in US law and culture. After the industrial revolution, free and productive labor became the primary currency of inclusion. Full membership, both cultural and legal, was determined on the basis of one's capacity and willingness to work. The link between labor and deservingness is carried through into the present with the 1996 Personal Responsibility and Work Opportunity Reconciliation Act, which, as part of the 1990s political focus on welfare reform, prevented immigrants with legal status from accessing various federal programs like Social Security, food stamps, and aid for the elderly, the blind, and the disabled, and barred them from participation in Medicaid for the first five years after their entry.[20]

Work is the central organizing principle in the lives of many Mexican immigrants. Take the very common political slogan, easily spotted at many immigrant rights actions: "We are workers, not criminals." Their subordination as an exploited and racialized class of workers is both a source of grievance and the foundation of a political claim for inclusion on the same terms as the requirements of political and cultural belonging. Immigrants force a legal and cultural reconciliation of their formal exclusion with their substantive performance of neoliberal citizenship. Though immigrants are the constitutive outside for legal citizens, they daily demonstrate their fitness for inclusion with the sweat equity they have already invested in the American Dream.

Second, many of the immigrants in this study wanted, as a result of their participation in political action, the trappings of a middle-class existence that would grant them stasis: a bulwark against the turbulence of precarity. Roberto wants to be able to access credit, build a home, and start a business. He is explicit in his recognition of Mexican immigrants' potential to do so and his indictment of the legal bars that prevent the realization of their full potential as middle-class citizen subjects. As I elaborated in Chapter 4, Mexican immigrant activism is instrumental in its focus on inhabiting norms. Many of the immigrants I encountered sought upward social mobility, as opposed to challenging the neoliberal terms upon which this mobility can be secured. While it is hardly the responsibility of immigrants to articulate a more radical claim, especially given the material exigencies of their precarity that I emphasize throughout this book, I noted that this invitation to a deeper criticism of citizenship is one potential outcome of their experience that is often not taken up. In their daily lives, they demonstrate their readiness for political inclusion using the criteria of neoliberal citizenship: hardworking noncriminals who prioritize family and self-sufficiency. I do not mean here to suggest that immigrants ought to pursue a more radical politics that questions the terms of their belonging or that they never do. The point is not to judge their choices, but to highlight the way their desires, of a potentially infinite range of possibilities, are articulated in terms that comport with the Dream.

The final way that Roberto's claims seek legal and cultural belonging is evident in how he describes doing Americanness better than Americans themselves. That he refuses to run from hard work suggests that, as a consequence of his undocumented status, Roberto is forced to understand what is required for American social mobility better than Americans themselves do. He is seeking legal inclusion in order to secure social mobility, and his strategy for pursuing this goal involves an utter devotion to work that he argues many Americans have forgotten or foregone. His place outside the privileged site of citizenship requires an unwavering fidelity to the conventions of neoliberal citizenship both to avoid the daily risks of dispossession, detention, and deportation and to present himself as worthy of the material benefits that attend legal belonging. In this formulation, Roberto understands best what being an American requires precisely because of his place outside citizenship. He understands this better than Americans themselves, who have grown complacent in their privilege.

Take another example, this time from a group interview:

R: And that's why [inaudible] they're spending millions [inaudible] feeding those bums in jails. And so with us, who are earning more money, they know very well that we pay because we work, so then that's why they take advantage of us a lot. . . . The police have power, supposedly, power to screw the people not to help us.

C: And us Mexicans are the ones that work, because there isn't another race that goes out to work hard in the fields of grapes or whatever. Nothing but Latinos, and if we run out of Latinos, we are left without food.

—Rosario, 50–60, and Cristina, 40–50

In this group interview, these respondents together enact a normative Mexican identity at whose heart is labor. Their opposition to their exploitation is buttressed by their hard work, something they claim other racial groups simply will not do. Note, however, the way that this indictment of the hypocrisy of US citizenship and the American Dream relies on another constitutive outside: those "bums" in jail, those incarcerated masses whose own failings have evidently landed them in the custody of the state. Excluded from formal membership, these Mexican immigrants demonstrate their fitness for inclusion by highlighting their performance of citizenship's requirements. Their exclusion is a symptom of the state's failure to reward their contributions, not their personal failings. They compare themselves to those who have formal membership, but have failed to earn it ("bums"). Their fitness for the Dream is demonstrated not only through their own labor and self-enterprise, but by identifying a negative referent group who has not demonstrated the same.[21] An inherent complexity of political claims making is that the articulation of one group's deservingness can come at the expense of another's, especially when articulated from within the fraught norms of the American Dream. Such a claim risks alienating Others on those same terms and with whom we might make common cause.

But if these immigrant politics seek to inhabit norms, in what ways do they extend out beyond these normative requirements? When undocumented immigrants make claims for inclusion and when documented immigrants demand equal protection commensurate with their legal standing, they make these claims from outside citizenship or from its lowest rungs. When claims are brought from the constitutive outside to legal and cultural belonging, immigrant politics represent a fundamentally democratic challenge that is marshaled by those who live at democracy's limit.[22] When "those appear who are not supposed to appear," we witness the most naked expression of democratic practice.[23] Immigrant acts force a reconciliation between their performance of the norms of legal belonging and their actual inclusion. Their politics represent an invitation to the American body politic to abide by its own norms of equal opportunity and work as worth. Indeed, it is an invitation to be more fully democratic.

Second, much has been made of the immigrant demand for mobility as a counterpoint to the permanence that citizenship implies. Fernandez and Olsen, for instance, argue, "To the extent that they do seek US citizenship, it is to facilitate locomotion rather than vice versa. They are thus demanding both less and more than liberal citizenship."[24] While I also encountered immigrant respondents who also sought the right to traverse the US-Mexico border freely, I see this claim as differing from Fernandez and Olsen's argument in two important ways. First, immigrants seek mobility *through* legal belonging. Their mobility is not counterposed to legal inclusion, but facilitated by it. Second, given the militarization of the US-Mexico border that began in earnest in the early 1990s, cyclical labor migration throughout the Southwest has been interrupted, trapping undocumented immigrants inside the United States. The unintended consequence of intensified border enforcement has been that immigrants have developed deeper roots than they otherwise would have if they were allowed to move freely across the border. US-born children, in particular, provide an incentive to stay in the United States. Maritza's perspective, from my interview with her and Roberto, was typical:

> I'd love to go back to Mexico. It's a beautiful place, but I would like to go on a tourist plan, if some day we obtain our documents I would like to go

and come back here. Maybe when I'm old I can go back there, stay there
for a while and come back here. My daughters live here and no matter
what we have to stay here, but I would like to go back for a visit.

Border enforcement strategies have transformed both migratory cycles
and the aspirations of immigrants now permanently settled in the
United States. Maritza's long-term prospects inside the United States
are not simply counterposed to an abiding desire for unbounded "locomotion," but are transformed as a consequence of her undocumented
status. She wishes to visit Mexico freely, but this mobility, it seems to
me, is secured through and not against legal inclusion. The notion that
immigrant mobility chafes against a territorially bounded definition of
citizenship is important, but such mobility may be secured by burrowing
into the conventions of citizenship. In this complex way, mobility may
be important though not central to the everyday experience and aspirations of immigrants in the United States who have themselves been
transformed over the course of their residence in the deportation nation.

A final way that immigrant politics extend out beyond the conventions
of the American Dream is evident in the collective and transnational quality of their political activity. One of the most consistent themes across interviews was sacrifice for family and community. Hometown associations,
for instance, facilitate the transmission of the fruits of immigrants' labor
back to their communities of origin. Hometown associations are transnational partnerships between communities on both sides of the border.
Money raised by immigrants in the north is often combined with funds
from local governments in the south to support various community and
public works projects. Reymundo and Osvaldo explain:

> R: When we know that someone from Mexico is sick and doesn't have
> the money, we come together and make dinner and call people to
> come and cooperate. If we make a meal and sell each serving for $5,
> everything that's collected is sent to help that person who is sick. . . .
> O: Like a while ago, there's a program to help people over there, they
> repaired the streets because they are not all okay. They repaired a
> street, a plaza, and a garden.
> —Reymundo and Osvaldo, undocumented, South County, 30–40,
> landscaping and construction

This transnational network of support is perhaps the clearest example of the way immigrant politics exceed the territorially bounded quality of the American Dream and the legal pathways that lead to it. On the one hand, this entrepreneurial activity is performed in the interests of community, not the individual. And its transnational character evidences the scope of immigrant communities beyond the territorially bounded nation-state. The breadth of their concern indicates a political imagination and a scope of empathy unbound by the sovereign limits of citizenship.

Latino immigration since the 1960s, driven largely by Mexican immigrants, has inaugurated a potentially transformative moment in American politics. If brown really is "the new white,"[25] what kinds of politics are being ushered in during this period of demographic change? I submit that immigrant politics, moored as they are to their social location as economically necessary, but socially undesirable, may both comport with and break from the conventions of the American Dream. The centrality of labor to normative Mexican immigrant identity, coupled with the instrumental quality of their activism and their faithful adherence to norms of hard work, noncriminality, and family evidence their worthiness precisely because these characteristics comport with the requirements of legal and cultural inclusion, of citizenship and the Dream.

And yet immigrant politics exceed these expectations in important ways. As cultural and legal outsiders, their experience illuminates the hypocrisies of the present arrangement in which immigrants are necessary, but unwanted. Their politics represent a potential democratization of citizenship by demanding a reconciliation of their daily performance of Americanness with their legal exclusion. The transnational and collective character of their claims for mobility exceeds the territorially bounded and individualistic scope of concern typical of the entrepreneurial neoliberal citizen. Immigrant politics contain elements of both pragmatism and liberation. Their simultaneity reflects the material moorings of immigrant politics, the exigency of exploitation in the present, their challenge to American hypocrisy, and hope for enhanced mobility and dignity in the future.

Movements and Moorings: The Horizons of Latino Politics

The primary contribution of this study lies in its effort to refine a growing current in the immigration literature that has focused explicitly on the shape and place of immigrant agency in the deportation nation. In the immigrant communities where I was privileged to work, the various forms of agency and action in which they were engaged oscillated from the elusive and everyday to the confrontational and dramatic. Staying indoors after receiving a text about a nearby *retén* was a rather quotidian occurrence. Gathering in a group of 200 to ask for leniency from the police chief in the execution of car impoundments was considerably more striking. Common to both kinds of activities, both expressions of agency, is their link to the material and quotidian concerns of the Mexican immigrants in this study. They "make history" in order to improve the conditions under which they can engage in their primary activity, their primary motivation for migration in the first place: making life.

Their demands were shaped by a wide variety of factors. The political commitments, tactical preferences, and long-term goals of the organizers who led these mobilization efforts influenced the shape of immigrant political action. These demands are also undoubtedly shaped by the socioeconomic location of immigrant laborers. As they are toiling in the lowest rungs of a stratified global economy, their visions for themselves and their families are shaped simultaneously by hope and deprivation, by an optimistic futurism and the present reality of exploitation. They asked for neighborhoods free from gang violence, an end to or a reduction in the severity of car impoundments, freedom from deportation, access to education for their children, broader civic engagement from their neighbors, and high-quality, steady work opportunities.

This connection between quotidian grievances and instrumental politics raises a dilemma, not one focused on the exploitative conditions migrants face, as in the formulation, we want your labor, but we don't want you. Instead this dilemma is related to the shape of immigrant agency and the horizons of Latino politics in the United States. What is the transformative potential of this increasingly politically significant bloc of voters, activists, and political subjects? What are the horizons of Latino politics? What are immigrants' goals, and what obstacles lie in the path to their attainment?

As I discuss throughout this book, there are many barriers to greater immigrant inclusion. Former President Obama and a cadre of Democratic senators, for instance, have imperiled substantive reform by treating enforcement as a "down payment" for immigration reform later. The result has been more deportations than any previous administration, with the predictable result that Republicans would not budge on reform anyway.[26] On the other end of the political spectrum, the Republican Party largely refuses a pathway to legalization, calling for ever more enforcement. Huge swaths of the American public continue to blame immigrants for everything from the state of the economy to increased crime and unemployment, despite ample evidence to the contrary.[27] More broadly, US structural economic dependence on migrant labor coupled with the state's collusion in sustaining their deportability maintains their exploitation in the lowest rungs of the economy and feeds a growing "immigration industrial complex."[28] Each of these repressive dynamics fetters any drive for substantive immigrant inclusion from comprehensive reform to deferred action.

There is, however, more to this dilemma. The transformative potential of Latino politics is also limited by the very source of its inspiration: its material mooring. By examining forms of survival and resistance among Mexican immigrants at the micro and meso levels, I have demonstrated the ways that immigrant political action both is inspired by and remains moored to everyday material conditions of deprivation and risk.

Xiomara exemplifies this linkage between political action and quotidian life. When I asked her if she felt as though she were a part of the community, she said that not being able to obtain a driver's license because she is undocumented made her feel like an outsider. She went on to say that she wanted

a lot less risk, more safety for everybody. If I had my driver's license . . . look, simply for going from my house to work to my children's school, that's all I would need a license for. Only for work and for my kids' school, I wouldn't ask for anything more. With only that, for me it would be a victory!

—Xiomara, Mexican, undocumented, South City, 40–50,
  housekeeper

Xiomara participated in the community forums with the police chief in order to seek relief from the impoundment of unlicensed drivers' vehicles. But she notes that this is all she wants, the basic mobility and dignity that come with having a driver's license. She continued to organize actively with La Unión during the fieldwork for this study. The goals she held for herself and for this movement remained moored to quotidian desires, even as they inspired her involvement in the first place.

The material concerns that both inspire and constrain collective mobilization lie, I submit, at the heart of Mexican immigrant politics in the United States. In this way, immigrant agency is neither the stuff of conventional assimilationist tales, nor the radical politics of a revolutionary vanguard. The instrumental moorings of the immigrant politics that I have examined in this study lie between these poles. And while the precise reach and significance of Latino political influence in the contemporary moment cannot be known, I expect this tension between the normative aspirations of a growing movement and its material moorings will continue to influence immigrant politics going forward.

Given the centrality of the dilemma of material moorings to Latino politics, two practical shifts are necessary if the liberatory vision immanent to immigrant rights social movements is to be realized. First, we need a reinvigoration of political imagination on the left that is not captive to the hegemony of immigration enforcement. Decades of social science research have demonstrated the positive effects of immigration on the economy and our communities. These empirical insights must be pitted against a Latino threat narrative that enjoys hegemonic status among many Americans, especially, at the time of writing, in the early days of the Trump administration. That Democrat and former President Barack Obama oversaw the deportations of more immigrants than any previous administration, Democrat or Republican, is telling evidence of the grip that the enforcement-first approach has on party politics.

Beyond political parties, this "anti-migrant hegemony" circulates in the broader public discourse on the immigration crisis and constrains the terms of the debate: "a type of fluid and disparate ideological power that normalizes state violence" by narrowing the issue to one of criminality and terrorism.[29] The question becomes not whether deportation and border fortification, but how much. Countering the enforcement consensus will require both an empirical and a moral reckoning with the concrete effects of immigration on US society and our ethical obligation to provide a meaningful pathway to membership commensurate with immigrants' contributions.[30]

Second, and if it's the case that immigrants are least available to combat their subordination, allies of the immigrant rights struggle, documented immigrants and the native-born, have a key role to play in these movements. The broad-based participation of all those who have been the beneficiaries of immigration and the prosperity made possible by immigrants' sacrifice will be critical, especially because those who enjoy legal and political inclusion are unfettered by the quotidian exigencies that characterize Mexican immigrant life in the United States. The invitation to a more radical politics is extended not just to immigrants, but to all of us who see in their dilemma a common political future that does not dole out abuse and precarity on the basis of national belonging, even as those same groups do the socially necessary work that sustains us.

The material moorings of immigrant social movements point toward a liberatory project that is as pragmatic as it is democratic. It is democratic, in novel ways, because immigrants overtly contest the boundaries of belonging in the United States, often doing this from outside formal membership in the nation-state. These politics are pragmatic because they are designed to secure the makings of decent and dignified lives that are not unlike the lives of their nonimmigrant counterparts. They are part of a pragmatic liberatory project moored to the concrete preoccupations of Mexican migrants, informed by the experience of subordination, and seeking to amplify the dignity and opportunity that immigrants have sought all along.

ACKNOWLEDGMENTS

This book is an expression of the wisdom and experience of the many people to whom I am connected personally and professionally. They are credited below, though the work's shortcomings are, of course, exclusively my own.

Early mentors and readers included Howie Winant, whose unique blend of criticism and care is rare and was always delivered right on time. Winddance Twine helped me work through various ethnographic dilemmas and provided line edits and sage wisdom at key junctures. Lisa Hajjar and John S. W. Park offered candid and valuable feedback at early stages of the project. I owe a debt of gratitude to Carolyn Pinedo Turnovsky and Jennifer Earl, who were consummate mentors: professional, razor sharp, and supportive. I hope to be the kind of mentor to my students that they have been to me.

For their feedback and encouragement at different points in this project, I am grateful to John Mohr, Verta Taylor, Denise Segura, Maria Charles, and Grace Chang. Victor Rios, now colleague and collaborator, has been an unrelenting advocate, advancing my thinking again and again. Michelle Camacho has provided the best possible reception at the University of San Diego and weighed in at the latter stages of this project. I count my lucky stars that, by whatever grace, I was placed in her orbit. Pierrette Hondagneu-Sotelo, co-editor (with Victor Rios) of the NYU Press Latina/o Sociology series, has been a gentle and thorough reviewer. Tanya Golash-Boza, who I first encountered through her blog, Get a Life Ph.D., provided incredibly thorough notes on all of the chapters in this book at a late stage in the project. Tanya went above and beyond in her expert and thoroughgoing feedback, which has much improved the quality and presentation of the ideas in this book. Julia Miller-Cantzler and Rachel Einwohner each helped me think more deeply about the project's connection to the field of social movements.

My thanks to Ilene Kalish, Executive Editor at NYU Press, who saw promise in the work and gave me a shot. Dorothea Halliday, Caelyn Cobb, and Maryam Arain ushered the project along. I thank them for their efficiency and for entertaining my many questions. I owe a debt of gratitude to Joseph Dahm, who provided careful and thorough copyediting.

This work has benefitted from the support of the Center for New Racial Studies, the UCSB Chicano Studies Institute, the Flacks Fund for the Study of Democratic Possibilities, the Diversity Initiative for Graduate Study in the Social Sciences, the UCSB Department of Sociology, the UCSB Graduate Division, and the National Science Foundation (Grant SES-1203714). An early version of Chapter 2 was published in *The Nation and Its Peoples: Citizens, Denizens, Migrants* (Routledge), while a version of Chapter 5 appears in the journal *Research in Social Movements, Conflicts and Change* (Emerald). Various iterations and pieces of this project were presented to the audiences of the meetings of the Law and Society Association, the Pacific Sociological Association, the American Sociological Association, the UC Center for New Racial Studies, the California Lutheran University Center for Equality and Justice, and the inaugural international conference of the social movements journal *Mobilization*. Feedback and questions from the participants at these meetings undoubtedly improved this study.

I owe my deepest thanks to those who participated in this study. It is no small debt that I have incurred in asking immigrant respondents to reveal their vulnerabilities, struggles, and aspirations, especially when I had so little to offer them in return. They shared more than any stranger could rightfully ask them to share, and I hope that I have adequately and faithfully represented their struggles, hopes, and power in these pages. Their sacrifices inspire my ongoing dedication to the immigrant rights movement.

This project would have been simply impossible without three primary informants. Antonio Rivera, Hazel Putney-Davalos, and the indefatigable Tere Jurado vouched for me. Without their trust, no one would have trusted me in turn. Tere, in particular, *torciendo brazos*, opened doors I could not have opened alone and convinced people to share with this *pocho* stranger the stories of survival and resilience that fill these pages. She is a hero, an institution in her community, and a friend to whom I will always be devoted. *Mil gracias, amiga mia.*

The staff and volunteers at the various community organizations with whom I worked supported this project and my personal development at critical moments, especially Anabel Merino, Belén Seara, Nayra Pacheco, Kristine Chong, Eme, Santa, Alena Marie, Jarrod Schwartz, and Esther Flores. Their influence cemented my commitment to linking knowledge production to political action. Feliciano and Laura shared their beautiful home with me and provided sanctuary on my many trips north.

Colleagues and friends near and far provided intellectual stimulation, emotional support, and company in the many days of writing that produced this book. Danny Olmos, Cesar "Che" Rodríguez, Alison Crossly, Veronica Montes, Cassandra Engeman, Pat Lopez-Aguado, Andy Pattison, Desiree LeBoeuf-Davis, Deborah Hobden, Anna Sorenson, and Elizabeth Rahilly were comrades and confidantes. Writing with Chandra Russo remains one of my favorite collaborative experiences. I would not be where I am had it not been for my academic coaches Maghbouleh and Childress. Neda and Clayton, I am so grateful to each of you.

To my oldest mentors at Whittier College—sal johnston and Elizabeth Sage—the prospect of a career in the academy was unimaginable without your influence. More than that, the time I spent under your tutelage utterly transformed the way I understand this world and myself. I can say without exaggeration that you changed my life.

Chosen family has been vital. To my sisters—Tara Uliasz, Alena Marie, Kristen Uliasz, Maria Zamudio, Raquel Bernaldo, Em Baraan, Vanessa Solis, Grecia Lima, and Adrian—you nourish me, you inspire me, you have seen me through. To my brothers—York Shingle, Rian Johnson, and Yoon Woo Nam—we have worked through it all together. You are all a miracle.

Sherry and Sam, none of this could have happened without you. Michelle, this is for you.

APPENDIX

Research Methods

La Unión originated as a coalitional project of Latino activists, union leaders, and other community leaders who mobilized Latinos for local electoral campaigns and workers' rights causes, in particular for a living wage ordinance. It grew, over time, into a multi-issue organization addressing grievances related to public transportation, affordable housing, and immigrant rights. The organization worked on these issues across one California county and maintained offices in two cities: one located in North City and the other in South City. The organization had two arms, one with a 501(c)(3) tax-exempt status and another with 501(c)(4) tax-exempt status. This organizational structure enabled La Unión organizers to engage in both the educational and civic engagement work typical of social movement organizations, and the electoral and lobbying work typical of political advocacy organizations, such as endorsing candidates, raising money for political campaigns, running phone banks, and precinct walking in support of one or another candidate.

On one of the very first occasions that I recorded field notes, I noted the aesthetics and the "feel" of the South City office. Perhaps like those in many nonprofit offices, employees share a small space and office supplies. Volunteers regularly come in and out of the building to work on this or that project, lending the space a welcoming and familiar feeling. Staff also regularly come and go, and I'm never quite sure if, when I'm arriving, the office will be full or nearly empty. Most of time, I'm at La Unión with two or three other staff members and/or volunteers.

Inside there are tables covered in pamphlets, fliers, petitions, and other materials highlighting various programs and partner organizations. The walls have many articles and pictures of various events, movement leaders, and newspaper clippings. The floors are carpeted with that indoor/outdoor carpet that's stain resistant. And around the entire office, pinned to the highest part of the wall, is a long timeline written on large pieces of butcher paper that chronicles the major achievements and annual highlights of the organization from its founding through the present. In this way, a broad organizational memory and history is literally written on the walls of the office.

ACCESS

The South City office closed approximately midway through my fieldwork due to budget cuts. Volunteer and primary informant Esmeralda led all South City organizing from that point forward. During this period, the North City office remained open and was staffed by primary informants Leticia and Lucero.

The fieldwork began in earnest as I supported La Unión organizers and key informants during a series of "house meeting" campaigns in South City and then in North City. A classic organizing strategy often used by Dolores Huerta, César Chávez, and the United Farm Workers, these house meetings involved going to the homes of local residents who had gathered together family, friends, and neighbors who were unconnected or weakly connected to La Unión in order to discuss major issues facing the immigrant community, including car impoundments, Secure Communities, and comprehensive immigration reform. We talked about their rights when they encountered police and the different ways they could become more involved with La Unión. My role in these meetings was largely to describe the contours of immigration enforcement programs, Secure Communities in particular, and to explain changes in state and federal laws that impact immigrants, especially related to car impoundments. Almost all meetings were conducted in Spanish. In the few instances where these house meetings involved critical masses of young people, they moved back and forth between Spanish and English.

The house meeting strategy differed markedly from meetings hosted at La Unión's offices to which community members were invited because it leveraged community members' personal relationships with one another and introduced into the organizing process a critical element of trust between the organizers and community members that was facilitated by the host. This trust facilitated recruitment to La Unión organizing activities.

The support of primary informants was critical in this study. I cultivated three primary informants during this fieldwork: Esmeralda in South City and Leticia and Lucero in North City. Esmeralda worked with La Unión as a longtime volunteer, while Leticia and Lucero were paid organizers based in North City. Organizers in both North City and South City urged meeting participants to "tell their stories" and vouched for my trustworthiness. Having unsuccessfully tried to approach immigrant residents on my own in other community settings, I was acutely aware of the importance of the word of a trusted community leader in securing their participation in this project. Over time and with the essential help of primary informants, I slowly developed trust with members of the Mexican immigrant community, which enabled me to build a snowball sample and to expand the number of participants, most of whom were not previously involved with social justice work. For instance, I attended a house meeting in North City for the very first time with La Unión organizer Leticia. The meeting was hosted at the home of a teachers' union representative who also taught at the local elementary school. Leticia had met this teacher and his wife on a coalitional campaign in support of the California tax initiative Proposition 30. The meeting was attended by a small group of white and Latino parents. They served food as we sat in chairs set in a circle around the living room and listened to Leticia make a presentation about La Unión's work and how others could become involved. As I listened, I noticed a Latino couple sitting across from me, near the kitchen table. They barely spoke, but were clearly engaged as they nodded along with the presentation. Later, during our interview, I learned that they were indigenous Mixteco immigrants from southern Mexico. Both were field-workers and their children attended local schools. They had become more involved in parent activities at their children's school, so this teacher had reached out to them, hoping they would attend his house meeting since they lived on his street.

After the meeting, I approached them and introduced myself. I squatted down next to the woman and across from the man so that my face was about level with the kitchen table where there were seated. In Spanish, I described my project and my time with La Unión, and asked if they would grant me an interview. Almost as soon as I had begun speaking, the woman lifted her chin skyward and looked up at the ceiling, avoiding eye contact with me as I looked from her to her husband. The gesture appeared as though she hoped to float away and cut short my pitch. As I finished speaking, she looked to her husband expectantly, still avoiding my gaze. At that moment, Leticia, who had overheard my solicitation and had recalled me saying that I might need her help to win potential respondents' trust, interjected. In rapid Spanish, she quickly reiterated that I had worked with La Unión for several years and emphasized the importance of telling "our" stories since part of our work was changing people's perceptions of immigrants. She said that I was a good guy and it would be a good idea for them to participate. As Leticia interjected, the woman's gaze shifted from the ceiling, skipped over me, and looked right to Leticia. As Leticia spoke, her gaze softened, the creases in her face relaxed, and she finally made eye contact with me. "Está bien," she said. I set a date with her and her husband and completed the interview the following week at their home.

I was struck by the immediate and dramatic change in this woman's demeanor as a result of Leticia's intervention. Her visage had visibly shifted in response to Leticia's vouching for me. Even though I had worked for several years with this organization, I did not know this woman, and she did not know me. Leticia, as a leader in this meeting, and much more familiar with this community and this work, played an essential role in brokering a sense of trust and security between this couple and me that led to them sharing their stories.

This same process unfolded in South City, where Esmeralda vouched for my trustworthiness and impressed upon the participants the importance of recording "our" history and our stories. Often asking each of the house meeting participants in turn to grant me an interview, she would take the reins after my pitch, often securing two or more interview appointments on my behalf per house meeting.

TIMELINE

The data for this study are derived from field notes collected over approximately three years beginning in November 2009 through August 2012, but most intensively in the eight-month period between January and August 2012. Though I had been involved with La Unión since approximately 2008 as part of my personal activism, I did not begin collecting field notes there until November 2009 when I decided to embark on this study. This period was also the time during which I collected the majority of the interviews for this study. Intensive interviewing in South City began with the initiation of a house meeting campaign led by one of my primary informants, Esmeralda. This campaign began at the end of December 2011 and lasted through the beginning of April 2012. During those house meetings, I collected field notes and, with Esmeralda's support, solicited interview respondents. All interviews in North City were completed one-on-one or in pairs with a husband and wife or with two family members in their homes. Just as this campaign ended in early April, an electoral campaign was beginning in North City.

From May 2012 through August 2012, I traveled regularly to North City, approximately a one-hour drive from my home, to attend La Unión's house meetings and rallies and generally to be present in their main office to observe similarities and differences in their work. As in South City, the majority of the interviews were solicited during these house meeting campaigns. Occasionally and because of my own travel constraints, these interviews were collected impromptu and immediately after a house meeting with groups ranging from three to five participants. All other interviews were scheduled during the house meetings and completed later in respondents' homes. Of the 34 interviews conducted in North City, four were conducted one-on-one, while the remaining interviews were conducted in groups of two to five. While these groups of three to five were more difficult to manage than interviews one-on-one or in pairs, they also produced interesting crosstalk as respondents spoke with each other and posed questions that I had not thought to ask. In this way, these interviews were more ranging in their scope, but also produced interesting interactions that I may not have witnessed without the benefit of the group context.

Although the bulk of the interviews were solicited from house meetings, a small minority of interviews were conducted through referrals from other community members and acquaintances. In addition, the field notes were derived from many different activities and were not limited to house meetings. These activities included marches, rallies, know-your-rights trainings, public forums, meetings with elected officials, precinct walks, campaign celebrations, community barbeques, and time spent in La Unión's offices to understand the flow of their average day and employee work responsibilities.

THE SAMPLE

Often La Unión organizers relied upon "core" La Unión members—immigrant community members who regularly attended meetings, could be relied upon to volunteer their time, and often had personal relationships with the organizers—to initiate the house meeting campaigns. They would solicit core leaders to gather together family members, friends, and neighbors for these meetings and from there would solicit future house meetings. In this way, both core members of La Unión and people who had been only sporadically involved or not involved in La Unión's social movement activities attended these house meetings.

I have qualitatively categorized each interview respondent in this study as an "activist," a "core leader," or a "community member." Activists were professional organizers, most of whom worked for La Unión. I categorized one of my primary informants, Esmeralda, as an activist even though she never worked for La Unión. Esmeralda works full-time as "family advocate" at a local elementary school. In this role she interacts primarily with Latino parents and Latino immigrant parents, connecting them to a host of local, state, and federal resources and running after-school and parent education programs, among other responsibilities. Having worked in this position for 18 years, Esmeralda was perceived by many as a community leader. When I first became involved with La Unión, her leadership in this organization, despite not being employed by them, was evident. She co-led meetings with paid organizers, recruited participants to organizing activities, and contributed to the design and shape of different events and campaigns. When the South City organizer was laid off in the fall of 2011, she stepped in to lead the house meeting campaign in the winter of 2012. Both of the activists in this sample served as primary informants, vouching for my trustworthiness, granting me access to the core leaders, as I describe above, and generally offering a "bird's-eye view" of community dynamics.

Core leaders were people whom I observed participate regularly in La Unión planning meetings. They could be relied upon to host house meetings, to staff phone banks, and to serve as precinct captains who coordinated volunteers from their neighborhood to *tocar puertas*, knock on doors to ask their neighbors to support various candidates. In making this distinction, I also asked in interviews whether they had been involved with La Unión in the past. If they had been substantially and recently involved, I assigned them to the core leader group.

Finally, community members were those whom I never observed or observed only rarely participating in La Unión organizing activities. These were immigrants who may have very occasionally given their time to La Unión or had done so at some time in the past, but had not done so recently or with any regularity. Of 61 respondents, 2 were activists, 17 were core leaders, and 42 were community members.

These categorical distinctions are important for addressing the sampling bias in this convenience sample that was cultivated from a single organization. The primary criticism is that the respondents in this study would be predisposed to participation in social movement activities or more likely to articulate oppositional political claims regarding immigrant rights issues because they had been previously exposed to or are already involved with the organizing work of La Unión activists. While this element of bias is present for activists and core leaders in this study, it is much less present for those whom I identify as "community members" or members of local immigrant communities who had rarely or never been involved in the organizing activities of La Unión. The house meeting model facilitated the collection of a broad sample and countered some of this selection bias precisely because these meetings were designed to recruit new members or those only marginally connected to La Unión's organizing activities. These numbers are necessarily imprecise, of course, since they are based on my observations and may diverge from activists' perceptions or the self-perceptions of respondents. Nonetheless, they reflect a qualitative typology that gauges respondents' predisposition to activism and oppositional claims making by estimating their distance from or closeness to the organization through which I executed this study.

Respondent demographics break down as follows. A total of 38 respondents presented or identified as women (62 percent); 23 presented or identified as men (38 percent). In regard to residency, 34 lived in North City (56 percent) and 27 in South City (44 percent), and respondents had been present in the United States from a minimum of 3 years to a maximum of 47 years. Of the respondents, 6 had lived in the United States their entire lives or most of their lives. The average length of US residency was approximately 17 years; the median was 15.[1] The ages of respondents were distributed as follows: 8 were between the ages of 20 and 30, 9 were between 30 and 40, 36 were between 40 and 50, 7 were between 50 and 60, and 1 respondent was over 60 years old.

Of the 61 respondents, all but 5 were Mexican immigrants hailing from various regions in Mexico. These 5 Mexican Americans all resided in North City, were born in the United States, and were second-generation US citizens,[2] although one lived for extended periods in Mexico and was herself a member of an immigrant family primarily composed of migrant farmworkers. Some immigrant respondents came from southern Oaxaca and Guerrero, but most respondents were concentrated in central Mexican states including Jalisco, Michoacán, and Zacatecas. Of the 56 immigrant respondents, 3 were legal residents (5 percent), 8 were naturalized citizens (14 percent), 23 were undocumented (41 percent), and the remaining 22 were immigrants of an unknown status (39 percent).

Due to the sensitive nature of the interviews, I almost never directly asked for a respondent's immigration status. I especially refrained from asking this question in group settings, since I did not know whether the individuals had shared their status with others in the group. This information often came up in our discussion of the substantive issues of the interviews. For instance, I often heard that respondents were fearful of driving. When I probed with follow-up questions, they often explained that they could not obtain a driver's license because they did not have "papers." While the immigrant status of a significant minority of respondents is unknown, I confirmed each had immigrated to the United States from Mexico. The stories that they shared dovetailed with the experiences of fear and resilience articulated by the other respondents in the sample.

INTERVIEWS

Interviews were conducted almost exclusively in respondents' homes in both one-on-one and groups settings, as I described above. The interview schedule focused on three major themes: (1) respondents' general sense of inclusion in or exclusion from the local community, (2) respondents' experiences with and feelings about police and immigration enforcement, and (3) respondents' strategies for coping with the risks associated with being an immigrant in the city and their history with or willingness to engage in collective action. Representative questions from each of these sections include "Do you feel like you're safe in this community?" "Do you feel like you can trust the police?" and "Do you do anything differently to protect yourself or your family from police/immigration enforcement?" Each of these sections contained between five and seven questions and a series of probing questions related to each. I concluded each interview with a final series of questions related to their ideal community: "What does your ideal community look like to you?"

I treated this interview schedule as a guide and not as a survey. Depending on the respondents' own time constraints and my own sense of the flow of the conversation, I sometimes hewed closely to this interview schedule and other times strayed from it. Regardless of the setting or time constraints, I was always sure to touch on the three main topics for the interview: feelings of inclusion and exclusion, relations with police, and the forms of agency in which respondents engaged.

In these 61 interviews, the average interview length was approximately 42 minutes; the minimum interview duration was 10 minutes, the maximum 90 minutes. Interview duration hinged most importantly on respondents' own availability. For instance, if respondents made mention of impending work obligations or child care responsibilities, I cut the interview short. For low-wage immigrant workers, time is scare, and I sought above all to respect that time in my interactions with them. Nonetheless, a high degree of saturation was achieved in the course of these interviews, oscillating, as I describe in the chapters of this book, from fear and immobility to resilience and action.

NOTES

INTRODUCTION

1 A related development in the emergence of Latino power is their growing electoral prominence. Of Latinos, 67 percent cast their votes for Obama in 2008 and 71 percent in 2012. The latter figure was the largest Latino vote share going to a Democratic candidate since 1996 when President Bill Clinton received 72 percent of the Latino vote. Lopez and Taylor, "Latino Voters in the 2012 Election." The common protest slogan "Hoy marchamos, mañana votamos" ("Today we march, tomorrow we vote") suggests that protest and voting are closely related prongs of a broader social movement struggle for immigrant rights.

2 Jimenez, *Replenished Ethnicity*.

3 Immigration remains an important issue among all Latinos, but more so among Latino immigrants. Of course, immigration is not the only issue about which this large and diverse demographic cares. See Krogstad, "Top Issue for Hispanics?"

4 This very dilemma opens Bloemraad, Voss, and Lee's introductory chapter on this topic, "Protests of 2006."

5 Pseudonyms are used to refer to all people, places, and organizations.

6 Dawson, *Behind the Mule*.

7 García Bedolla argues that political efficacy, the belief that politic action is meaningful and worthwhile, is experienced by Latinos who exhibit positive group attachment, which she found was more common in immigrant rich East LA and less so in the more assimilated communities of Montebello that lie to the east. García Bedolla, *Fluid Borders*.

8 Johnson, "On Agency," 118.

9 Nancy Naples and Vicki Ruiz both stress the role of neighborhood and family in facilitating organizing among women community workers and among Mexican and Mexican American women cannery workers. See Naples, *Grassroots Warriors*; Ruiz, *Cannery Women, Cannery Lives*.

10 Ngai, *Impossible Subjects*.

11 Fitzgerald and Cook-Martín, "Geopolitical Origins of the U.S. Immigration Act of 1965"; Ngai, "Lost Immigration Debate."

12 See the "Origins of the U.S. Immigrant Population, 1960–2015" table in López and Radford, "Facts on U.S. Immigrants, 2015."

13 See Figure 4 in Pew Research Center, "Modern Immigration Wave."

14 Hussar and Bailey, "Projections of Education Statistics to 2022."

15 Ruben Navarrette has called Latinos a cheap date for the Democrats since, in election after election, they break for the Democratic candidate and yet have seen little in the way of attention to the issues that matter to them, like immigration. Navarrette, "Latino Voters Can Take More Power."

16 Increased enforcement coincided with the devaluation of the Mexican peso in 1994 and the economic fallout from NAFTA; see Andreas, *Border Games*; Bacon, "How US Policies Fueled Mexico's Great Migration"; Gonzalez, *Harvest of Empire*; Johnson, "Free Trade and Closed Borders." Which is to say that at the very moment that economic push factors in Mexico became especially acute, the pathway to the United States, and consequently economic survival, became more treacherous.

17 Cornelius et al., "Controlling Unauthorized Immigration from Mexico"; Massey, Durand, and Pren, "Why Border Enforcement Backfired."

18 Devolution has its origins in a series of jail check programs established in 1988 in response to the Immigration Reform and Control Act of 1986 (IRCA) mandate to prioritize the deportation of criminal aliens, though the federal government did not begin to use this authority extensively until after 9/11. Immigration enforcement also has regional dimensions, extending not only into the interior of the country, but beyond its borders as well. The Programa Frontera Sur, an agreement developed in June 2014, commits tens of millions of dollars of US funding to Mexican immigration enforcement in the form of equipment, surveillance technology, and training. See Castillo, "Programa Frontera Sur." For a perspective that centers immigrants' experiences of the changes brought on by the Programa Frontera Sur, see Nolen, "Southern Exposure." This program has led to the interception of large numbers of Central American child migrants, largely accounting for the drop off in the numbers of unaccompanied minors arriving on the US southern border. Swanson et al., "A Year After Obama Declared a 'Humanitarian Situation.'" Coleman cites this program as evidence of the regionalization of immigration enforcement. Coleman, "Geopolitics of Engagement."

19 Gonzales, *Reform without Justice*.

20 For a review, see Ruszczyk and Barbosa, "Second Generation of Immigrant Illegality Studies."

21 For a detailed theoretical specification of the meaning of agency, see Emirbayer and Mische, "What Is Agency?"

22 Jacques Derrida introduced the metaphor of haunting to describe the way that he anticipated Marxism would haunt Western capitalism until well after Marx's Death in *Specters of Marx*.

23 Foucault, *Discipline and Punish*; Foucault, *History of Sexuality*.

24 Gordon, *Ghostly Matters*, 4.

25 Menjívar and Abrego, "Legal Violence."

26 Kanstroom, *Deportation Nation*.

27 Genova, *Working the Boundaries*; see also Genova and Peutz, *Deportation Regime*.

28 Stumpf, "Crimmigration Crisis."

29 Golash-Boza, *Deported*; Genova and Peutz, *Deportation Regime*; Hagan, Rodriguez, and Castro, "Social Effects of Mass Deportations"; Kanstroom, *Deportation Nation*; Brotherton and Barrios, *Banished to the Homeland*; Golash-Boza and Hondagneu-Sotelo, "Latino Immigrant Men and the Deportation Crisis."

30 Hernandez, "Pursuant to Deportation"; Feliciano and Rumbaut, "Gendered Paths"; Macías-Rojas, *From Deportation to Prison*.

31 Light, Massoglia, and King, "Citizenship and Punishment."

32 Dunn, *Militarization of the U.S.-Mexico Border*; Falcón, "Rape as a Weapon of War"; Andreas, *Border Games*; Maril, *Patrolling Chaos*; Nevins, *Operation Gatekeeper*; Luibheid, *Entry Denied*.

33 Robinson, "Aqui Estamos y No Nos Vamos!"; Massey, "Why Does Immigration Occur?"; Golash-Boza, *Deported*; Ong, *Neoliberalism as Exception*; Gonzalez, *Harvest of Empire*; Sadowski-Smith, "Introduction."

34 Coleman, "Geopolitics of Engagement"; Coleman, "What Counts as the Politics and Practice of Security, and Where?"; Esbenshade and Obzurt, "Local Immigration Regulation"; Varsanyi, "Rescaling the 'Alien,' Rescaling Personhood"; Varsanyi et al., "Multilayered Jurisdictional Patchwork"; Coleman, "'Local' Migration State"; Armenta, "From Sheriff's Deputies to Immigration Officers"; Pham and Van, "Economic Impact of Local Immigration Regulation"; Provine et al., "Growing Tensions"; Provine and Lewis, "Shades of Blue"; Steil and Vasi, "New Immigration Contestation."

35 Dreby, *Everyday Illegal*; Willen, "Toward a Critical Phenomenology of 'Illegality.'"

36 Gleeson, "Labor Rights for All?"; Menjívar, "Intersection of Work and Gender."

37 Tirman, *Maze of Fear*; Gerstle, "Immigrant as Threat to American Security."

38 Gonzales and Chavez, "'Awakening to a Nightmare'"; Gonzales and Vargas, *Lives in Limbo*; Menjívar, "Educational Hopes, Documented Dreams."

39 Hondagneu-Sotelo and Avila, "'I'm Here but I'm There'"; Levitt, *Transnational Villagers*; Ong, *Buddha Is Hiding*; Slack et al., "In the Shadow of the Wall"; Parreñas, *Children of Global Migration*.

40 Heyman, "Grounding Immigrant Rights Movements," 197.

41 Campbell and Heyman, "Slantwise."

42 Scott, *Weapons of the Weak*; Scott, *Domination and the Arts of Resistance*.

43 Ellerman, "Undocumented Migrants and Resistance in the Liberal State."

44 Coutin, *Legalizing Moves*; Ramakrishnan and Bloemraad, *Civic Hopes and Political Realities*; Ramakrishnan and Viramontes, "Civic Spaces"; Brettell and Reed-Danahay, *Civic Engagements*; Terriquez, "Schools for Democracy"; Terriquez, "Civic Inequalities?"; Varsanyi, "Paradox of Contemporary Immigrant Political Mobilization"; Ebert and Okamoto, "Social Citizenship, Integration and Collective Action."

45 Gálvez, *Guadalupe in New York*; Gonzales, "Left Out but Not Shut Down"; Gonzales, *Reform without Justice*; Das Gupta, *Unruly Immigrants*; Laubenthal, "Emergence of Pro-Regularization Movements"; Nicholls, *DREAMers*; Okamoto and Ebert, "Beyond the Ballot"; Ruiz, *Cannery Women, Cannery Lives*; Coddou,

"Institutional Approach to Collective Action"; Zepeda-Millán, "Weapons of the (Not So) Weak"; Zlolinski, *Janitors, Street Vendors, and Activists*; Nyers, "Abject Cosmopolitanism"; see the collections from Ramakrishnan and Bloemraad, *Civic Hopes and Political Realities*; Voss and Bloemraad, *Rallying for Immigrant Rights*.

46 García, "Hidden in Plain Sight."

47 Voss and Bloemraad, *Rallying for Immigrant Rights*.

48 Bloemraad, Voss, and Lee, "Protests of 2006."

49 Ibid., 33; Coddou, "Institutional Approach to Collective Action"; Fox and Bada, "Migrant Civic Engagement." See also Minkoff, "From Service Provision to Institutional Advocacy."

50 Garcia, *Operation Wetback*, 126.

51 Campbell and Heyman, "Slantwise," 13; Hollander and Einwhoner, "Conceptualizing Resistance."

52 Scott, *Weapons of the Weak*, 295.

53 Ibid.

54 Campbell and Heyman, "Slantwise."

55 See Bloemraad and Trost, "It's a Family Affair."

56 It is worth noting that I do not conceptualize participation as a dichotomous outcome variable. I am not seeking to identify those individual characteristics that predict social movement participation or not. Often respondents moved between periods of participation and not, and so their answer to the question of whether they participate in social movements is not stable and fluctuates over time. The objective for this study is to identify the conditions of everyday life that inspire and constrain movement emergence among Mexican immigrants in a particular locale. The answer to this question must go beyond yes or no to the identification of a dynamic, dialectic, or tension between the everyday and the historic that immigrants will negotiate in different ways not only due to their individual propensities for activism, but in response to overtures from social movement organizations and to changing opportunities to press their claims in the context of massive demographic change and unprecedented levels of immigration enforcement.

57 Tilly, *From Mobilization to Revolution*; McAdam, *Political Process and the Development of Black Insurgency 1930–1970*.

58 See Benford and Snow, "Framing Processes and Social Movements."

59 Snow et al., "Frame Alignment Processes."

60 See Snow et al., "Disrupting the 'Quotidian.'"

61 Ruiz, *Cannery Women, Cannery Lives*, 19–20; see also Naples, *Grassroots Warriors*; Zavella, *Women's Work and Chicano Families*.

62 Bayat, "From 'Dangerous Classes' to 'Quiet Rebels'"; Bayat, *Life as Politics*; Bayat, "Un-civil Society."

63 Bayat, "Un-civil Society," 57.

64 Ibid., 64.

65 See, e.g., Martinez, "Mobilizing Marchers in the Mile High City"; Okamoto and Ebert, "Beyond the Ballot."

66 Observers often point to the role of spontaneity and emotion in the spring 2006 immigrant rights marches, driven by Spanish-language media and the Catholic Church, when explaining the unprecedented outpouring of immigrants and their allies. These qualities of social movement organizing are often left out of social movement theory, though of course there are notable exceptions. See Robnett, *How Long?*; Snow and Moss, "Protest on the Fly." Bloemraad et al. argue the dynamics of these marches, critical as they are, "reinforce social movement scholars' argument about the importance of organizations for contentious politics." Bloemraad, Voss, and Lee, "Protests of 2006," 4–5.

67 Flacks, *Making History.*

68 Ibid., 90.

69 Ibid., 3–4.

70 See García Bedolla, *Fluid Borders.*

71 Flacks, *Making History*, 73.

72 Kandel, "Interior Immigration Enforcement"; Cantor, Noferi, and Martínez, "Enforcement Overdrive."

73 Varsanyi et al., "Multilayered Jurisdictional Patchwork."

74 Abrego, "Legal Consciousness of Undocumented Latinos."

75 McAdam, "Recruitment to High-Risk Activism."

76 See Flores, "Citizens vs. Citizenry."

77 Lee and Miller, "Current Fiscal Impact of Immigrants and Their Descendants"; Lee and Miller, "Immigration, Social Security, and Broader Fiscal Impacts"; National Academies of Sciences, Engineering, and Medicine, *Economic and Fiscal Consequences of Immigration.*

78 Camacho, *Migrant Imaginaries*; Fernandez and Olsen, "To Live, Love and Work Anywhere You Please: Critical Exchange on Arizona and the Struggle for Locomotion"; Das Gupta, *Unruly Immigrants.*

79 Felstiner, Abel, and Sarat, "Emergence and Transformation of Disputes."

80 See Zlolinski, *Janitors, Street Vendors, and Activists*, chap. 5.

81 Though there is certainly an argument to be made that the simultaneous social reality and legal impossibility of undocumented immigrants itself represents an undermining of the nation-state. See Ngai, *Impossible Subjects.*

82 Walzer, *Spheres of Justice.*

83 Johnson, "On Agency," 118.

84 Dawson, *Behind the Mule.*

85 García Bedolla, *Fluid Borders.*

86 Chavez, *Latino Threat.*

87 Carbado, "Racial Naturalization"; Carbado, "(E)racing the Fourth Amendment."

CHAPTER 1. GHOST IN THE DEPORTATION MACHINE

1 Genova, "Spectacles of Migrant 'Illegality.'"

2 Ibid., 1180.

3 Martin, "Immigration in the United States"; Martin, "United States."

4 Genova and Peutz, *Deportation Regime.*

5 Schrag, *Not Fit for Our Society.*

6 Ibid., 6.

7 See Horsman, *Race and Manifest Destiny.*

8 Higham, *Strangers in the Land*, 6.

9 Anderson, *Imagined Communities.*

10 Ngai, *Impossible Subjects*, 23–24.

11 Ibid., 25.

12 Omi and Winant, *Racial Formation in the United States.*

13 Daniels, *Guarding the Golden Door*, 52.

14 Briggs, "'Albatross' of Immigration Reform."

15 Ngai, *Impossible Subjects*, 55.

16 Balderrama and Rodriguez, *Decade of Betrayal.*

17 Ibid., 74.

18 Driscoll, *Tracks North.*

19 Almaguer argues that as the Chinese steadily replaced blacks as the primary source of "unfree labor" in the wake of abolition, the Chinese were met with widespread resentment and racial violence. Proletarian whites jealously guarded their precarious class position in the new capitalist economic order against the Chinese, whom they perceived as fundamentally different in terms of race, language, culture, and religion. Mexicans, on the other hand, were incorporated into the lowest rungs of a stratified economic system due, in part, to their racial palatability: they spoke a romance language, were of mixed European ancestry, largely practiced Catholicism, and were from political and economic institutions not unlike those on the American frontier. See Almaguer, *Racial Fault Lines.*

20 Driscoll, *Tracks North*, 51–52.

21 Genova, *Working the Boundaries.*

22 See Fitzgerald and Cook-Martín, "Geopolitical Origins of the U.S. Immigration Act of 1965."

23 Chinese exclusion was repealed in 1943, although their quota allotment remained very small. The War Brides Act of 1945 allowed for the immigrant spouses and children of military personnel to enter the United States; over 100,000 did so. In the contemporary period, the 1986 Immigration Reform and Control Act (IRCA) offered amnesty to some undocumented immigrants, the 1990 Immigration Act raised the annual ceiling for some categories of immigrants and increased the number of employment visas, and a variety of targeted programs have created accelerated pathways to belonging for some immigrant groups whose migration is permitted to the extent that it advances US foreign policy objectives. The 1966 Cuban Refugee Adjustment Act, for instance, created an expedited pathway to lawful permanent resident (LPR) status for approximately 300,000 Cubans refugees fleeing Fidel Castro's communist regime. Applicants were required to have been present in the United States for one year. This benefit was extended to the spouses and children of the Cuban applicants regardless of their nationalities.

They did not need to apply for a family-based or employment-based visa, nor did being a "public charge" serve as a bar to LPR eligibility. Similar refugee adjustment programs have been created for Vietnamese, Laotians, and refugees from Soviet Russia.

24 Genova, *Working the Boundaries*, 230–31. Mexico continues to send the greatest number of immigrants to the United States compared to all other countries.

25 In general, see Bell, *Faces at the Bottom of the Well*; Tushnet, "Critique of Rights"; Williams, *Alchemy of Race and Rights*.

26 See Harvey, *Brief History of Neoliberalism*.

27 Under the Refugee Act of 1980, the United States adopted the UN definition of refugee and raised the annual cap on refugee admissions from 17,400 to 50,000. The Immigration Act of 1990 raised the previous worldwide annual ceiling on immigration from 270,000 a year plus immediate relatives to 675,000 including relatives plus refugees, and more than doubled the number of immigration visas granted for economic and employment reasons to 140,000 a year. The Anti-Terrorism and Effective Death Penalty Act of 1996 allowed for the expedited removal of foreigners seeking asylum who arrived at US airports without proper documents.

28 Ngai, "Civil Rights Origins of Illegal Immigration."

29 Martin, "United States," 67.

30 Gonzales, *Reform without Justice*.

31 Gordon, *Ghostly Matters*.

32 Kanstroom, *Deportation Nation*.

33 The 1996 Antiterrorism and Effective Death Penalty Act and the 1996 Illegal Immigration Reform and Immigrant Responsibility Act effected several important changes that expanded the post-entry social control of all noncitizens (Kanstroom, *Deportation Nation, 10*):
  • They radically changed many grounds of exclusion and deportation,
  • Retroactively expanded criminal grounds of deportation,
  • Eliminated some and limited other discretionary waivers of deportability,
  • Created mandatory detention for many classes of noncitizens,
  • Expedited deportation procedures for certain types of cases,
  • Eliminated judicial review of certain types of deportation (removal) orders,
  • Authorized increased state and local law enforcement involvement in deportation,
  • Created a new type of streamlined removal proceeding—permitting the use of secret evidence—for noncitizens accused of terrorist activity.

34 Armenta, "From Sheriff's Deputies to Immigration Officers."

35 The Criminal Alien Program or CAP functions as an umbrella program that links federal immigration enforcement to local law enforcement agencies. As part of CAP, the Prioritized Enforcement Program (formerly Secure Communities) allows for fingerprint sharing between federal and local agencies, the identification of immigrants who are out of status, and a mechanism for issuing detainers

or requests to hold those suspected of an immigration violation so that they can be transferred into federal custody. This information can also be gleaned during interrogations with detained immigrants, booking information, and access to local jail databases. The 287(g) program allows for federal immigration officials to specially train local police and sheriff's deputies to operate as federal immigration enforcement officers. Together CAP accounts for between two-thirds and three-fourths of all removals from within the United States. See Kandel, "Interior Immigration Enforcement"; Cantor, Noferi, and Martínez, "Enforcement Overdrive."

36   As Monica Varsanyi details, immigration enforcement before the 1990s largely adhered to the strictures of the preemption clause of Article 6 of the US Constitution, which mandates states' deference to uniform federal regulation on a range of issues, including immigration. The policy architecture for the current immigration enforcement regime, distinguished by devolution, was developed under the Illegal Immigration Reform and Immigrant Responsibility Act of 1996. Among other things, this act established a memorandum of understanding (MOU) process, referred to by the subsection of the law where it can be found: 287(g). Individual agencies can enter into an agreement with the federal government that offers training and funding to support local police agencies' efforts to enforce federal immigration law. Initially not a very popular program, these agreements proliferated in a post-9/11 moment in which national security came to be conflated with immigration enforcement. Varsanyi, "Rescaling the 'Alien,' Rescaling Personhood." See also Tirman, *Maze of Fear*.

37   S-Comm is a collaborative local-federal immigration enforcement program that is deployed in 100 percent of the 3,181 jurisdictions in the United States and has been responsible for the deportation of 266,137 immigrants nationwide since its deployment in 2008. Immigration and Customs Enforcement, "Activated Jurisdictions." Initially pitched as a voluntary program from which local municipalities could opt-out, it became the first systematic and mandatory immigration enforcement program operating in all counties in the United States. Secure Communities officially rolled out in 2008 and was functioning in every US county by 2013. This program screens all detainees booked in local jails through an Immigration and Customs Enforcement (ICE) database (in addition to the standard FBI criminal background database). If the database produces a hit, or a match between the booked detainee and an out-of-status person in the database, ICE issues a "detainer," or a request to the local jail to hold the detainee for a 48-hour period beyond the resolution of their case during which time ICE officials can arrive to take the person into custody. Immigration restrictionists have hailed the program as an effective force multiplier that contributes to "attrition through enforcement." In other words, if the daily lives of immigrants are made so inhospitable by the proliferation of the risks associated with deportation at *all* levels of government, immigrants will simply choose, in a rational cost-benefit analysis, to deport themselves. Opponents of the program fault it for operating as a dragnet, indiscriminately deporting serious criminal offenders and immigrants with no criminal his-

tory (Gardner and Kohli, "C.A.P. Effect"; Human Rights Watch, "Forced Apart"; Office of the Inspector General, "Performance of 287(g) Agreements"; Schriro, "Immigration Detention"), expending scarce local tax dollars that go unremunerated by the federal government, eroding trust between immigrant communities and local police, separating families, and fomenting fear and insecurity in the Latino community (Bobb and Police Assessment Resource Center, "Los Angeles County Sheriff's Department 28th Semiannual Report"; Prieto, Russo, and Winant, "(Mis)Trusting the Police"). Though S-Comm has now been replaced by the Prioritized Enforcement Program, during the time I conducted fieldwork for this book it was still in effect. Though the Prioritized Enforcement Program was rolled out in response to the well-established claim that S-Comm was not, in fact, prioritizing the deportation of serious, violent offenders, it remains to be seen whether this new iteration will differ substantially from the original program.

38 Scholars have linked this shift in the geography of immigration enforcement to the maintenance of neoliberal economic policy. Local enforcement, Mathew Coleman argues, allows the state to preserve the flow of commerce across the border, while still aggressively pursuing immigration enforcement at different of geographic levels. New immigration enforcement strategies are *rolled out* in order to maintain the neoliberal *rolling back* of government intervention in the economic sphere. Coleman, "Geopolitics of Engagement," 615; see also Varsanyi, "Rescaling the 'Alien,' Rescaling Personhood."

39 Varsanyi et al., "Multilayered Jurisdictional Patchwork"; see also Walker and Leitner, "Variegated Landscape of Local Immigration Policies."

40 Coleman, "What Counts as the Politics and Practice of Security, and Where?"; Coleman, "'Local' Migration State"; Provine et al., "Growing Tensions"; Willen, "Toward a Critical Phenomenology of 'Illegality.'"

41 See Esbenshade and Obzurt, "Local Immigration Regulation"; Garni and Miller, "Localized Immigration Policy and Migrant Life Experiences"; Varsanyi et al., "Multilayered Jurisdictional Patchwork."

42 Laglagaron et al., "Regulating Immigration at the State Level," 3. Interestingly, this flurry of local regulatory activity is driven by the dominant local political ideology, progressive or conservative, and less by the demographic shifts and economic changes spurred by immigration. See Chavez and Provine, "Race and the Response of State Legislatures to Unauthorized Immigrants"; Ebert and Okamoto, "Legitimating Contexts, Immigrant Power, and Exclusionary Actions"; Ramakrishnan and Wong, "Immigration Policies Go Local"; Steil and Vasi, "New Immigration Contestation."

43 Anderson, "How Many More Deaths?," 1.

44 Cornelius et al., "Controlling Unauthorized Immigration from Mexico."

45 Shear, "Advocates Push Obama to Halt Aggressive Deportation Efforts."

46 At the time of writing, the year 2015 marked the most recent deportation data made available by the US Department of Homeland Security. Technically, the term "deportation" was made obsolete after 1996. Before that time, immigration

law distinguished between those excluded (never permitted entry) and those deported (or expelled after entering). The operative legal distinction today is between removals and returns (and a variety of subcategories contained within each). A removal refers to a court-ordered expulsion of an immigrant from the United States that carries with it a bar to reentry from between 5 and 20 years and additional penalties if the removed individual attempts reentry. A return refers to the expulsion of an immigrant without a court order. Returns may be applied only to Mexicans apprehended at the southern border and Canadians at the northern border. As I use the term in this book, a deportation refers to a removal, which under the Obama administration reached a historic peak in 2013, but then steadily declined through 2015. See Table 39 of US Department of Homeland Security, "Yearbook of Immigration Statistics," 103. Scholars debate the causes of the decline, though it is likely the combined effects of President Obama's deprioritization of the removal of noncriminal aliens, formalized in programs like DACA; some local and state law enforcement agencies' refusal to cooperate with interior enforcement programs, such as the now-defunct Secure Communities program; and lower levels of both documented and undocumented immigration (evidenced in the steadily declining number of apprehensions at the border), owing to the Great Recession of 2008, ramped up border enforcement, and a decline in Mexican birth rates. Notably, returns were lower under the Obama administration than under previous administrations, reflecting both lower levels of unauthorized immigration in general and a shift in emphasis in enforcement practice, beginning under the Bush administration and continuing under Obama, that emphasized removals, not returns, for all undocumented immigrants in order to deter their future reentry. The choice to report returns versus removals is a largely political and theoretical one. For more on this distinction, see Law, "Lies, Damned Lies, and Obama's Deportation Statistics." My emphasis on removals in this text mirrors the rationale advanced by Dara Lind at Vox, who argues, "Returns are partly dependent on the state of the economy. Removals, on the other hand, tell the story of the deliberate policy choices made over the last decade that are having lasting consequences for the people being expelled." Lind, "Research That Made Me Take Donald Trump Seriously."

47 Golash-Boza and Hondagneu-Sotelo, "Latino Immigrant Men and the Deportation Crisis."
48 Passel and Taylor, "Unauthorized Immigrants and Their U.S.-Born Children."
49 Freed Wessler, "Shattered Families," 6.
50 Hondagneu-Sotelo and Avila, "'I'm Here but I'm There'"; Nazario, *Enrique's Journey*; Parreñas, *Children of Global Migration*.
51 Falcón, "Rape as a Weapon of War"; Luibheid, *Entry Denied*.
52 Gonzales and Chavez, "'Awakening to a Nightmare'"; Menjívar, "Educational Hopes, Documented Dreams."
53 Gleeson, "Labor Rights for All?"
54 Organista, Organista, and Soloff, "Exploring AIDS-Related Knowledge."

55 Light, Massoglia, and King, "Citizenship and Punishment."

56 Kanstroom, *Deportation Nation*, 5.

57 Lopez et al., "On Immigration Policy."

58 Gerstle, "Immigrant as Threat to American Security."

59 Falcón, "Rape as a Weapon of War"; Genova, *Working the Boundaries*; Luibheid, *Entry Denied*; Ong, *Buddha Is Hiding*.

60 López and Radford, "Facts on U.S. Immigrants, 2015."

61 Ibid.

62 Ibid.

63 Passel and Cohn, "Unauthorized Immigrant Population."

64 Massey, "America's Immigration Policy Fiasco," 8. For an empirical analysis of the way the militarization of the border contributed to the rise in the undocumented population, see Massey, Durand, and Pren, "Why Border Enforcement Backfired."

65 Passel and Cohn, "Overall Number of U.S. Unauthorized Immigrants."

66 Massey, "America's Immigration Policy Fiasco," 9–10.

67 Kanaiaupuni, "Reframing the Migration Question."

68 Foner, *In a New Land*; Levitt, *Transnational Villagers*; Menjívar, "Intersection of Work and Gender."

69 Feliciano and Rumbaut, "Gendered Paths."

70 Kohli, Markowitz, and Chavez, "Secure Communities by the Numbers," 5–6.

71 Lopez and Gonzalez-Barrera, "Latino Voters Support Obama."

72 Glenn, *Unequal Freedom*.

73 Mezzadra, "Gaze of Autonomy."

CHAPTER 2. "THE SENSE OF LAW IS LOST"

1 Carbado, "(E)racing the Fourth Amendment"; Carbado, "Racial Naturalization."

2 Gabrielson, "Sobriety Checkpoints Catch Unlicensed Drivers"; Gabrielson, "Car Seizures at DUI Checkpoints Prove Profitable." Though car impoundments were on the rise at the beginning of the study period (November 2009–December 2012), two events since the conclusion of the study period contributed to a decline in their frequency. In January 2012, California state law SB 353 went into effect, mandating that local police offer unlicensed drivers a grace period when stopped at a DUI checkpoint to allow for an authorized, licensed driver to collect the unlicensed driver's vehicle. Later in January 2015, another law, AB 60, went into effect allowing undocumented immigrants to obtain driver's licenses marked "federal limits apply," indicating that the license is not proof of legal residence. As a consequence, the numbers of car impoundments has likely declined, and the discrepancy between car impoundments for drunk drivers and those for unlicensed drivers has also likely diminished. Consequently, the problem of car impoundments for undocumented drivers is no longer as pressing today as it was during this study.

I attempted to secure updated figures from the California Office of Traffic Safety (OTS) and the Berkeley Safe Transportation Research and Education

Center. After corresponding with the OTS Marketing and Public Affairs Division, I learned that car impoundment data were not reported to the OTS after 2011, when grant funding for DUI checkpoints ceased. They confirmed, based on anecdotal evidence only, that SB 353 likely reduced the number of impounds at DUI checkpoints, but had no anecdotal evidence regarding AB 60. They also cautioned that no uniform standards were used when local enforcement agencies reported impoundments; therefore, the data should be evaluated critically. They further cautioned that they identified factual errors in the data reported in Gabrielson's *California Watch* article that were not corrected thereafter. While Gabrielson suggests, for instance, that many if not all impoundments were for unlicensed, undocumented drivers, OTS, in a sample of 298 checkpoints conducted between October and December 2009, found that just over half (55 percent) of all impoundments were for unlicensed drivers. Another 31 percent of impoundments were from drivers with a suspended or revoked driver's license and 14 percent of vehicles were impounded from DUI drivers, drivers with outstanding warrants, and so on. Though the general claim remains the same—impoundments at DUI checkpoints largely affect undocumented drivers—there may be more variation in the distribution of legal justifications for vehicle impoundments than Gabrielson presents. OTS provided a summary of factual errors from the article. This summary is on file with the author and can be made available to interested readers.

3 Gabrielson, "Sobriety Checkpoints Catch Unlicensed Drivers."

4 Ibid.

5 Ibid.

6 The concept is coined by Juliet Stumpf, "Crimmigration Crisis." For a short primer on this issue, see the useful roundtable interview with Tanya Golash-Boza, Ryan King, and Yolanda Vázquez: McElrath, Mahadeo, and Suh, "'Crimmigration.'"

7 In the absence of firsthand experience, Menjívar and Bejarano note the importance of immigrants' social networks in the formation of their opinions about police. "Latino Immigrants' Perceptions of Crime and Police Authorities."

8 Epp, Maynard-Moody, and Haider-Markel, *Pulled Over*.

9 Carbado, "Racial Naturalization," 637.

10 Ibid., 638.

11 Ibid., 642.

12 Volpp, "Citizen and the Terrorist," 1594.

13 Luibheid, *Entry Denied*; Falcón, "Rape as a Weapon of War"; Rich, "Compulsory Heterosexuality and Lesbian Existence."

14 Glenn, *Unequal Freedom*.

15 Genova, *Working the Boundaries*; Genova, "Spectacles of Migrant 'Illegality.'"

16 See Gardner and Kohli, "C.A.P. Effect"; Kohli, Markowitz, and Chavez, "Secure Communities by the Numbers"; Golash-Boza and Hondagneu-Sotelo, "Latino Immigrant Men and the Deportation Crisis."

17 Foucault, *Discipline and Punish*.

18 See Cornelius et al., "Controlling Unauthorized Immigration from Mexico."

19 See Epp, Maynard-Moody, and Haider-Markel, *Pulled Over*.

20 California State Assembly Bill 60 (AB 60), which went into effect on January 1, 2015, restores the ability of undocumented drivers to obtain a driver's license. During the data collection period for this book, undocumented immigrant respondents had no such relief available to them. Their narratives reflect this now-outdated prohibition.

21 Gordon, *Ghostly Matters*.

22 This figure was reported in Gabrielson, "Sobriety Checkpoints Catch Unlicensed Drivers."

23 California Vehicle Code 26708 subdivision (a)(2): a person shall not drive a car with any object or material placed, affixed, or installed on the vehicle that obstructs or reduces the driver's clear view through the windshield or side windows. www.leginfo.ca.gov.

24 Carbado and Harris, "Undocumented Criminal Procedure."

25 Vila, *Crossing Borders, Reinforcing Borders*, 200.

26 Epp, Maynard-Moody, and Haider-Markel, *Pulled Over*.

27 Du Bois, *Souls of Black Folk*.

28 Drake, "Divide between Blacks and Whites on Police Runs Deep."

29 Althusser introduces the idea of interpellation to refer to the way that identity is given or called into being by another. To be "hailed" by another is part of the process by which we come to have identities in the first place. *Lenin and Philosophy and Other Essays*.

30 Tyler, "Procedural Justice."

31 Epp, Maynard-Moody, and Haider-Markel, *Pulled Over*.

32 Menjívar and Bejarano, "Latino Immigrants' Perceptions of Crime and Police Authorities," 136–37.

33 Crenshaw, "Mapping the Margins"; Menjívar and Salcido, "Immigrant Women and Domestic Violence."

CHAPTER 3. THE SHELL

1 Terriquez identifies the school as a central site for immigrants' civic engagement even in the face of exclusionary measures. Citizenship is not predictive of involvement, though language barriers do predict participation. "Civic Inequalities?" In a separate study, she found that engagement at schools is also informed by civic engagement in other sites, like labor unions, where immigrant participants develop leadership skills that foster more critical engagement with teachers and administrators. "Schools for Democracy."

2 See Gleeson, "Labor Rights for All?"

3 Bayat, "From 'Dangerous Classes' to 'Quiet Rebels.'"

4 See Snow et al., "Disrupting the 'Quotidian.'"

5 Flacks, *Making History*, 50.

6 In a different context, Matthew Desmond, in a sweeping ethnographic examination of eviction and poverty, takes up the question of the relationship between economic deprivation and culture. Examining the sometimes-harsh parenting of poor mothers, he explains that mothers have to again and again confront the failure to adequately provide for their children. They may respond with irritability and harshness both because they are coping with the stress of parenting in poverty and because they are preparing their children for the harshness of growing up poor and black in America. This approach is affirmed by a range of social actors from pastors to social workers who advise parents, "Do not spare the rod." Desmond explains, "What began as survival carried forward in the name of culture." *Evicted*, 241, 382. A parallel process unfolds in the case of Mexican immigrants. What begins as the necessary work of avoidance and isolation is carried through into a habituated mode of managing problems: to keep one's head down. Over time, recourse to the protective strategies of the shell are folded into immigrants' common sense about how to manage problems in a more general way.

7 See Gleeson, "Labor Rights for All?," 591.

8 See ibid., 591–92.

9 Weber, *Protestant Ethic*.

10 Sayer, *Capitalism and Modernity*, 144.

11 Ibid., 144.

12 Weber famously noted the role of an extreme work ethic in his seminal study of the religious and cultural underpinnings of early capitalism. *Protestant Ethic*.

13 Contrast Ricardo's experience to that of adult immigrants who have endured a longer naturalization process, such as Manuel in Menjívar and Lakhani's "Transformative Effects of Immigration Law," 1841–42. Manuel's civic engagement is incentivized by a prolonged interaction with the state. Though Ricardo votes, his civic engagement stops there since, as he suggests, he adjusted his status very soon after arriving in the United States. It is also worth noting that many of the forms of civic engagement discussed in Menjívar and Lakhani's piece are a lower risk than some of what La Unión organizers were asking of prospective immigrant activists. To participate in a church group or volunteer with a blood drive is decidedly a form of engagement, but of a rather different nature than attending a public protest or a "dialogue" with a city police chief.

14 Gálvez, *Guadalupe in New York*; Gonzales, "Left Out but Not Shut Down"; Gonzales, *Reform without Justice*; Das Gupta, *Unruly Immigrants*; Laubenthal, "Emergence of Pro-Regularization Movements"; Nicholls, *DREAMers*; Okamoto and Ebert, "Beyond the Ballot"; Ruiz, *Cannery Women, Cannery Lives*; Varsanyi, "Paradox of Contemporary Immigrant Political Mobilization"; Terriquez, "Schools for Democracy." See also the collections by Ramakrishnan and Bloemraad, *Civic Hopes and Political Realities*; Voss and Bloemraad, *Rallying for Immigrant Rights*.

CHAPTER 4. INSTRUMENTAL ACTIVISTS

1   Mahmood, "Feminist Theory, Embodiment, and the Docile Agent."

2   I confirmed these approximate figures with my primary informant Esmeralda.

3   Women of color often play a central role in social movement organizations by serving as a bridge between formal social movement organizations (SMOs) and the community. Zlolinski, *Janitors, Street Vendors, and Activists*, 166. See also Oliver, "If You Don't Do It."

4   California Vehicle Code 26708 subdivision (a)(2), http://leginfo.legislature.ca.gov.

5   Lupita's experience mirrors what Veronica Terriquez found in a Los Angeles–based survey project of Latina immigrant mothers. English language ability and time spent in the United States are predictive of school involvement, while citizenship and legal status are not. Terriquez, "Civic Inequalities?"

6   Hiroshi Motomura explains what rights undocumented immigrants retain. "Rights of Others."

7   Menjívar and Lakhani find that enduring personal transformations, like Lupita's, often occur as a result of attaining legal status. "Transformative Effects of Immigration Law."

8   This saying is attributed to Mother Teresa of Calcutta and is often stated "el que no vive para servir, no sirve para vivir." The phrase does not translate easily into English, but may be rendered as "those who do not live to serve, are not fit to live." My thanks to Gerardo Ayala, Tanya Golash-Boza, Alena Marie, Nayra Pacheco, and Maria Zamudio for their assistance in translating this phrase.

9   For more on hometown associations, see Ramakrishnan and Viramontes, "Civic Spaces."

10 Organizations with 501(c) status are not required to pay federal income taxes or other kinds of taxes. Those designated 501(c)(3) differ from 501(c)(4) organizations in a number of ways. For the purposes of this study, their most important difference is that the latter type may engage in electoral organizing including making campaign contributions and endorsing electoral candidates, while the former type can do this only in a very limited way. Consequently, charitable contributions to a 501(c)(4) organization are not tax-deductible.

11 Zlolinski, *Janitors, Street Vendors, and Activists*, chap. 5.

12 In addition to cultivating activists in ways that aligned with their own political philosophies and organizing strategies, organizational context mattered in another way. Social movement scholars have long demonstrated the importance of organizations to the longevity and sustainability of social movements; see, e.g., McAdam, *Political Process and the Development of Black Insurgency*, 44–47. In the wake of the Great Recession of 2008, La Unión experienced a sharp drop in foundation support—the largest portion of its funding portfolio—forcing them to close their South City office and rely on volunteers, like primary informant Esmeralda, to lead the South City house meeting campaign. And while Esmeralda was able to organize a vibrant house

meeting campaign with my limited support, La Unión's long-term organizing capacity dwindled and many of the initiatives and much of the momentum established in South City by prior organizers faded. In this way, the absence of robust institutional support for this social movement work impeded mobilization efforts.

13 Contrast the organizing work of La Unión with the efforts of four respondents in South City, including Evelinda and Ignacio (mentioned above). They had, for instance, established a "club" or hometown association (HTA) and, with the support of the local Mexican consul's office, the mayor of their hometown in Mexico, state officials, and the local community north of the border, raised funds for local community projects and emergency medical care for neighbors and family living in their hometown. See Fox and Bada, "Migrant Civic Engagement"; Ramakrishnan and Viramontes, "Civic Spaces." They report that in total they raised $500,000 for several community projects. This activity directly addressed the need of members from the sending community and was led by community members themselves who had secured the cooperation of local officials and diplomats. This activity stands in marked contrast to the work that I observed with La Unión, which was led primarily by community organizers.

14 Tilly, "Getting It Together"; Tilly, "Contentious Repetoires in Great Britain."

15 Introjection is a psychoanalytic term used by Freud, among others, to describe the way that external inputs from the world outside the subject are folded into the ego.

16 See Agrawal, "Environmentality."

17 Flacks, *Making History*, 86–87.

18 Sidney Tarrow refers to these oscillations as cycles of protest. *Power in Movement*.

19 Mahmood, "Feminist Theory, Embodiment, and the Docile Agent," 212.

20 Critical observers (US feminists for Mahmood) often regard the situation of pious Muslim women, to take Mahmood's example, or poor white Republicans in Appalachia, to take another, as working against their own interests. Pious women, subordinating themselves to the religious authority of men, or poor whites, voting for a political party that exploits their ideological convergence on social issues like opposition to gay marriage and drug crime but leverages that convergence to mask conservative economic policies that further impoverish them, are presumably examples of people undermining their own political interests. Mahmood's point, however, is that this formulation makes sense only if the "interests" of the group under observation are inferred by the observers themselves. While these various subject positions and political aspirations may not make sense to critical observers, their "interests" may in fact function within a cosmology that outsiders misunderstand or ignore. So in one way, these groups may very well be working against their own interests, but only to the extent that the observers define what those interests are in the first place. Within the cosmology of these subjects themselves, there very well may not be any conflict.

CHAPTER 5. OPPORTUNITY AND THREAT

1 Bloemraad, Voss, and Lee, "Protests of 2006," 36; Chavez and Provine, "Race and the Response of State Legislatures to Unauthorized Immigrants"; Laglagaron et al., "Regulating Immigration at the State Level"; Ramakrishnan and Wong, "Immigration Policies Go Local"; Steil and Vasi, "New Immigration Contestation."

2 See Varsanyi et al., "Multilayered Jurisdictional Patchwork."

3 The letter, of course, raises a variety of legal issues, not the least of which is whether a mayor can expel a foreign diplomat from a city in the first place. Notwithstanding the legality of such a maneuver, the more practical issue is that immigrants would be made vulnerable to impoundments and potentially arrest, a move the city is legally empowered to undertake, even if the consul were able to successfully host its mobile consulate events and were on firm legal ground to do so. In the end, the Mexican consulate simply hosted its events in the next town over.

4 McAdam, "Framing Function of Movement Tactics."

5 The presence of conservative elected officials, like the North City mayor whose letter opens this chapter, and conservative electorates are critical factors explaining the emergence of anti-immigrant mobilization and the adoption of anti-immigrant legislation. Rapid demographic changes, especially growing numbers of Latinos and immigrants, also spur conservative backlash. See Chavez and Provine, "Race and the Response of State Legislatures to Unauthorized Immigrants"; Ebert and Okamoto, "Legitimating Contexts, Immigrant Power, and Exclusionary Actions"; Ramakrishnan and Wong, "Immigration Policies Go Local"; Steil and Vasi, "New Immigration Contestation."

6 Latino refers to all those who marked Hispanic or Latino on the US census for 2010, the year that falls in the middle of the data collection period for this book. White refers to those who indicated not Hispanic Latino and "white alone." US Census Bureau, "American FactFinder."

7 Ibid.

8 See note 6 above.

9 The term *la corrida* literally means "the run" or "the circuit" and is used to refer to the way migrant farmworkers follow the work opportunities that each season's harvest brings. For an excellent ethnographic account of farmworker migration, see Holmes, *Fresh Fruit, Broken Bodies*; Holmes, "'Oaxacans Like to Work Bent Over.'"

10 The Minutemen are a citizen militia dedicated to enforcing immigration laws that they believe the federal government will not enforce themselves. See Molina, "Minutemen and Neoliberal State Activity."

11 California Secretary of State, "Voter Registration Statistics."

12 A late version of this chapter was reviewed by a primary informant to confirm the accuracy of the below narratives.

13 Gabrielson, "Sobriety Checkpoints Catch Unlicensed Drivers."

14 Esmeralda fits the definition of an active contributor and leader as defined by
    Pamela Oliver. She was interested and involved in local issues, knew many people
    in the community, and, though I do not elaborate this point in this chapter, was
    generally pessimistic about immigrant community members' willingness to get
    involved without prompting from organizers and other volunteer leaders: a pro-
    cess she often referred to as *torciendo brazos*, or twisting arms. See Oliver, "If You
    Don't Do It."

15 Beat officers are distinct from other patrol officers in their community policing
    approach. They work exclusively in one or two neighborhoods or "beats" for sev-
    eral years and are tasked with forming relationships with key community mem-
    bers and institutions in order to facilitate a more cooperative policing strategy.

16 Threat and opportunity have been explicitly theorized together as with opportu-
    nity/threat spirals or "sequences of environmental change, interpretation of that
    change, action, and counteraction, repeated as one action alters another actor's
    environment." McAdam, Tarrow, and Tilly, *Dynamics of Contention*, 243; see also
    Karapin, "Opportunity/Threat Spirals." Political opportunity and threat compose
    part of a broader political approach in the social movement literature, which, in
    addition to political opportunity, explains the emergence of protest with reference
    to mobilizing structures (like social movement organizations) and framing pro-
    cesses. McAdam, *Political Process and the Development of Black Insurgency*; Tilly,
    "Contentious Repetoires in Great Britain."

17 Though threat was initially theorized alongside opportunity, threat has been "an
    underemphasized corollary of the model." McAdam, Tarrow, and Tilly, *Dynam-
    ics of Contention*, 43. For instance, Tilly's political process approach assigned
    "equal weight to threat and opportunity as stimulants to collective action."
    McAdam, "Revisiting the U.S. Civil Rights Movement," 205. Nevertheless, an
    overemphasis on opportunity yielded the perception that expanding opportuni-
    ties are the primary precursors to mobilization. Tarrow, *Power in Movement*,
    17–18. See, e.g., Eisinger, "Conditions of Protest Behavior in American Cities";
    McAdam, *Political Process and the Development of Black Insurgency*; Reese,
    Giedraitis, and Vega, "Mobilization and Threat," 305; Tilly, *From Mobilization to
    Revolution*.

18 On threat in authoritarian settings, see Alimi, "Mobilizing under the Gun"; Al-
    meida, "Opportunity Organizations and Threat-Induced Contention"; Einwohner,
    "Opportunity, Honor, and Action in the Warsaw Ghetto Uprising of 1943";
    Loveman, "High-Risk Collective Action"; Maher, "Threat, Resistance, and Col-
    lective Action"; Shriver, Adams, and Longo, "Environmental Threats and Political
    Opportunities"; White, "From Peaceful Protest to Guerrilla War." On threat in
    Western democracies, see Goldstone and Tilly, "Threat (and Opportunity)";
    Johnson and Frickel, "Ecological Threat"; Kitschelt, "Political Opportunity Struc-
    tures and Political Protest"; Meyer, "Peace Protest and Policy"; Tester, "Resources,
    Identity, and the Role of Threat"; Tilly and Tarrow, *Contentious Politics*; Van Dyke
    and Soule, "Structural Social Change and the Mobilizing Effect of Threat." Wright

argues this overemphasis on opportunity may be a result of the literature's lack of coverage of right-wing movements, where threat is often a powerful motivator. Wright, *Patriots, Politics, and the Oklahoma City Bombing*, 29.

19 Reese, Giedraitis, and Vega, "Mobilization and Threat," 289.

20 Bloemraad, Voss, and Lee, "Protests of 2006," 28–29.

21 Okamoto and Ebert, "Beyond the Ballot," 550.

22 Meyer argues that the concept is fraught because of (1) major differences in the operationalization of the dependent variable, political opportunity (e.g., mobilization, policy change, social movement organization formation, etc.), (2) a lack of clarity in the selection of the opportunity variables that matter (e.g., elite allies, divisions among the elite, opportunities for institutionalized political participation, movement-countermovement interaction, etc.), and (3) a lack of clarity about exactly *how* political opportunities change in response to social movement activity. See Meyer, "Protest and Political Opportunities"; see also Meyer and Minkoff, "Conceptualizing Political Opportunity"; Meyer and Staggenborg, "Movements, Countermovements, and the Structure of Political Opportunity."

23 Not merely a matter of style or tone, tactics play an important role in broader movement dynamics. "Tactical innovation," for instance, is often what affords less powerful challengers the leverage to initiate new cycles of protest. See McAdam, "Tactical Innovation and the Pace of Insurgency"; see also Miller Cantzler, "Translation of Indigenous Agency and Innovation."

24 Taylor and Van Dyke, "'Get Up, Stand Up.'"

25 Staggenborg argues that organizations can be critical for sustaining movement coalitions when public interest in an issue fades. See "Consequences of Professionalization and Formalization," 602–4. Coalitions of organizations, in addition to Spanish-language media, were a critical factor in the emergence of the unprecedented immigrant marches in spring 2006. See Martinez, "Mobilizing Marchers in the Mile High City." Organizations can sustain movements from one protest wave to another; Almeida, "Opportunity Organizations and Threat-Induced Contention." They can promote protest across movements; see Minkoff, "Sequencing of Social Movements." Organizations are also critical for sustaining a movement while it is in "abeyance"; Taylor, "Social Movement Continuity."

26 Piven and Cloward, *Poor People's Movements*, xii.

27 Staggenborg, "Consequences of Professionalization and Formalization." Similarly, while Walker, Martin, and McCarthy find that the involvement of social movement organizations (SMOs) in mobilization decreases the likelihood of civil disobedience and increases the likelihood of conventional tactics, "organizational presence appears also to support certain radical tactics (strikes, sit-ins, pickets, boycotts) and to decrease the usage of certain tactics that are more conventional (rallies, demonstrations, marches)." "Confronting the State, the Corporation, and the Academy," 67.

28 Piven and Cloward, *Poor People's Movements*, chap. 2; McAdam, "Recruitment to High-Risk Activism."

29 Walker, Martin, and McCarthy, "Confronting the State, the Corporation, and the Academy."

30 See, e.g., Alimi, "Mobilizing under the Gun."

31 See, e.g., White, "From Peaceful Protest to Guerrilla War," 1297.

32 See, e.g., Reese, Giedraitis, and Vega, "Mobilization and Threat," 298.

33 To be clear, the absence of opportunity is not synonymous with threat. To take a classic element of political opportunity—elite allies—we can imagine a situation in which political actors have clear elite allies (opportunity), another in which they do not (no opportunity or closure), and finally another in which political elites actively seek to erode the rights, safety, or resources of a group (threat). Threat is related to opportunity, but is not the same as the absence of opportunity or closure.

34 For more on repression and protest, the work of Jennifer Earl on this topic is particularly nuanced and informative. See Earl, "'You Can Beat the Rap, But You Can't Beat the Ride'"; Earl, "Protest Arrests and Future Protest Participation."

35 Various studies have documented the positive effect of conservative political power on anti-immigrant legislative activity. See Chavez and Provine, "Race and the Response of State Legislatures to Unauthorized Immigrants"; Ebert and Okamoto, "Legitimating Contexts, Immigrant Power, and Exclusionary Actions"; Ramakrishnan and Wong, "Immigration Policies Go Local."

36 Staggenborg, "Consequences of Professionalization and Formalization," 587.

37 Ethnographic methods uniquely provide methodological leverage over the analysis advanced in this chapter because they are attuned to micro-level processes of meaning making and inclusive of nonconfrontational tactics undercounted in or excluded from quantitative studies relying on newspaper reports. See Earl et al., "Use of Newspaper Data"; see also McAdam et al., "'There Will Be Fighting in the Streets.'"

38 Walker, Martin, and McCarthy, "Confronting the State, the Corporation, and the Academy."

39 Tilly, "Getting It Together."

CONCLUSION

1 Walzer, *Spheres of Justice*, 61.

2 Associated Press, "Mexico Got More Money from Remittances."

3 The problem of the country cap is especially acute for those coming from the top four immigrant-sending countries: Mexico, India, China, and the Philippines. See Ngai, "Civil Rights Origins of Illegal Immigration"; Massey, Durand, and Pren, "Why Border Enforcement Backfired." An additional unanticipated consequence of the constriction of avenues for legal migration and growing enforcement was defensive naturalization by those with legal permanent status. To safeguard their place in the United States and because naturalized citizens are able to bring spouses, minor children, and parents, who are exempt from the numerical limits

of the country cap, legal migration from Mexico also surged over this period. See Massey, "America's Immigration Policy Fiasco," 9–10.

4 For more on the expanded grounds for deportation for legal immigrants, see Kanstroom, *Deportation Nation*. In *Latino Threat*, Chavez argues, "Their social identity has been plagued by the mark of illegality, which in much public discourse means that they are criminals and thus illegitimate members of society undeserving of social benefits, including citizenship. Latinos are an alleged threat because of this history and social identity, which supposedly make their integration difficult and imbue them, particularly Mexicans, with a desire to remain socially apart as they prepare for a reconquest of the U.S. Southwest." Chavez, *Latino Threat*, 3.

5 Heyman, "'Illegality' and the U.S.-Mexico Border," 117. In Heyman's analysis the localization of enforcement at the border, far from work sites, demonstrates the way the risks of immigration are placed on migrants and not on those who employ them. His analysis may be complicated by the fact of increasing interior and regional enforcement. Though devolution might bring the site of enforcement closer to the workplace, it remains true that employer sanctions are the least well-funded tactic among all enforcement practices.

6 Genova, *Working the Boundaries*.

7 Ta-Nehisi Coates, in his acclaimed *Between the World and Me*, 11, writes of a similar Dream:

> It is perfect houses with nice lawns. It is Memorial Day cookouts, block associations, and driveways. The Dream is treehouses and the Cub Scouts. The Dream smells like peppermint but tastes like strawberry shortcake. And for so long I have wanted to escape into the Dream, to fold my country over my head like a blanket. But this has never been an option because the Dream rests on our back, the bedding made from our bodies.

> Of course, African Americans were not immigrants, and so their history in this country is not directly comparable with the history Mexican immigration. But their relationship to what Coates calls simply the Dream is an important source of solidarity. Roberto's comments indicate both what his aspirations are reaching toward—a certain material security—and the barriers that impede their realization. Coates's conceptualization of the Dream reflects what I see as the currents running through Roberto's comments: the Dream is both a goal and something of an impossibility since the prosperity at the heart of the Dream functions not in spite of but because of the subordination of his racialized labor.

8 Menjívar, "Liminal Legality."

9 According to Voss and Bloemraad, "more successful framing strategies appealed to bedrock American values: family and work. Appeals to America's experience with immigration, to immigrants' home country pride, or even to human rights stood out as too 'foreign'; such discourses found little purchase and often significant mainstream opposition." "Protests of 2006," 31.

10 Emirbayer and Mische offer a carefully elaborated theorization of agency comprising iterational, projective, and practical evaluative elements. Emphasis on one or another of these elements fluctuates over time and reshapes the actor's relationship to structure. Emirbayer and Mische, "What Is Agency?"

11 Gonzales, *Reform without Justice*.

12 Das Gupta, *Unruly Immigrants*.

13 Ibid., 19.

14 Ibid., 22.

15 Fernandez and Olsen, "To Live, Love and Work Anywhere You Please," 416; see also Camacho, *Migrant Imaginaries*.

16 Baker-Cristales, "Mediated Resistance," 78.

17 Barvosa, *Wealth of Selves*, 45–47.

18 Mahmood, *Politics of Piety*.

19 See Isin, "Citizenship in Flux."

20 Martin calls the PRWORA the third biggest shift in immigration policy after the establishment of national origins in 1924 and their elimination in 1965, creating a "sharp distinction between US citizens and immigrants in terms of access to a social safety net." Martin, "United States," 67.

21 De Genova finds a similar dynamic in his ethnography of Mexican factory workers in Chicago. He describes the way that Mexican immigrants readily understand that while they cannot assimilate to whiteness or "Americanness," they still distinguish themselves from blacks who are *flojo* or lazy. While the excerpt above does not identify blacks explicitly, their challenge to exclusionary citizenship relies on the reinscription of a hierarchy of deservingness in which those who conform to a racialized politics of respectability are worthy of full inclusion (though they may be legally barred from it), while those others, those bums, are not (they may have formal membership, but have squandered it). Genova, *Working the Boundaries*, chap. 5.

22 Peter Nyers refers to this dynamic as "abject cosmopolitanism," or the way refuges and migrants are "reinvigorating democratic politics" by demanding a moratorium on deportations and a pathway to regularize their status. Nyers, "Abject Cosmopolitanism," 440; see also Brettell and Reed-Danahay, *Civic Engagements*. In a similar vein, Isin redefines citizenship not as legal status, but as acts. "The emerging figure of the activist citizen," he explains, "calls into question the givenness of that body politic and opens its boundaries wide." Isin, "Citizenship in Flux," 384.

23 Butler, "Reflections on Trump."

24 Fernandez and Olsen, "To Live, Love and Work Anywhere You Please," 418.

25 Phillips, *Brown Is the New White*.

26 See Toobin, "American Limbo."

27 Generally, see the collection of studies from Smith and Edmonston, *Immigration Debate*. On economic impacts, see Card, "Is the New Immigration Really So Bad?"; Hinojosa-Ojeda, "Raising the Floor for American Workers"; US Council of Economic Advisers, "US Council of Economic Advisers on Immigration's

Economic Impact." On fiscal impacts, see Lee and Miller, "Current Fiscal Impact of Immigrants and Their Descendants"; Lee and Miller, "Immigration, Social Security, and Broader Fiscal Impacts." On wages, see Ottaviano and Peri, "Rethinking the Effect of Immigration on Wages"; Ottaviano, Peri, and Wright, "Immigration, Offshoring and US Jobs." On crime, see Hagan and Palloni, "Sociological Criminology and the Mythology of Hispanic Immigration and Crime"; Martinez, "Coming to America"; Rumbaut et al., "Immigration and Incarceration"; Sampson, "Rethinking Crime and Immigration."

28 Golash-Boza, "Immigration Industrial Complex."
29 Gonzales, *Reform without Justice*, 6.
30 See Wendland, "What Do We Owe Each Other?"; Benhabib, "Morality of Migration."

APPENDIX

1 Data are missing for four respondents.
2 Respondents' Latino heritage is defined as follows: first-generation respondents are of foreign birth, second-generation respondents have at least one parent of foreign birth, and third-generation respondents are of native birth and native parentage. Portes and Rumbaut, *Immigrant America*.

BIBLIOGRAPHY

Abrego, Leisy J. "Legal Consciousness of Undocumented Latinos: Fear and Stigma as Barriers to Claims-Making for First- and 1.5-Generation Immigrants." *Law and Society Review* 45, no. 2 (June 1, 2011): 337–70.

Agrawal, Arun. "Environmentality: Community, Intimate Government, and the Making of Environmental Subjects in Kuamon, India." *Current Anthropology* 46, no. 2 (2005): 161–90.

Alimi, Eitan. "Mobilizing under the Gun: Theorizing Political Opportunity Structure in a Highly Repressive Setting." *Mobilization* 14, no. 2 (June 1, 2009): 219–37. doi:10.17813/maiq.14.2.u210745765568737.

Almaguer, Tomás. *Racial Fault Lines: The Historical Origins of White Supremacy in California*. Berkeley: University of California Press, 1994.

Almeida, Paul D. "Opportunity Organizations and Threat-Induced Contention: Protest Waves in Authoritarian Settings." *American Journal of Sociology* 109, no. 2 (September 2003): 345–400.

Althusser, Louis. *Lenin and Philosophy and Other Essays*. New York: Monthly Review Press, 1971.

Anderson, Benedict. *Imagined Communities: Reflections on the Origin and Spread of Nationalism*. New York: Verso, 1983.

Anderson, Stuart. "How Many More Deaths? The Moral Case for a Temporary Worker Program." National Foundation for American Policy, March 2013.

Andreas, Peter. *Border Games: Policing the U.S.-Mexico Divide*. Ithaca, NY: Cornell University Press, 2001.

Armenta, Amada. "From Sheriff's Deputies to Immigration Officers: Screening Immigrant Status in a Tennessee Jail." *Law & Policy* 34, no. 2 (2012): 191–210.

Associated Press. "Mexico Got More Money from Remittances Than from Oil Revenues in 2015." *NBC News*, February 3, 2016. www.nbcnews.com.

Bacon, David. "How US Policies Fueled Mexico's Great Migration." *The Nation*, January 4, 2012. www.thenation.com.

Baker-Cristales, Beth. "Mediated Resistance: The Construction of Neoliberal Citizenship in the Immigrant Rights Movement." *Latino Studies* 7, no. 1 (Spring 2009): 60–82. doi:10.1057/lst.2008.55.

Balderrama, Francisco E., and Raymond Rodriguez. *Decade of Betrayal: Mexican Repatriation in the 1930s*. Albuquerque: University of New Mexico Press, 1995.

Barvosa, Edwina. *Wealth of Selves: Multiple Identities, Mestiza Consciousness, and the Subject of Politics.* College Station: Texas A&M University Press, 2008.

Bayat, Asef. "From 'Dangerous Classes' to 'Quiet Rebels': Politics of the Urban Subaltern in the Global South." *International Sociology* 15, no. 3 (2000): 533–57.

———. *Life as Politics: How Ordinary People Change the Middle East.* Palo Alto, CA: Stanford University Press, 2010.

———. "Un-civil Society: The Politics of the 'Informal' People." *Third World Quarterly* 18, no. 1 (2010): 53–72.

Bell, Derrick A. *Faces at the Bottom of the Well: The Permanence of Racism.* New York: Basic Books, 1992.

Benford, Robert D., and David A. Snow. "Framing Processes and Social Movements: An Overview and Assessment." *Annual Review of Sociology* 26 (2000): 611–39.

Benhabib, Seyla. "The Morality of Migration." *New York Times Opinionator,* July 29, 2012. http://opinionator.blogs.nytimes.com.

Bloemraad, Irene, and Christine Trost. "It's a Family Affair: Intergenerational Mobilization in the Spring 2006 Protests." In Voss and Bloemraad, *Rallying for Immigrant Rights,* 180–97.

Bloemraad, Irene, Kim Voss, and Taeku Lee. "The Protests of 2006: What Were They? How Do We Understand Them, Where Do We Go?" In Voss and Bloemraad, *Rallying for Immigrant Rights,* 3–43.

Bobb, Merrick, "The Los Angeles County Sheriff's Department 28th Semiannual Report." PARC, October 2009.

Brettell, Caroline, and Deborah Reed-Danahay. *Civic Engagements: The Citizenship Practices of Indian and Vietnamese Immigrants.* Palo Alto, CA: Stanford University Press, 2011.

Briggs, Vernon M. "The 'Albatross' of Immigration Reform: Temporary Worker Policy in the United States." *International Migration Review* 20 (1986): 995–1019.

Brotherton, David, and Luis Barrios. *Banished to the Homeland: Dominican Deportees and Their Stories of Exile.* New York: Columbia University Press, 2011.

Butler, Judith. "Reflections on Trump." *Cultural Anthropology,* January 18, 2017. http://culanth.org.

California Secretary of State. "Voter Registration Statistics." 2016. www.sos.ca.gov.

Camacho, Alicia. *Migrant Imaginaries: Latino Cultural Politics in the U.S.-Mexico Borderlands.* New York: New York University Press, 2008.

Campbell, Howard, and Josiah Heyman. "Slantwise: Beyond Domination and Resistance on the Border." *Journal of Contemporary Ethnography* 36, no. 3 (2007): 3–30.

Cantor, Guillermo, Mark Noferi, and Daniel E. Martínez. "Enforcement Overdrive: A Comprehensive Assessment of ICE's Criminal Alien Program | Immigration Policy Center." American Immigration Council, October 23, 2015. http://immigrationpolicy.org.

Carbado, Devon W. "(E)racing the Fourth Amendment." *Michigan Law Review* 100, no. 5 (March 2002): 946–1044. doi:10.2307/1290502.

———. "Racial Naturalization." *American Quarterly* 57, no. 3 (2005): 633–58.

Carbado, Devon W., and Cheryl I. Harris. "Undocumented Criminal Procedure." *UCLA Law Review* 58 (August 23, 2011). http://papers.ssrn.com.

Card, David. "Is the New Immigration Really So Bad?" Discussion Paper Series. Bonn, Germany: Institute for the Study of Labor, April 2004.

Castillo, Alejandra. "Programa Frontera Sur: The Mexican Government's Faulty Immigration Policy." Washington, DC: Council on Hemispheric Affairs, October 26, 2016. www.coha.org.

Chavez, Jorge M., and Doris Marie Provine. "Race and the Response of State Legislatures to Unauthorized Immigrants." *Annals of the American Academy of Political and Social Sciences* 623 (2009): 78–92.

Chavez, Leo R. *The Latino Threat: Constructing Immigrants, Citizens, and the Nation.* Palo Alto, CA: Stanford University Press, 2008.

Coates, Ta-Nehisi. *Between the World and Me.* New York: Spiegel & Grau, 2015.

Coddou, Marion. "An Institutional Approach to Collective Action: Evidence from Faith-Based Latino Mobilization in the 2006 Immigrant Rights Protests." *Social Problems* 63, no. 1 (February 1, 2016): 127–50. doi:10.1093/socpro/spv023.

Coleman, Mathew. "A Geopolitics of Engagement: Neoliberalism, the War on Terrorism, and the Reconfiguration of Immigration Enforcement." *Geopolitics* 12 (2007): 607–34.

———. "The 'Local' Migration State: The Site-Specific Devolution of Immigration Enforcement in the U.S. South." *Law & Policy* 34, no. 2 (April 1, 2012): 159–90. doi:10.1111/j.1467–9930.2011.00358.x.

———. "What Counts as the Politics and Practice of Security, and Where? Devolution and Immigrant Insecurity after 9/11." *Annals of the Association of American Geographers* 99, no. 5 (2009): 904–13.

Cornelius, Wayne, Scott Borger, Adam Sawyer, David Keyes, Clare Appleby, Kristen Parks, Gabriel Lozada, and Jonathan Hicken. "Controlling Unauthorized Immigration from Mexico: The Failure of 'Prevention through Deterrence' and the Need for Comprehensive Reform." San Diego: Center for Comparative Immigration Studies, June 10, 2008.

Coutin, Susan Bibler. *Legalizing Moves: Salvadoran Immigrants' Struggle for US Residency.* Ann Arbor: University of Michigan Press, 2000.

Crenshaw, Kimberle. "Mapping the Margins: Intersectionality, Identity Politics, and Violence against Women of Color." *Stanford Law Review* 43, no. 6 (July 1991): 1241–99.

Daniels, Roger. *Guarding the Golden Door: American Immigration Policy and Immigrants since 1882.* New York: Hill & Wang, 2004.

Das Gupta, Monisha. *Unruly Immigrants: Rights, Activism, and Transnational South Asian Politics in the United States.* Durham, NC: Duke University Press, 2006.

Dawson, Michael C. *Behind the Mule: Race and Class in African-American Politics.* Princeton, NJ: Princeton University Press, 1994.

Derrida, Jacques. *Specters of Marx: The State of the Debt, the Work of Mourning and the New International.* Translated by Peggy Kamuf. New York: Routledge, 1993.

Desmond, Matthew. *Evicted: Poverty and Profit in the American City*. New York: Crown, 2016.

Drake, Bruce. "Divide between Blacks and Whites on Police Runs Deep." Pew Research Center, April 28, 2015. www.pewresearch.org.

Dreby, Joanna. *Everyday Illegal: When Policies Undermine Immigrant Families*. Berkeley: University of California Press, 2015.

Driscoll, Barbara A. *The Tracks North: The Railroad Bracero Program of World War II*. Austin: University of Texas Press, 1999.

Du Bois, W. E. B. *The Souls of Black Folk*. New York: Bedford/St. Martin's, 1903.

Dunn, Timothy J. *The Militarization of the U.S.-Mexico Border, 1978–1992: Low-Intensity Conflict Doctrine Comes Home*. Austin: University of Texas Press, 1997.

Earl, Jennifer. "Protest Arrests and Future Protest Participation: The 2004 Republican National Convention Arrestees and the Effects of Repression." In "Social Movements/Legal Possibilities," edited by Austin Sarat, special issue, *Studies in Law, Politics, and Society* 54 (2011): 141–73.

———. "'You Can Beat the Rap, But You Can't Beat the Ride': Bringing Arrests Back into Research on Repression." *Research in Social Movements, Conflicts and Change* 26 (December 20, 2005): 101–39. doi:10.1016/S0163-786X(05)26004-4.

Earl, Jennifer, Andrew Martin, John D. McCarthy, and Sarah A. Soule. "The Use of Newspaper Data in the Study of Collective Action." *Annual Review of Sociology* 30 (August 2004): 65–80. doi:10.1146/annurev.soc.30.012703.110603.

Ebert, Kim, and Dina G. Okamoto. "Legitimating Contexts, Immigrant Power, and Exclusionary Actions." *Social Problems* 62 (February 7, 2015): 40–67. doi:10.1093/socpro/spu006.

———. "Social Citizenship, Integration and Collective Action: Immigrant Civic Engagement in the United States." *Social Forces* 91, no. 4 (June 1, 2013): 1267–92. doi:10.1093/sf/sot009.

Einwohner, Rachel L. "Opportunity, Honor, and Action in the Warsaw Ghetto Uprising of 1943." *American Journal of Sociology* 109, no. 3 (2003): 650–75. doi:10.1086/379528.

Eisinger, Peter K. "The Conditions of Protest Behavior in American Cities." *American Political Science Review* 67, no. 1 (1973): 11–28.

Ellerman, Antje. "Undocumented Migrants and Resistance in the Liberal State." *Politics and Society* 38, no. 3 (2010): 408–29.

Emirbayer, Mustafa, and Ann Mische. "What Is Agency?" *American Journal of Sociology* 103, no. 4 (January 1998): 962–1023.

Epp, Charles R., Steven Maynard-Moody, and Donald P. Haider-Markel. *Pulled Over: How Police Stops Define Race and Citizenship*. Chicago: University of Chicago Press, 2014.

Esbenshade, Jill, and Barbara Obzurt. "Local Immigration Regulation: A Problematic Trend in Public Policy." *Harvard Journal of Hispanic Policy* 20 (2008): 33–47.

Falcón, Sylvanna. "Rape as a Weapon of War: Advancing Human Rights for Women at the U.S.-Mexico Border." *Social Justice* 28, no. 2 (2001): 31–50.

Feliciano, Cynthia, and Rubén G. Rumbaut. "Gendered Paths: Educational and Occupational Expectations and Outcomes among Adult Children of Immigrants." *Ethnic and Racial Studies* 28, no. 6 (November 2005): 1087–1118. doi:10.1080/01419870500224406.

Felstiner, William L. F., Richard L. Abel, and Austin Sarat. "The Emergence and Transformation of Disputes: Naming, Blaming, Claiming. . . ." *Law and Society Review* 15, nos. 3/4 (1980–81): 631–54.

Fernandez, Luis, and Joel Olsen. "To Live, Love and Work Anywhere You Please: Critical Exchange on Arizona and the Struggle for Locomotion." *Contemporary Political Theory* 10 (2011): 412–19.

Fitzgerald, David S., and David Cook-Martín. "The Geopolitical Origins of the U.S. Immigration Act of 1965." Migration Policy Institute, February 5, 2015. www.migrationpolicy.org.

Flacks, Richard. *Making History: The American Left and the American Mind*. New York: Columbia University Press, 1988.

Flores, William V. "Citizens vs. Citizenry: Undocumented Immigrants and Latino Cultural Citizenship." In *Latino Cultural Citizenship: Claiming Identity, Space, and Rights*, edited by William V. Flores and Rina Benmayor, 255–77. Boston: Beacon, 1997.

Foner, Nancy. *In a New Land: A Comparative View of Immigration*. New York: New York University Press, 2005.

Foucault, Michel. *Discipline and Punish: The Birth of the Prison*. New York: Vintage, 1975.

———. *The History of Sexuality: Volume 1. An Introduction*. New York: Vintage, 1976.

Fox, Jonathan, and Xóchitl Bada. "Migrant Civic Engagement." In Voss and Bloemraad, *Rallying for Immigrant Rights*, 142–60.

Freed Wessler, Seth. "Shattered Families: The Perilous Intersection of Immigration Enforcement and the Child Welfare System." Applied Research Center, November 2011.

Gabrielson, Ryan. "Car Seizures at DUI Checkpoints Prove Profitable for Cities, Raise Legal Questions." *California Watch*, February 13, 2010. http://californiawatch.org.

———. "Sobriety Checkpoints Catch Unlicensed Drivers." *New York Times*, February 14, 2010. www.nytimes.com.

Gálvez, Alyshia. *Guadalupe in New York: Devotion and the Struggle for Citizenship Rights among Mexican Immigrants*. New York: New York University Press, 2009.

García, Angela S. "Hidden in Plain Sight: How Unauthorised Migrants Strategically Assimilate in Restrictive Localities in California." *Journal of Ethnic and Migration Studies* 40, no. 12 (December 2, 2014): 1895–1914. doi:10.1080/1369183X.2014.883918.

Garcia, Juan Ramon. *Operation Wetback: The Mass Deportation of Mexican Undocumented Workers in 1954*. Westport, CT: Greenwood, 1980.

García Bedolla, Lisa. *Fluid Borders: Latino Power, Identity, and Politics in Los Angeles*. Berkeley: University of California Press, 2005.

Gardner, Trevor, and Aarti Kohli. "The C.A.P. Effect: Racial Profiling in the ICE Criminal Alien Program." Policy Brief. Berkeley: Chief Justice Earl Warren Institute on Race, Ethnicity, and Diversity, University of California, Berkeley Law School, September 2009.

Garni, Alisa, and Arpi Miller. "Localized Immigration Policy and Migrant Life Experiences: The Case of Mexican Migrants in Southern California." *Journal of Immigrant and Refugee Studies* 6, no. 3 (2008): 435–50.

Genova, Nicholas De. "Spectacles of Migrant 'Illegality': The Scene of Exclusion, the Obscene of Inclusion." *Ethnic and Racial Studies* 36, no. 7 (2013): 1180–98. doi:10.1080/01419870.2013.783710.

———. *Working the Boundaries: Race, Space, and Illegality in Mexican Chicago.* Durham, NC: Duke University Press, 2005.

Genova, Nicholas De, and Nathalie Peutz, eds. *The Deportation Regime: Sovereignty, Space, and the Freedom of Movement.* Durham, NC: Duke University Press, 2010.

Gerstle, Gary. "The Immigrant as Threat to American Security: A Historical Perspective." In Tirman, *Maze of Fear*, 87–108. New York: The New Press, 2004.

Gleeson, Shannon. "Labor Rights for All? The Role of Undocumented Immigrant Status for Worker Claims Making." *Law & Social Inquiry* 35, no. 3 (2010): 561–602.

Glenn, Evelyn Nakano. *Unequal Freedom: How Race and Gender Shaped American Citizenship and Labor.* Cambridge, MA: Harvard University Press, 2004.

Golash-Boza, Tanya. *Deported: Policing Immigrants, Disposable Labor and Global Capitalism.* New York: New York University Press, 2015.

———. "The Immigration Industrial Complex: Why We Enforce Immigration Policies Destined to Fail." *Sociology Compass* 3, no. 2 (2009): 1–15.

Golash-Boza, Tanya, and Pierrette Hondagneu-Sotelo. "Latino Immigrant Men and the Deportation Crisis: A Gendered Racial Removal Program." *Latino Studies* 11, no. 3 (2013): 271–92. doi:10.1057/lst.2013.14.

Goldstone, Jack A., and Charles Tilly. "Threat (and Opportunity): Popular Action and State Response in the Dynamics of Contentious Action." In *Silence and Voice in the Study of Contentious Politics*, edited by Ronald Aminzade, 179–94. New York: Cambridge University Press, 2001.

Gonzales, Alfonso. *Reform without Justice: Latino Migrant Politics and the Homeland Security State.* New York: Oxford University Press, 2013.

Gonzales, Roberto G. "Left Out but Not Shut Down: Political Activism and the Undocumented Student Movement." *Northwestern Journal of Law and Social Policy* 3, no. 2 (2008): 219–39.

Gonzales, Roberto G., and Leo R. Chavez. "'Awakening to a Nightmare': Abjectivity and Illegality in the Lives of Undocumented 1.5 Generation Latino Immigrants in the United States." *Current Anthropology* 53, no. 3 (2012): 255–81.

Gonzales, Roberto G. *Lives in Limbo: Undocumented and Coming of Age in America.* Berkeley: University of California Press, 2015.

Gonzalez, Juan. *Harvest of Empire: A History of Latinos in America.* 2nd ed. New York: Viking, 2000.

Gordon, Avery F. *Ghostly Matters: Haunting and the Sociological Imagination*. 2nd ed. Minneapolis: University of Minnesota Press, 2008.

Hagan, Jacqueline Maria, Nestor Rodriguez, and Brianna Castro. "Social Effects of Mass Deportations by the United States Government, 2000–10." *Ethnic and Racial Studies* 34, no. 8 (2011): 1374–91.

Hagan, John, and Alberto Palloni. "Sociological Criminology and the Mythology of Hispanic Immigration and Crime." *Social Problems* 46, no. 4 (November 1, 1999): 617–32.

Harvey, David. *A Brief History of Neoliberalism*. Oxford: Oxford University Press, 2007.

Hernandez, David Manuel. "Pursuant to Deportation: Latinos and Immigrant Detention." *Latino Studies* 6 (2008): 35–63.

Heyman, Josiah McC. "Grounding Immigrant Rights Movements in the Everyday Experience of Migration." *International Migration* 45, no. 3 (2007): 197–202.

———. "'Illegality' and the U.S.-Mexico Border." In *Constructing Immigrant "Illegality": Critiques, Experiences, and Responses*, edited by Cecilia Menjívar and Daniel Kanstroom, 111–35. New York: Cambridge University Press, 2013.

Higham, John. *Strangers in the Land: Patterns of American Nativism, 1860–1925*. New Brunswick, NJ: Rutgers University Press, 1965.

Hinojosa-Ojeda, Raul. "Raising the Floor for American Workers: The Economic Benefits of Comprehensive Immigration Reform." Center for American Progress and the Immigration Policy Center, January 2010. www.americanprogress.org.

Hollander, Jocelyn A., and Rachel L. Einwhoner. "Conceptualizing Resistance." *Sociological Forum* 19, no. 4 (2004): 533–54.

Holmes, Seth M. *Fresh Fruit, Broken Bodies: Migrant Farmworkers in the United States*. Berkeley: University of California Press, 2013.

———. "'Oaxacans Like to Work Bent Over': The Naturalization of Social Suffering among Berry Farmworkers." *International Migration* 45, no. 3 (2007): 39–63.

Hondagneu-Sotelo, Pierrette, ed. *Gender and U.S. Immigration: Contemporary Trends*. Berkeley: University of California Press, 2003.

Hondagneu-Sotelo, Pierrette, and Ernestine Avila. "'I'm Here but I'm There': The Meanings of Latina Transnational Motherhood." In Hondagneu-Sotelo, *Gender and U.S. Immigration*, 317–40.

Horsman, Reginald. *Race and Manifest Destiny: The Origins of American Racial Anglo-Saxonism*. Cambridge, MA: Harvard University Press, 2009.

Human Rights Watch. "Forced Apart (by the Numbers): Non-citizens Deported Mostly for Nonviolent Offenses." Human Rights Watch, April 15, 2009. www.hrw.org.

Hussar, William J., and Tabitha M. Bailey. "Projections of Education Statistics to 2022: Forty-First Edition." Washington, DC: National Center for Education Statistics, U.S. Department of Education, February 2014. http://nces.ed.gov.

Immigration and Customs Enforcement. "Activated Jurisdictions." 2013. http://www.ice.gov.

Isin, Engin. "Citizenship in Flux: The Figure of the Activist Citizen." *Subjectivity* 29 (2009): 367–88.

Jiménez, Tomás R. *Replenished Ethnicity: Mexican Americans, Immigration, and Identity*. Berkeley: University of California Press, 2009.

Johnson, Erik W., and Scott Frickel. "Ecological Threat and the Founding of U.S. National Environmental Movement Organizations, 1962–1998." *Social Problems* 58, no. 3 (August 1, 2011): 305–29. doi:10.1525/sp.2011.58.3.305.

Johnson, Kevin R. "Free Trade and Closed Borders: NAFTA and Mexican Immigration to the United States." *U.C. Davis Law Review* 27 (1994): 937–78.

Johnson, Walter. "On Agency." *Journal of Social History* 37, no. 1 (2003): 113–24.

Kanaiaupuni, Shawn Malta. "Reframing the Migration Question: An Analysis of Men, Women, and Gender in Mexico." *Social Forces* 78, no. 4 (June 2000): 1311–47.

Kandel, William A. "Interior Immigration Enforcement: Criminal Alien Programs." Washington, DC: Congressional Research Service, September 6, 2016. http://fas.org.

Kanstroom, Daniel. *Deportation Nation: Outsiders in American History*. Cambridge, MA: Harvard University Press, 2007.

Karapin, Roger. "Opportunity/Threat Spirals in the U.S. Women's Suffrage and German Anti-immigration Movements." *Mobilization* 16, no. 1 (February 1, 2011): 65–80. doi:10.17813/maiq.16.1.y1007j0n837p5p45.

Kitschelt, Herbert P. "Political Opportunity Structures and Political Protest: Anti-nuclear Movements in Four Democracies." *British Journal of Political Science* 16 (1986): 57–85.

Kohli, Aarti, Peter L. Markowitz, and Lisa Chavez. "Secure Communities by the Numbers: An Analysis of Demographics and Due Process." Chief Justice Earl Warren Institute on Law and Social Policy, University of California, Berkeley Law School, October 2011.

Krogstad, Jens Manuel. "Top Issue for Hispanics? Hint: It's Not Immigration." Washington, DC: Pew Research Center, June 2, 2014. www.pewresearch.org.

Laglagaron, Laureen, Cristina Rodríguez, Alexa Silver, and Sirithon Thanasombat. "Regulating Immigration at the State Level: Highlights from the Database of 2007 Immigration Legislation and Methodology." Washington, DC: Migration Policy Institute, October 2008.

Laubenthal, Barbara. "The Emergence of Pro-regularization Movements in Western Europe." *International Migration* 45, no. 3 (2007): 101–33.

Law, Anna O. "Lies, Damned Lies, and Obama's Deportation Statistics." *Washington Post*, April 21, 2014. www.washingtonpost.com.

Lee, Ronald D., and Timothy W. Miller. "The Current Fiscal Impact of Immigrants and Their Descendants: Beyond the Immigrant Household." In Smith and Edmonston, *Immigration Debate*, 183–205.

———. "Immigration, Social Security, and Broader Fiscal Impacts." *American Economic Review* 90, no. 2 (2000): 350–54.

Levitt, Peggy. *The Transnational Villagers*. Berkeley: University of California Press, 2001.

Light, Michael T., Michael Massoglia, and Ryan D. King. "Citizenship and Punishment: The Salience of National Membership in U.S. Criminal Courts." *American Sociological Review* 79, no. 5 (October 1, 2014): 825–47. doi:10.1177/0003122414543659.

Lind, Dara. "The Research That Made Me Take Donald Trump Seriously." *Vox*, May 4, 2016. www.vox.com.

López, Gustavo, and Jynnah Radford. "Facts on U.S. Immigrants, 2015." Washington, DC: Pew Research Center, May 3, 2017. www.pewhispanic.org.

Lopez, Mark Hugo, and Ana Gonzalez-Barrera. "Latino Voters Support Obama by 3–1 Ratio, but Are Less Certain Than Others about Voting." Washington, DC: Pew Research Center, October 11, 2012. www.pewhispanic.org.

Lopez, Mark Hugo, and Paul Taylor. "Latino Voters in the 2012 Election." Washington, DC: Pew Research Center, November 7, 2012. www.pewhispanic.org.

Lopez, Mark Hugo, Paul Taylor, Cary Funk, and Ana Gonzalez-Barrera. "On Immigration Policy, Deportation Relief Seen as More Important Than Citizenship." Washington, DC: Pew Research Center, December 19, 2013. www.pewhispanic.org.

Loveman, Mara. "High-Risk Collective Action: Defending Human Rights in Chile, Uruguay, and Argentina." *American Journal of Sociology* 104, no. 2 (September 1998): 477–525. doi:10.1086/210045.

Luibheid, Eithne. *Entry Denied: Controlling Sexuality at the Border*. Minneapolis: University of Minnesota Press, 2002.

Macías-Rojas, Patrisia. *From Deportation to Prison: The Politics of Immigration Enforcement in Post–Civil Rights America*. New York: New York University Press, 2016.

Maher, Thomas V. "Threat, Resistance, and Collective Action: The Cases of Sobibór, Treblinka, and Auschwitz." *American Sociological Review* 75, no. 2 (2010): 252–72.

Mahmood, Saba. "Feminist Theory, Embodiment, and the Docile Agent: Some Reflections on the Egyptian Islamic Revival." *Cultural Anthropology* 16, no. 2 (2001): 202–36.

———. *Politics of Piety: The Islamic Revival and the Feminist Subject*. Princeton, NJ: Princeton University Press, 2005.

Maril, Robert Lee. *Patrolling Chaos: The US Border Patrol in Deep South Texas*. Lubbock: Texas Tech University Press, 2004.

Martin, Philip L. "Immigration in the United States." University of California, Davis, 2002.

———. "The United States: The Continuing Immigration Debate." In *Controlling Immigration: A Global Perspective*, edited by Wayne A. Cornelius, Takeyuki Tsuda, Philip L. Martin, and James F. Hollifield, 51–85. Palo Alto, CA: Stanford University Press, 2004.

Martinez, Lisa. "Mobilizing Marchers in the Mile High City." In Voss and Bloemraad, *Rallying for Immigrant Rights*, 123–41.

Martinez, Ramiro, Jr. "Coming to America: The Impact of the New Immigration on Crime." In Martinez and Valenzuela, *Immigration and Crime*, 1–19.

Martinez, Ramiro, Jr., and Abel Valenzuela Jr., eds. *Immigration and Crime: Race, Ethnicity, and Violence*. New York: New York University Press, 2006.

Massey, Douglas S. "America's Immigration Policy Fiasco: Learning from Past Mistakes." *Dædalus* 142, no. 3 (2013): 5–15.

————. "Why Does Immigration Occur? A Theoretical Synthesis." In *The Handbook of International Migration: The American Experience*, edited by Charles Hirschman, Josh Dewind, and Philip Kasinitz, 34–52. New York: Russell Sage Foundation, 1999.

Massey, Douglas S., Jorge Durand, and Karen A. Pren. "Why Border Enforcement Backfired." *American Journal of Sociology* 121, no. 5 (2016): 1557–1600.

McAdam, Doug. "The Framing Function of Movement Tactics: Strategic Dramaturgy in the American Civil Rights Movement." In *Comparative Perspectives on Social Movements*, edited by John D. McCarthy and Mayer N. Zald, 338–55. Cambridge Studies in Comparative Politics. Cambridge: Cambridge University Press, 1996. doi:10.1017/CBO9780511803987.014.

————. *Political Process and the Development of Black Insurgency 1930–1970*. Chicago: University of Chicago Press, 1982.

————. "Recruitment to High-Risk Activism: The Case of Freedom Summer." *American Journal of Sociology* 92, no. 1 (1986): 64–90.

————. "Revisiting the U.S. Civil Rights Movement: Toward a More Synthetic Understanding of the Origins of Contention." In *Rethinking Social Movements*, edited by Jeff Goodwin and James M. Jasper, 201–32. Lanham, MD: Rowman & Littlefield, 2004.

————. "Tactical Innovation and the Pace of Insurgency." *American Sociological Review* 48, no. 6 (1983): 735–54. doi:10.2307/2095322.

McAdam, Doug, Robert Sampson, Simón Weffer-Elizondo, and Heather MacIndoe. "'There Will Be Fighting in the Streets': The Distorting Lens of Social Movement Theory." *Mobilization* 10, no. 1 (2005): 1–18.

McAdam, Doug, Sidney Tarrow, and Charles Tilly. *Dynamics of Contention*. Cambridge: Cambridge University Press, 2001.

McElrath, Suzy, Rahsaan Mahadeo, and Stephen Suh. "'Crimmigration,' with Tanya Golash-Boza, Ryan King, and Yolanda Vázquez." *The Society Pages*, February 24, 2014. http://thesocietypages.org.

Menjívar, Cecilia. "Educational Hopes, Documented Dreams: Guatemalan and Salvadoran Immigrants' Legality and Educational Prospects." *Annals of the American Academy of Political and Social Science* 620 (2008): 177–93.

————. "The Intersection of Work and Gender: Central American Immigrant Women and Employment in California." In Hondagneu-Sotelo, *Gender and U.S. Immigration*, 101–26. Berkeley: University of California Press, 2003.

————. "Liminal Legality: Salvadoran and Guatemalan Immigrants' Lives in the United States." *American Journal of Sociology* 111, no. 4 (2006): 999–1037. doi:10.1086/499509.

Menjívar, Cecilia, and Leisy J. Abrego. "Legal Violence: Immigration Law and the Lives of Central American Immigrants." *American Journal of Sociology* 117, no. 5 (March 2012): 1380–1421. doi:10.1086/663575.

Menjívar, Cecilia, and Cynthia Bejarano. "Latino Immigrants' Perceptions of Crime and Police Authorities in the United States: A Case Study from the Phoenix Metropolitan Area." *Ethnic and Racial Studies* 27, no. 1 (2004): 120–48.

Menjívar, Cecilia, and Sarah M. Lakhani. "Transformative Effects of Immigration Law: Immigrants' Personal and Social Metamorphoses through Regularization." *American Journal of Sociology* 121, no. 6 (May 2016): 1818–55.

Menjívar, Cecilia, and Olivia Salcido. "Immigrant Women and Domestic Violence Common Experiences in Different Countries." *Gender & Society* 16, no. 6 (December 1, 2002): 898–920. doi:10.1177/089124302237894.

Meyer, David S. "Peace Protest and Policy." *Policy Studies Journal* 21, no. 1 (1993): 35–51. doi:10.1111/j.1541–0072.1993.tb01452.x.

———. "Protest and Political Opportunities." *Annual Review of Sociology* 30 (2004): 125–45.

Meyer, David S., and Debra C. Minkoff. "Conceptualizing Political Opportunity." *Social Forces* 82, no. 4 (2004): 1457–92.

Meyer, David S., and Suzanne Staggenborg. "Movements, Countermovements, and the Structure of Political Opportunity." *American Journal of Sociology* 101, no. 6 (1996): 1628–60.

Mezzadra, Sandro. "The Gaze of Autonomy: Capitalism, Migration, and Social Struggles." In *The Contested Politics of Mobility: Borderzones and Irregularity*, edited by Vicki Squire, 121–42. London: Routledge, 2011.

Miller Cantzler, Julia. "The Translation of Indigenous Agency and Innovation into Political and Cultural Power: The Case of Indigenous Fishing Rights in Australia." *Interface* 5, no. 1 (2013): 69–101.

Minkoff, Debra C. "From Service Provision to Institutional Advocacy: The Shifting Legitimacy of Organizational Forms." *Social Forces* 72, no. 4 (1994): 943–69.

———. "The Sequencing of Social Movements." *American Sociological Review* 62, no. 5 (1997): 779–99.

Molina, Devin T. "The Minutemen and Neoliberal State Activity: Towards an Understanding of Private Border Patrols." *New Proposals: Journal of Marxism and Interdisciplinary Inquiry* 4, no. 2 (April 11, 2011): 59–66.

Motel, Seth, and Eileen Patten. "Statistical Portrait of the Foreign-Born Population in the United States, 2011." Pew Hispanic Center, January 29, 2013. www.pewhispanic.org.

Motomura, Hiroshi. "The Rights of Others: Legal Claims and Immigration outside the Law." *Duke Law Journal* 59 (2010): 1723–86.

Naples, Nancy A. *Grassroots Warriors: Activist Mothering, Community Work, and the War on Poverty*. New York: Routledge, 1998.

National Academies of Sciences, Engineering, and Medicine. *The Economic and Fiscal Consequences of Immigration*. Washington, DC: National Academies Press, 2016. www.nap.edu.

Navarrette, Ruben, Jr. "Latino Voters Can Take More Power." *USA Today*, October 13, 2016. www.usatoday.com.

Nazario, Sonia. *Enrique's Journey*. New York: Random House Trade Paperbacks, 2007.

Nevins, Joseph. *Operation Gatekeeper: The Rise of the "Illegal Alien" and the Remaking of the U.S.-Mexico Boundary*. New York: Routledge, 2002.

Ngai, Mae M. "The Civil Rights Origins of Illegal Immigration." *International Labor and Working-Class History* 78, no. 1 (2010): 93–99.

———. *Impossible Subjects: Illegal Aliens and the Making of Modern America*. Princeton, NJ: Princeton University Press, 2004.

———. "The Lost Immigration Debate." *Boston Review*, September 6, 2006. http://bostonreview.net.

Nicholls, Walter. *The DREAMers: How the Undocumented Youth Movement Transformed the Immigrant Rights Debate*. Palo Alto, CA: Stanford University Press, 2013.

Nolen, Stephanie. "Southern Exposure: The Costly Border Plan Mexico Won't Discuss." *Globe and Mail*, August 31, 2016. www.theglobeandmail.com.

Nyers, Peter. "Abject Cosmopolitanism: The Politics of Protection in the Anti-Deportation Movement." In Genova and Peutz, *Deportation Regime*, 413–42.

Office of the Inspector General. "The Performance of 287(g) Agreements." Washington, DC: Department of Homeland Security, Office of the Inspector General, March 2010.

Okamoto, Dina, and Kim Ebert. "Beyond the Ballot: Immigrant Collective Action in Gateways and New Destinations in the United States." *Social Problems* 57, no. 4 (2010): 529–58.

Oliver, Pamela E. "If You Don't Do It, Nobody Will: Active and Token Contributors to Local Collective Action." *American Sociological Review* 49, no. 5 (1984): 601–10. doi:10.2307/2095418.

Omi, Michael, and Howard Winant. *Racial Formation in the United States: From the 1960s to the 1990s*. 2nd ed. New York: Routledge, 1986.

Ong, Aihwa. *Buddha Is Hiding: Refugees, Citizenship, the New America*. Berkeley: University of California Press, 2003.

———. *Neoliberalism as Exception: Mutations in Citizenship and Sovereignty*. Durham, NC: Duke University Press, 2006.

Organista, Pamela Balls, Kurt C. Organista, and Pearl R. Soloff. "Exploring AIDS-Related Knowledge, Attitudes, and Behaviors of Female Mexican Migrant Workers." *Health & Social Work* 23, no. 2 (May 1, 1998): 96–103. doi:10.1093/hsw/23.2.96.

Ottaviano, Gianmarco I. P., and Giovanni Peri. "Rethinking the Effect of Immigration on Wages." *Journal of the European Economic Association* 10, no. 1 (February 1, 2012): 152–97. doi:10.1111/j.1542–4774.2011.01052.x.

Ottaviano, Gianmarco I. P., Giovanni Peri, and Greg C. Wright. "Immigration, Offshoring and US Jobs." London: Centre for Economic Policy Research, November 18, 2010. www.voxeu.org.

Parreñas, Rhacel Salazar. *Children of Global Migration: Transnational Families and Gendered Woes*. Palo Alto, CA: Stanford University Press, 2005.

Passel, Jeffrey S., and D'Vera Cohn. "Overall Number of U.S. Unauthorized Immigrants Holds Steady since 2009." Washington, DC: Pew Research Center, September 20, 2016. www.pewhispanic.org.

———. "Unauthorized Immigrant Population: National and State Trends, 2010." Pew Hispanic Center, February 1, 2011. www.pewhispanic.org.

———. "Unauthorized Immigrant Totals Rise in 7 States, Fall in 14." Washington, DC: Pew Research Center, November 17, 2014. www.pewhispanic.org.

Passel, Jeffrey S., and Paul Taylor. "Unauthorized Immigrants and Their U.S.-Born Children." Washington, DC: Pew Hispanic Center, August 11, 2010. www.pewhispanic.org.

Pew Research Center. "Modern Immigration Wave Brings 59 Million to U.S., Driving Population Growth and Change through 2065." Washington, DC: Pew Research Center, September 2015. www.pewhispanic.org.

Pham, Huyen, and Pham Van. "The Economic Impact of Local Immigration Regulation: An Empirical Analysis." *Cardozo Law Review* 32 (2010): 485–518.

Phillips, Steve. *Brown Is the New White: How the Demographic Revolution Has Created a New American Majority*. New York: New Press, 2016.

Piven, Frances Fox, and Richard A. Cloward. *Poor People's Movements: Why They Succeed, How They Fail*. New York: Vintage, 1978.

Portes, Alejandro, and Ruben Rumbaut. *Immigrant America: A Portrait*. 3rd ed. Berkeley: University of California Press, 2006.

Prieto, Greg, Chandra Russo, and Howard Winant. "(Mis)Trusting the Police: Gauging Levels of Confidence between the Latina/O Community and the Santa Barbara Police." Santa Barbara, CA: UC Center for New Racial Studies, June 2012. www.uccnrs.ucsb.edu.

Provine, Doris Marie, and Paul G. Lewis. "Shades of Blue: Local Policing, Legality, and Immigration Law." In *Constructing Illegality in America: Immigrant Experiences, Critiques, and Resistance*, edited by Cecilia Menjívar and Daniel Kanstroom, 298–324. New York: Cambridge University Press, 2014.

Provine, Doris Marie, Monica Varsanyi, Paul G. Lewis, and Scott H. Decker. "Growing Tensions between Civic Membership and Enforcement in the Devolution of Immigration Control." In *Punishing Immigrants: Policy, Politics, and Injustice*, edited by Charis E. Kubrin, Marjorie S. Zatz, and Ramiro Martínez, 42–61. New York: New York University Press, 2012.

Ramakrishnan, S. Karthick, and Irene Bloemraad, eds. *Civic Hopes and Political Realities: Immigrants, Community Organizations, and Political Engagement*. New York: Russell Sage Foundation, 2011.

Ramakrishnan, S. Karthick, and Celia Viramontes. "Civic Spaces: Mexican Hometown Associations and Immigrant Participation." *Journal of Social Issues* 66, no. 1 (2006): 155–73.

Ramakrishnan, S. Karthick, and Tom Wong. "Immigration Policies Go Local: The Varying Responses of Local Government to Low-Skilled and Undocumented Immigration." In *Taking Local Control: Immigration Policy Activism in US Cities and States*. Palo Alto, CA: Stanford University Press, 2010.

Reese, Ellen, Vincent Giedraitis, and Eric Vega. "Mobilization and Threat: Campaigns against Welfare Privatization in Four Cities." *Sociological Focus* 38, no. 4 (2005): 287–309.

Rich, Adrienne. "Compulsory Heterosexuality and Lesbian Existence." *Signs* 5, no. 4 (July 1, 1980): 631–60.

Robinson, William. "Aqui Estamos y No Nos Vamos! Global Capital and Immigrants' Rights." *Global and International Studies* 48, no. 2 (2006): 77–91.

Robnett, Belinda. *How Long? How Long? African-American Women in the Struggle for Civil Rights*. New York: Oxford University Press, 1997.

Ruiz, Vicki L. *Cannery Women, Cannery Lives: Mexican Women, Unionization, and the California Food Processing Industry, 1930–1950*. Albuquerque: University of New Mexico Press, 1987.

Rumbaut, Rubén G., Roberto G. Gonzales, Golnaz Komaie, Charlie V. Morgan, and Rosaura Tafoya-Estrada. "Immigration and Incarceration: Patterns and Predictors of Imprisonment among First- and Second-Generation Young Adults." In Martinez and Valenzuela, *Immigration and Crime*, 64–89.

Ruszczyk, Stephen P., and Guillermo Yrizar Barbosa. "A Second Generation of Immigrant Illegality Studies." *Migration Studies* 5, no. 3 (2017): 445–56.

Sadowski-Smith, Claudia. "Introduction: Border Studies, Diaspora, and Theories of Globalization." In *Globalization on the Line: Culture, Capital, and Citizenship at U.S. Borders*, edited by Claudia Sadowski-Smith, 1–27. New York: Palgrave, 2002.

Sampson, Robert J. "Rethinking Crime and Immigration." *Contexts*, January 9, 2008.

Sayer, Derek. *Capitalism and Modernity: An Excursus on Marx and Weber*. New York: Routledge, 1991.

Schrag, Peter. *Not Fit for Our Society: Nativism and Immigration*. Berkeley: University of California Press, 2010.

Schriro, Dora. "Immigration Detention: Overview and Recommendations." Department of Homeland Security, Immigration and Customs Enforcement, October 6, 2009.

Scott, James C. *Domination and the Arts of Resistance: Hidden Transcripts*. New Haven, CT: Yale University Press, 1990.

———. *Weapons of the Weak: Everyday Forms of Peasant Resistance*. New Haven, CT: Yale University Press, 1985.

Shear, Michael D. "Advocates Push Obama to Halt Aggressive Deportation Efforts." *New York Times*, February 22, 2013. www.nytimes.com.

Shriver, Thomas E., Alison E. Adams, and Stefano B. Longo. "Environmental Threats and Political Opportunities: Citizen Activism in the North Bohemian Coal Basin." *Social Forces* 94, no. 2 (May 20, 2015): 699–722. doi:10.1093/sf/sov072.

Slack, Jeremy, Daniel E. Martínez, Scott Whiteford, and Emily Peiffer. "In the Shadow of the Wall: Family Separation, Immigration Enforcement and Security." Tucson: Center for Latin American Studies, University of Arizona, 2013.

Smith, James P., and Barry Edmonston, eds. *The Immigration Debate: Studies on the Economic, Demographic, and Fiscal Effects of Immigration*. Washington, DC: National Academies Press, 1998.

Snow, David A., David M. Cress, Liam Downey, and Andrew W. Jones. "Disrupting the 'Quotidian': Reconceptualizing the Relationship between the Breakdown and the Emergence of Collective Action." *Mobilization* 3, no. 1 (1998): 1–22.

Snow, David A., and Dana M. Moss. "Protest on the Fly: Toward a Theory of Spontaneity in the Dynamics of Protest and Social Movements." *American Sociological Review* 79, no. 6 (December 1, 2014): 1122–43. doi:10.1177/0003122414554081.

Snow, David A., E. Burke Rochford, Steven K. Worden, and Robert D. Benford. "Frame Alignment Processes, Micromobilization, and Movement Participation." *American Sociological Review* 51, no. 4 (1986): 464–81. doi:10.2307/2095581.

Staggenborg, Suzanne. "The Consequences of Professionalization and Formalization in the Pro-Choice Movement." *American Sociological Review* 53, no. 4 (1988): 585–605. doi:10.2307/2095851.

Steil, Justin Peter, and Ion Bogdan Vasi. "The New Immigration Contestation: Social Movements and Local Immigration Policy Making in the United States, 2000–2011." *American Journal of Sociology* 119, no. 4 (2014): 1104–55.

Stumpf, Juliet. "The Crimmigration Crisis: Immigrants, Crime, and Sovereign Power." *American University Law Review* 56, no. 2 (2006): 367–419.

Swanson, Kate, Rebecca Torres, Amy Thompson, Sarah Blue, and Óscar Misael Hernández Hernández. "A Year after Obama Declared a 'Humanitarian Situation' at the Border, Child Migration Continues." *NACLA*, August 27, 2015. http://nacla.org.

Tarrow, Sidney G. *Power in Movement: Social Movements and Contentious Politics*. 3rd ed. New York: Cambridge University Press, 1994.

Taylor, Verta. "Social Movement Continuity: The Women's Movement in Abeyance." *American Sociological Review* 54, no. 5 (1989): 761–75. doi:10.2307/2117752.

Taylor, Verta, and Nella Van Dyke. "'Get Up, Stand Up': Tactical Repertoires of Social Movements." In *The Blackwell Companion to Social Movements*, edited by David A. Snow, Sarah A. Soule, and Hanspeter Kriesi, 262–93. Oxford: Blackwell, 2004.

Terriquez, Veronica. "Civic Inequalities? Immigrant Incorporation and Latina Mothers' Participation in Their Children's Schools." *Sociological Perspectives* 55, no. 4 (2012): 663–82.

———. "Schools for Democracy: Labor Union Participation and Latino Immigrant Parents' School-Based Civic Engagement." *American Sociological Review* 76, no. 4 (August 2011): 581–601. doi:10.1177/0003122411414815.

Tester, Griff M. "Resources, Identity, and the Role of Threat: The Case of AIDS Mobilization, 1981–1986." *Research in Political Sociology* 13 (2004): 47–75.

Tilly, Charles. "Contentious Repetoires in Great Britain, 1758–1834." In *Repertoires and Cycles of Collective Action*, edited by Mark Traugott, 15–42. Durham, Duke University Press, 1995.

———. *From Mobilization to Revolution*. Reading, MA: Addison-Wesley, 1978.

———. "Getting It Together in Burgundy: 1675–1975." *Theory and Society* 4, no. 4 (1977): 479–504.

Tilly, Charles, and Sidney G. Tarrow. *Contentious Politics*. Oxford: Oxford University Press, 2007.

Tirman, John, ed. *The Maze of Fear: Security and Migration after 9/11*. New York: New Press, 2004.

Toobin, Jeffrey. "American Limbo." *New Yorker*, July 27, 2015. www.newyorker.com.

Tushnet, Mark. "A Critique of Rights." *Texas Law Review* 62 (1984): 1363–1403.

Tyler, Tom R. "Procedural Justice." In *The Blackwell Companion to Law and Society*, edited by Austin Sarat, 435–52. Malden, MA: Blackwell, 2004.

US Census Bureau. "US Census." 2010. http://factfinder.census.gov.

US Council of Economic Advisers. "The US Council of Economic Advisers on Immigration's Economic Impact." *Population & Development Review* 33, no. 3 (2007): 641–46.

US Department of Homeland Security. "Yearbook of Immigration Statistics: 2015." Washington, DC: U.S. Department of Homeland Security, Office of Immigration Statistics, December 2016. www.dhs.gov.

Van Dyke, Nella, and Sarah A. Soule. "Structural Social Change and the Mobilizing Effect of Threat: Explaining Levels of Patriot and Militia Organizing in the United States." *Social Problems* 49, no. 4 (2002): 497–520.

Varsanyi, Monica W. "The Paradox of Contemporary Immigrant Political Mobilization: Organized Labor, Undocumented Migrants, and Electoral Participation in Los Angeles." *Antipode* 37, no. 4 (2005): 775–95.

———. "Rescaling the 'Alien,' Rescaling Personhood: Neoliberalism, Immigration, and the State." *Annals of the Association of American Geographers* 98, no. 4 (2008): 877–96.

Varsanyi, Monica W., Paul G. Lewis, Doris Marie Provine, and Scott Decker. "A Multilayered Jurisdictional Patchwork: Immigration Federalism in the United States." *Law & Policy* 34, no. 2 (2011): 138–58.

Vila, Pablo. *Crossing Borders, Reinforcing Borders: Social Categories, Metaphors and Narrative Identities on the U.S.-Mexico Frontier*. Austin: University of Texas Press, 2000.

Volpp, Leti. "The Citizen and the Terrorist." *Immigration and Nationality Law Review* 23 (2002): 1575–1600.

Voss, Kim, and Irene Bloemraad, eds. *Rallying for Immigrant Rights: The Fight for Inclusion in 21st Century America*. Berkeley: University of California Press, 2011.

Walker, Edward T., Andrew W. Martin, and John D. McCarthy. "Confronting the State, the Corporation, and the Academy: The Influence of Institutional Targets on Social Movement Repertoires." *American Journal of Sociology* 114, no. 1 (2008): 35–76.

Walker, Kyle E., and Helga Leitner. "The Variegated Landscape of Local Immigration Policies in the United States." *Urban Geography* 32, no. 2 (February 1, 2011): 156–78. doi:10.2747/0272-3638.32.2.156.

Walzer, Michael. *Spheres of Justice: A Defense of Pluralism and Equality*. New York: Basic Books, 1983.

Weber, Max. *The Protestant Ethic and the Spirit of Capitalism with Other Writings on the Rise of the West*. New York: Oxford University Press, 1905.

Wendland, Aaron James. "What Do We Owe Each Other?" *New York Times Opinionator*, January 18, 2016. http://opinionator.blogs.nytimes.com.

White, Robert W. "From Peaceful Protest to Guerrilla War: Micromobilization of the Provisional Irish Republican Army." *American Journal of Sociology* 94, no. 6 (1989): 1277–1302.

Willen, Sarah S. "Toward a Critical Phenomenology of 'Illegality': State Power, Criminalization, and Abjectivity among Undocumented Migrant Workers in Tel Aviv, Israel." *International Migration* 45, no. 3 (2007): 8–38.

Williams, Patricia J. *The Alchemy of Race and Rights.* Cambridge, MA: Harvard University Press, 1991.

Wright, Stuart A. *Patriots, Politics, and the Oklahoma City Bombing.* New York: Cambridge University Press, 2007.

Zavella, Patricia. *Women's Work and Chicano Families: Cannery Workers of the Santa Clara Valley.* Ithaca, NY: Cornell University Press, 1987.

Zepeda-Millán, Chris. "Weapons of the (Not So) Weak: Immigrant Mass Mobilization in the US South." *Critical Sociology* 42, no. 2 (March 1, 2016): 269–87. doi:10.1177/0896920514527846.

Zlolinski, Christian. *Janitors, Street Vendors, and Activists: The Lives of Mexican Immigrants in Silicon Valley.* Berkeley: University of California Press, 2006.

INDEX

abject cosmopolitanism, 206n22
Abrego, Leisy, 26
action: disruption as motivation to, 18, 20, 91; grievances spurring, 16; scope of agency and, 12–13. *See also* collective action; political action
activism, 2–3, 8; conceptualizing, 21; democratic visions and, 159–61; emergence of, 29; focus on inhabiting norms, 162; individual propensities for, 188n56; instrumental quality of, 166; legacy of, 15; material moorings of immigrant, 9, 11, 16, 20, 26, 85, 105, 108, 129, 158; motivation for, 15–16; participation in, 128, 178–79; precarity linked to, 29; predisposition to, 181; SMOs shaping, 122–26
activists, 2–3; cultivating, 111–17, 125, 199n12; emergence of, 106; inviting of, 109–11; moved to participation, 91; opportunity perceived by, 100, 147; resonating with, 17; sacrifice of, 94; SMOs influence on, 146; social movement organizing engaging, 108. *See also* instrumental activists
agency, 10, 132; avoidance as, 89; examples of, 14–16; expression of, 151; as inhabiting norms, 160; insulation as, 89; relationship between forms of, 18, 106; respondents engagement in forms of, 182–83; scope of action and, 12–13; shape and place of, 167; shaping of, 30, 157; within the shell, 18; theorization of, 206n10

agriculture, 24, 41, 42, 135, 155
American Dream, 153–57, 162–66, 205n7
American Native Party, 38
Americanness, 60, 62, 162, 166, 206n21
amnesty, 44–45, 190n23
Anti-Terrorism and Effective Death Penalty Act (1996), 191n27, 191n33
Asiatic Barred Zone, 39
avoidance, 2, 8, 13, 54, 157; of confrontation, 96; engaging in, 108; fear managed through, 26; as form of agency, 89; as habit, 85, 96; insulation, the shell and, 26, 76, 81, 101–3; as insulation from risk, 14–16; isolation and, 18; phone networks and, 88–89; as protection strategy, 86–88; of trouble, 69–70; undermining of, 115

Baker-Cristales, Beth, 160
Balderrama, Francisco E., 41–42
Bayat, Asef, 18–19, 89
Bedolla, García, 185n7
belonging, 9, 61, 156; benefits of, 162–63; as citizenship, 160; norms of, reconciliation with inclusion, 164; requirements for, 161; seeking of, 79
Bloemraad, Irene, 13
border control, 12, 165
border crossing, 47, 48, 64, 73
Border Patrol, 48, 56, 69
Bracero Program (1942–1964), 15, 42, 44
Brown, Jerry, 4
"browning of America," 7, 27, 51–53

cage of gold ("La Jaula de Oro"), 84
California Dream Act, 4
Campbell, Howard, 12, 14
CAP. *See* Criminal Alien Program
Carbado, Devon, 31, 60, 69
car impoundments, 5, 55, 90, 141; com-
    monality of, 47–48, 56–57; costs asso-
    ciated with, 57–58; crimmigration and,
    63–66; ending of, 113, 136, 167; experi-
    ences of, 66–71; frequency of, 195n2; as
    informal immigration enforcement, 31,
    58, 79–80; as institutionalized practice,
    68; limiting of, 148–49; physical mobil-
    ity constrained by, 64; as primary risk,
    86; as racial naturalization, 66–71, 81;
    testimonies of, 113–14, 144; threat of,
    13, 64; as unfair, 74
Chávez, César, 2, 109, 117, 176
Chinese Exclusion Act (1882), 38, 190n23
citizenship, 159, 197n1; belonging as,
    160; benefits attending, 30, 205n4;
    consequences of legal shift in, 35–36;
    democratization of, 166; eligibility for,
    40; engaging in, 161–62; hypocrisy of,
    163; labor as qualification for, 61–62;
    legal protections guaranteed by, 60–61,
    69; norms of, 29; permanence implied
    by, 164; sovereign limits to, 166. *See
    also* liberal citizenship
civic engagement, 32, 81, 167, 197n1, 198n13
civic participation, 12, 120
civil disobedience, 26, 158, 203n27
Clinton, Bill, 185n1
Cloward, Richard A., 146
Coates, Ta-Nehisi, 156, 205n7
Cohn, D'Vera, 51–52
collaboration, 8; adoption of, 150; contes-
    tation and, for immigrant rights, 147;
    culture of, 143
collective action, 1, 6, 16, 54–55, 89; ben-
    efits gained through, 28; desire of, 108;
    efficacy of, 157; grievances transformed
    into, 111; participation in, 20–21, 95,

105; power of, 112; stimulating, 202n17;
    as unstructured, 19
collective memory, 43
collective mobilization, 2–3, 12, 106, 169;
    benefits of, 100; of communities, 126;
    emergence of, 8–9, 17, 21; exploitation
    contested through, 53; family repro-
    duction weighed against, 157; obstacles
    to, 105; political climate relationship
    with, 132; threat not repressing, 32
community: collective mobilization
    of, 126; commitment to, 110; com-
    munication between police and, 142;
    dynamics of, 180; landscapes of, 27;
    Latino immigrants permanence in,
    136; marginalization of immigrant, 37;
    physical presence in, 135; pride from
    involvement in, 120; racialization of,
    28; representation for, 124–25; respon-
    sibility of, 114–16
community forums, 143–44, 147–48, 169
comparative ethnography, 23–25, 159,
    204n37
complex personhood, 10–12
conformism, 160
confrontation, 167; avoidance of, 96; tactic
    of, 32, 137, 147–51
contention, 158–59
contestation, 30, 130, 133–37; collabora-
    tion and, for immigrant rights, 147; as
    varied, 151
coping, 85–89, 96–98
Criminal Alien Program (CAP), 23, 46,
    191n35
criminalization, 41, 54, 62–66, 74, 79–81,
    169–70
crimmigration, 58, 60, 63–66
Cuban Refugee Adjustment Act (1966),
    190n23
culture, 161, 198n6; caution as, 91; of
    collaboration, 143; developing of, 17;
    of noninvolvement, 96; as organiza-
    tional, 142–43, 150; of subordination,

fear, 6, 182; of asking for support, 118; of authority, 76, 114; of deportation, 24, 83; of driving, 120; as facet of racial naturalization, 79; as immobilizing, 16; managed through avoidance, 26; participation impeded by, 90; of police, 13, 77, 120–21
Fernandez, Luis, 159–60, 164
Flacks, Richard, 19–20, 95
flojera (laziness), 93–98, 206n21

Gabrielson, Ryan, 58, 195n2
García, Angela, 12–13
gender: immigration influenced by, 53; race, sexuality and, 50, 59; social boundaries of, 61. *See also* women
Genova, Nicholas de, 36, 69
Ghostly Matters (Gordon), 10
global capitalism, 6, 12, 37, 44–45. *See also* neoliberal capitalism
Gonzales, Alfonso, 158
Gordon, Avery F., 10, 65
Great Depression, 41–42
Great Recession (2008), 20, 52, 92–93, 150, 193n46

Haider-Markel, Donald P., 75
Heyman, Josiah, 12, 14, 155, 205n5
Holder, Eric, 72
homeownership, 51, 157
hometown associations (HTAs), 165–66, 200n13
house meetings, strategy of, 176–81
HTAs. *See* hometown associations
Huerta, Dolores, 2, 109, 176
hypocrisy, 153–59, 163, 166

ICE. *See* Immigration and Customs Enforcement
identification card (*matrícula consular*), 5, 131
Illegal Immigration Reform and Immigrant Responsibility Act (1996), 191n33, 192n36

immigrant politics, 11–12, 19, 32–33; emergence of, 27; as exceeding territory, 166; grounding analysis in, 161; horizons of, 167–70; inhabiting norms sought by, 164; material moorings and, 27–30; as not radical, 29; as remedy, 29–30; social location of, 21; transnational and transformative radicalism in, 160
immigrants. *See specific topics*
immigration, 185n3; benefits of, 153; countries excluded from, 39–40; creating everyday life as motivation for, 167; as crisis, 7–8; demographic composition of, 7, 24, 51, 193n42; economic development changing, 41; federal regulation of, 192n36; gender influencing, 53; increase in, 191n27; legal compared to illegal, 41; placement of risks of, 205n5; positive economic influence of, 169; pressure for unauthorized, 44; quantitative limit on, 43–44; sociology of, 8; status of, related to police, 50
Immigration Act (1882), 38
Immigration Act (1917), 40–41
Immigration Act (1990), 190n23, 191n27
Immigration and Customs Enforcement (ICE), 2, 4–5, 56, 118; cooperation with, 135–36; database for, 192n37; hiding from, 83–84; presence of, 47
Immigration and Nationality Act (1965), 6–7, 43
Immigration and Naturalization Service (INS), 42
immigration enforcement (*la migra*), 2, 4–5, 150, 192n36; anxiety created from, 48; car impoundments as informal, 31, 58, 79–80; consequences to transformations in, 48–50; embracing of, 119; geographic shift in, 46, 193n38; increase in, 186n16, 188n56; local and federal collaboration of, 144; organizations for, 8; police as, 75–76, 154,

Massey, Douglas, 52
material moorings, 97–98, 156, 160–61;
centrality of, 168–70; dilemma of, 33;
of immigrant activism, 9, 11, 16, 20,
26, 85, 105, 108, 129, 158; immigrant
politics and, 27–30
matrícula consular (identification card),
5, 131
May Day marches (2006), 105, 107, 160
Maynard-Moody, Steven, 75
McAdam, Doug, 17, 26, 132
McCarthy, John D., 147, 203n27
media: border crossing presented in, 47;
Latino immigrants portrayed in, 36;
negative influence of, 54
Mexican immigrants, 2, 6, 191n24; benefits
sought by, 30; experience of, 11, 155–56;
generational difference in, 26; labor of,
40; police as threat to, 58–59; population of, 51–52, 53; repatriation of,
41–43; resistance organizing by, 109;
responsibility felt by, 119, 121–22; social
location of, 63; vulnerability of, 62
Mexican Revolution, 41
Mezzadra, Sandro, 54–55
micromobilization, 17, 146
la migra. See immigration enforcement
militarization, of US-Mexico border, 164
Minutemen, 136, 201n10
mobile consulate, 130–32, 201n3
mobility, 31; car impoundments con-
straining physical, 64; characteristics
of, 166; constraints on, 50, 81; demand
for, 164; denial of, 65; as economic, 28,
36, 153; in education, 25, 49, 103; in occupation, 30; securing of, 108, 158, 165
mobilization, 3; as anti-immigrant, 201n5;
as cultivated, 19; emergence of, 21; as
national, 22; as political, 90, 126; political opportunity structures influencing,
132; protecting right to, 158; of resources, 17; SMOs involvement in, 203n27;
of social movements, 128; stimulating,

149; study of, 145–46; targets for efforts
of, 137. *See also* collective mobilization
multi-sited ethnography, 22

Naples, Nancy, 185n9
National Day Organizing Network, 45–46
nationalism, 28
National Origins Act (1924), 39–40, 43
nativism, 45
naturalization, 52, 63, 198n13, 204n3
Naturalization Act (1790), 38
Navarrette, Ruben, 186n15
neoliberal capitalism, 93. *See also* global
capitalism
neoliberal citizenship, 32–33, 161–62, 166
Ngai, Mae M., 40, 45
nonparticipation, 1, 93–98

Obama, Barack, 1, 45–46, 168, 169, 185n1,
193n46
Okamoto, Dina, 145–46
Oliver, Pamela, 202n14
Olsen, Joel, 159–60, 164
Operation Wetback, 14

el pajarito (the little bird), 112
participation, 188n56; in activism, 128,
178–79; activists moved to, 91; in
collective action, 105; deterrents to,
90–92; of Latino immigrants, 1; in
La Unión, 107, 117; laziness as barrier
to, 93–98; in political action, 100; as
pragmatic, 107–9; predisposition to
social movement, 181; the shell as
encumbrance to, 95; in social movement organizing, 32, 104, 158; in social
movements, 22, 109; status as barrier
to, 98–100; stimulating of, 91; trust
critical for influencing, 177; of undocumented immigrants in social movements, 100; in La Unión, 122. *See also*
civic participation; nonparticipation
Passel, Jeffrey S., 51–52

CHIASMUS

When even a stranger's
face has too much history about
the eyes and mouth, I open

the book to FERNS I, II, and III,
UMBELLIFERS, LOVE-IN-A-MIST,
TIPS OF TWIGS, pods, cones, petals

arrayed in grids, some dissected
so far from their given forms
as to be mineral or animal.

CHESTNUT SHOOTS aren't just phallic,
they're actual cocks! And so on,
through the last, strenuous display.

HENBANE, KNAPWEED, SAXIFRAGE.
I climb the spiral staircase of brown gelatin,
silver bromide. HORSETAIL stems dizzy,

there is no backing down. Leaf through
SELF-HEAL, BUTTERBUR, SCABIOUS SEEDS.
What counts as seduction? Why

does the photographer's red X
set one MONKSHOOD apart from
its more deeply bent double,

unfurling arms of each raised
in alarm, leaves flexed, shading
the averted, bulbous tip?

Both plants strain to be themselves
in space, the sensing spills into
the sensed.

One hand starts
at the touch
of the other.

ONE

Macondo

And the shapes nosed onto the sand,
were drawn back in and under, nudged up again
as if by their own flailing,
flayed and stifled

I kept my brain under my tongue,
salt gathered in a sinus
paying out for days in tiny echoes,
throat roughed, ready as flypaper

Opened my arms to what
moved my way, wings half-spread,
brown feathers now black, slack pouch
sealed shut, one web pulling through the crude,
a black eye bright in a face of black sheen

Pinned to my lap the small throb

                              Around us
men like lost farmers scattered straw,
raked away the straw they had scattered,
scattered more

And So the Hairy Vetch Burrowed with the Wheat

nick by nick,
until the fire flush.

I like to a chair
was, spindle spine

upright retro-
fitted broke yet

breathing. Backstory —
four seedlings fought

their little histories
of drought and flood,

raw throats open to all
slakers. He stole—bag-eyed,

rune-strewn with weasel tail
and one worn creel from which

bad seeds were broadcast. We sat
cobbler-style in the low-slung snarl,

common oaks stunted to our scale
roofing the granite clitter.

No one else that day, nothing
but humus, whortleberry, fronds

resurrecting in crevice and crotch.
We staved with flame and billow

and again we stove in. I, one stave
among them, slender bundle.

I pried apart the pages,
soles of my feet.

It is Possible to Live Justly and Happily and Do Good Things for Men

The force of the middle voice often cannot
be reproduced in translation...
— Smyth, Greek Grammar

One syllable turns a word in on its subject
like a duck who tucks her beak
and sleeps in wing's fold
doing the less translatable,

dreaming what self a duck can dream.
Words pulled to their centers,
neither active nor passive
with the same black hair only blacker
and a tendency to stare into mirrors:

> *What did it beseem the city to do when it saw*
> *Philip compassing for himself dominion*
> *and despotic sway over the Greeks?*

That's the way to put a question,
flattened of panic, extracting from
another's throttled cries the poise it takes to name
the enemy and the reach of his power.

Weed by the wall,
I desire now to mercy myself.

Good to Go

You get yourself to the point where
you're sketching on napkins—
altimeter, penknife, jerky, CB,
LA County map, question mark,
question mark. If you should plummet, slash
the water jugs rigged to the frame
light as a bird's bones. Christening:
Inspiration. The end of lists.

Calm in your lawn chair, tilting slightly,
tethered to forty-two weather balloons,
you're vaulted two miles up, into
the third busiest airspace in North America,
saying, *Wow, man! Unreal!*
All the gear secured except the pellet gun
that lurches from your lap and falls
toward the motherboard of a city
until your eye can't parse the splinter.

No way in heck. Machines of rising and descent.
No way. You plunge, raining spring water
until your chair parts the power lines and
you hang there like something the stork brought.
Fifteen years later you will shoot yourself
in the San Gabriel Mountains,
above a place called Idlehour.

But if the Santa Anas had claimed you,
gusts wheeling off the canyons? Soaring
over Highway One, over the spine of sand
keeping everything we do from all we wish for
and can never know. Streaks of sapphire and beryl stone,
rusting bands of kelp, clarity to a point, silhouettes,
depth. Skim off the top fathom. No bright fishes,
just primitive stuff getting by in the dark.

Eye strain, soreness in the neck, easing back
in your sling of waffle webbing.
Time to consider objections, a sip of Coke.
Reverting to verses marked
in mind alone, *Remove by day*
in their sight, in their sight. Sigh,
but not aloud. Transistor falls,
unremarkable plash.

Showdown

Let's interpellate the trees,
"That reddish-orange one over there,
beyond the barn? It's almost like it's — "
No, please — "like it's on fire!"
Called out, maple displays

the diffidence of a straightedge.
I balance on my palm a curl of gingko,
stem through which sap once
ran unsentimental.

Overdetermined sumac rims the field,
each torch fused by centaur's blood.

There was a woman who rebuked her child,
"Don't point at the mountain, it's rude!"
What's this then, actionable?

The trees shed just so much rustle
beneath my old friend Deineira's
high-stacked boot soles.
Sky, visible at last to the two of us,
is known again to exist, a fact

that makes it easier for her
to breathe, yet all those branches cinch
the space, cinch the dark grove sure
as heredity. She's in my face, "You, you are
my mother, your mother, someone's — "

She can hail me till we're ashen,
watch me shake my head from birch
to birch as our voices wane, blacken,
surge *It is grey we need to begin with,*
because of what it is and of what it can do,
made of bright and black

To Saint Hubert, Wonderworker of the Ardennes, Patron of Hunters and Mathematicians, Protector from Rabies

Woozy raccoon slogs gutter
to culvert, hears my *Oh!* turns

Eyes molten, fish-pale, snagged up
from where the leaf mulm churns

Her eyes, what stray sickness
what stillness turned stiff

I eye the pond, lips parting
Come Saint Hubert Come
why rush why wait why

Nick me, cut this tongue's
thin anchor, heat the nail head

red to white, brand me here and
here, why water why spit why dry

Keep me Keep me

from this bruised, this bruising
fur made to matter

At the Riverbank

the consonance, the math, the more than three
kinds of cry from each of my mouths, the quavers,
the swallowings

from the one slipping over the lip into snowmelt roil,
her whoops opening into an O of woe of worry of too
too sorry, so wet, so *how?* bowled over, gulping
then righted, face angled skyward while current yanks her,
feet first, frail bark, knothole mouth whisked from sight

of the vulture who humps the wind in the cleft between
her claws tucked close for lift, *where I caught her,*
where I lost her, how I tracked her, opening her mouth
with my tail, stroking her lips with a drop to make suck,
a ringing, a striking of beak on beak,
signs of succor, of distress *tocsin, tocsin, tocsin*

to the boy on the bank, unsinging his faith.
No, lips clamped, a sweetness seeping from between the brows,
No. She bobs, she floats, she needs no saving

I do the voices for my lover who straddles, who hovers
close to the curling, drawn down by the belly's puff
and hollow, whom I beg now to please, please fill
my dreamspent mouth

Milagro

The sun off the snowfields is too much today.
I live in a cathedral whose interior reaches
cannot be taken in, not now,

with the scaffolding risen
and these walkways of fragrant plywood.
A cathedral is a world, clusters of people

doing things together, some singly,
tower of crutches stone-torqued into sheaves of wheat.
There are no fixed pews. Chairs may be dragged

or carried to where they're needed.
What if five or six people want to sit facing one another
in a circle or in a line knee to knee

before one of the lesser windows
or the still wet fresco?
I see them there where they've been

for days, the vigilants.
Behind them, our cabinet of reliquaries,
several splinters and one gray bone —
the woods.

I believe but cannot prove
that the sun will begin to lower
later today than yesterday.

May one less soul plummet
in this hill-town tomorrow.

A ray passes over the golden foot of Christ
There! a fish shimmers,

                             animate

There now,
softening

      the mountain

TWO

Egg Tooth

Chalkseed vellum,
wall's matter
no matter,
no where
but here

Conforming palm
of inside's
inside,
heretofore
herein

Bud!
bit
to bore
the air

Little nothing
to worry
worry
with

First Mow, with Walking Meditation

Twenty-seven bones in each grip,
radius, ulna, humerus doubled —
shock's math among the fumes.

I can't shake the chive shred
flooding this two-cycle brain.
Foot to ground, foot to ground.

My little gleaners stay one step ahead,
clearing from the Husqvarna's path
the swamp willow's wretched trash —

handspring, grumble, cartwheel.
I circle the mower ever tighter,
green overlapping greens.

Soon I will wrap right hand around
left hand's fist, as my teacher does.
A lotus will blossom in the wake of every step.

But first there are questions to field:
When exactly *afternoon* begins?
Just try doing this with a soft belly.

Project Grizzly

Ursus Ferox, Ursus Horribilis —
Mr. Grizzly, I'm here for you,
this armor seven years in the making —
rubber, titanium, chain mail,
plastic, titanium, plastic,
buffer of space between suit and shoulder.
You get that far, Old Man,
I'm yours for your trouble.

That day our stenches mixed
over the ten meters you threw me,
blade drawn half out of sheath,
half out of sheath,
you caught the infraction,
eyes deep in thumbhole caves.
Son of a bitch you turned away.

Old Man, King Shit, fifty times
my fucking prowess.
I'm here for you, waiting,
waiting to be rolled again,
plowed over, rammed, raked —
Come on now, I'm here for you.

FIVE LESSONS

[BOX]

Ficelle of steel,
        cigar box, barrel

stave, pernambuco,
        river-shipped

Spruce gauged for ear,
        maple gauged for eye,

flames mounting toward button of neck,
        its tender, backward slant

Compare Bergonzi's f-hole
        to that of Gasparo da Salo

how each seems about
        to fall forward, seahorses

flanking the belly's arch
        itself shadowed by the bridge,

ponticello of spotted maple
        with feet ears heart

It will take years of daily playing
        before the instrument begins to speak properly,

before sound moves through
        as sap once did

[GUT]

Armour Factory, Chicago 1922

Men work quickly over steaming tables scraping
      pencil thin lengths of sheep intestine

to be soaked in cold then tepid water
      scraped again with the split and beveled briar cane

steeped further scraped
      steeped again in the next room

workers wear rubber gloves ring on index
      copper thimble on thumb

taking one membrane from the stone jar on his left
      each man worries it as his mother her rosary

places it in the jar to his right
      every few hours jar to jar

solution by solution the thing reduced
      to cleanest shred then

the sorting splitting with the narrow *soutil*
      stringing on frames twisting bleaching with smoke

of sulfur freshening on the rooftop
      above the city's shambles

torsion more torsion — *Does someone sigh?*
      arms outstretched finish men grip

the lines of gut cushion of horsehair
            in each hand they pace the aisles of looms

All asperities shall be removed
            placed now in folds of soft cloth

wiped with olive oil
            and powdered glass or pumice

dried seasoned cut
            graded coiled

into its lovely
            paper envelope

[GUM]

Knob of sound

rosin resin distillate
of Venetian terebrinth

turpentine's
transparence

citron lozenge
friction powder

wrapped in flannel

[BOW]

Muscle memory,
fretless — each tone
a slowed-down finding

     Ribbon of rounded hairs
     bound with waxed silk
     is thrust into wedge box of nut.

Don't worry about the sound,
he said *Moving from wrong*
to right must entail discomfort

     Heat is increased, screws are
     tightened, mother of pearl is slid
     into its groove.

Down-bow, of course, has advantage
but up-bow plays into weight of hand
and arm
         The movement forward sits in
the lap of the attack

That gesture —
         like threading something into something

[PROVENANCE]

Bow's flash and cloud,
infinite cabinet.

Amber washes:
dragon blood, saffron, sweat-
stripped swath where first his father's,
then his own, and now my palm

homes. My chest,
a resonator.

I worry the chain of reprises
and compensations,

each of the six dusts
stirred. When they settle

they will stick, they will
wonder, they will sound.

BOURRÉE, FROM THE THIRD UNACCOMPANIED SUITE

Throughout he held my eyes,
a dancer spotting. Father,
grid of face, its refusal finally
to ironize —

assemblages of taut string set swirling
paint, cardboard or a rag,
nails studding the canvas
of Picasso's Guitar. He would
rim this one with

razor blades,
steel points
puncturing the space
where oscillation happens.

Anchises, Aeneas, Ascanius

Father holds fast to the porch rail
Go on without me, I'll stay
in this dark havoc collating
fragments of disaster.

From above the grand mosaic a red star
rockets by *Okay so I'll go with*, he says.
We falter at the gambit
Faster they're upon us!

> His conversion thoughtless as a button
> through its slit. I stoop and hoist him,
> handing back the household gods.
> Following behind us

> my Creusa, our course cobbled of quiet
> turns set by the shifting load and this child
> I pull along. The ruin we move through,
> cool as a humidor.

> At Ceres's grove, the tally of losses
> and back into the looting. *Let it go,*
> her ghost says, *The wailing, the walls.*
> My grief towers into

> > *Defeat? But Papa, the miracles of flame,*
> > *my sweet face wreathed in warning,*
> > *refugees ready —*

COROLLARY

Breadth of tree crown and rhizome, loose symmetry thereof
Each branch, twig and dwindle are doubled eighty feet below,
adventitious root-hair nursed within the drip-line.

A root may bear fire as a root bears water
Methods of delivery, circumference, tanglement,
stoma shallower than winds, fire
as seed of fire.

One need not understand to explain
Now I ply the ground, my stove. The recipe
called for a subterranean fire. I waited
for the heat to snake its way, unseen.

Ransack

They go to the dam nightly, one after the other, and as they pass along
its margins each upon his own motion does such work
as he chooses to perform.

The American Beaver and His Works (1868)

We are getting to know the makers,
the neighbor girl and I, smoothing
the splinterless wood as we talk.
They mate for life, one family to a pond,
eating what they work with — as if we dined
on plaster, *or built our homes of bread.* Last fall
when they drained the pond the lodge rose slowly,
lifting from the receding water, tempering,
waiting, it seemed, for anything, for us.
For now we're driven, seeking fence posts, bean poles, cudgels longer
and lighter, javelins! silver logs
with which to line my garden or to edge
the bed she has planted at her mother's grave,
To keep them from mowing it over
like they always do.
One more load, once more across the field,
past the row of hay bales that rims the muck, along
the path we've tamped between the shallows of mud,
strong sucking, black, deeper than every spear we've fed it.
The thatching holds us: caulked earth, density of timbers
unmoved by our prying. For us it's simply
that the beavers are elsewhere.
Today we opened their hollow to the light,
knelt down, put our faces to the hole,
took in the air they breathed together, stale,
saw the pallet of cut grasses now brown
beside the cavern's shore of dust,

its own small tides sealed inside.
        It is very old in here,
    inside, where we lodge our griefs
  among our grievances,
those exacted by others,
    those exacted by ourselves,
        each upon her own motion doing such work
            as she is able to perform,
                moving through marsh and sinuous burrow,
            throwing ourselves upon the beds
        we've made from what edges
    the still evaporating pond.

THREE

The Marmiton

*It seemed to me a strange thing that anyone could be so great in an art
for which he felt nothing but contempt.*

Isak Dinesen, OUT OF AFRICA

[I]

Ngong Hills

I am the best dog-boy, I retrieve.
I stand on three legs.
The stoutest, smoothed of bark,
doubles as sheep-staff.
Pains gather to me from the hills,
run down my open skin
like a dream of rain,
gathering again, swelling, necessary.

I stand on three legs
to the side of the terrace
where the sick gather around her,
wanting.

Nairobi

I hear her voice in the corridor.
"I am on the verge of mastery," she says.
"I trust your care of this *toto.*"

Ngong Hills

Back from the time of city-sleep, the time
of creosote, of needles, of wet cloths
wound and unwound, wrapped
and rewrapped like time itself
to the farm: she is here.

37

Our Saviour is risen, I say.
She answers, "He is risen indeed."

Lump of mutton fat,
dust dense as stone,
I am alive.

[II]

Ngong Hills

At the stove she teaches me the dishes,
each with its story of origin,
each guinea fowl in its own coffin.
She is charmed by the flash
of my weed-knife.

"'Sauce of lightning that struck the tree,'"
she repeats with a smile.
"'Sauce of the grey horse that died.'"
If I must taste, I do.
I make my mouth
her mouth, I tongue
the spoon's oily silt
until she is moved by a new smell
to bend from my side
and I am saved

All afternoon she grieves aloud for the old man.
"We would sit before his kilns for hours," she says.
"Charcoal burners see things in a different light.
They are given to taradiddle and poetry."

I swirl the new lettuces in the basin.

"But tell me, Kamante.
Here we work, side by side.
What do you make of this art to which I —
to which we are so perversely devoted?"

I will name the dish
I perfect for the Prince tonight:
sauce of the bird of the third body we bore together
(white man with soles like hippo hide)
along the mushroom path.
She, the old man's head, I, the feet.

Daphne

roved the pathless woods patted the mullein
straddled the odd felled maple cutting it like bread

to clear a stripling's way moved through boughs
arms of trees braiding herself into thickets

gauged hollows old wounds mouths large enough
to hold her if water that pooled there

stood too long she scooped it out every standing tree
a narrow boat in peril she nicked cork from oak

axe blade scoring trunk from base to highest reach
handle as lever to pry soft gold in strips

pressed herself against the nuded oak in thanks
her own skin an organ of agitation

life then was motion

Emperor Select

Question is how many
oolong buds I can snatch

from the bauxite cliffs before you,
craning, recall me to the verge.

Cypress shade, you
make my rest.

Task me, trapeze me,
more fetch and trove,

clamor, reach, fingertip tweeze,
not one bruised leaf, never.

Pay day basket bulge,
crooked way home where I,

sleeping, dream the steeps you,
steeping, wait to sip.

Unorthodox Itinerary of the Molasses City Express

Leaned into the charm
of beloved after beloved, purring
diminutives as mantra, floating
to the next innocent skin, on into
       the umbra of promise,
       total, without divigation

Envisioned the yabyum
spinning, hovering above fontanel,
its downward issue
liquid, looping,
       at once warm and blue
       and the other opposite of hard

The blue bathed the eyes, all three,
pooled in the bend of knee's bound angles
and then, by waft, by osmosis
was drawn up again

Zoomed through
places thickly settled
and others more or less barren

Was reminded at every whistle-stop
of what was widely espoused
to be the relevant trope,
       whiff of the five Ws and one
       enormous How

Fingered the strand
of lapis fastened at the throat,
       as insurance,
       as signal to sing upon arrival

KOOKABURRA

I stump through the woods on wooden limbs
dragging my didgeridoo, each hollow I pass
snarling lipped and gap-toothed a promise
empty only if I discount the soft decay that makes for

the hollow itself once a volunteer from that very tree
rooted in its own hollow like the day I found a pea crab
small as a speck nestled in the mantle of every mussel
except this was maple within maple
fed on maple shale and shadow
                                 Son who spiraled out of me
toggling near farther lower than the lowing my air
makes blown through the gum tree hollowed by mites long gone
I put my mouth to the beeswax seal flutter living tissue
against what hosts the breath but cannot breathe

I stir this narrow tree I cut it free I hum
make what leaves me turn back grasp the other end
take into his palms the hardwood drone
kingfisher call my son my son

Four Weathercocks

[MOTTO]

Lunch again beneath the Spanish lime.
Cocks and hens hunt around the tables,
house cat ignores the scrambling chicks,
floating her tail along my ankles,
making the small hairs stand.
On this island the roosters crow at dawn,
and then more or less incessantly all day.

Evenings Vanna
pulls the wheel down hard, steps back,
claps until the spinning stops.
In such a mood each opinion feels sudden,
unbidden after all.

From the rooftop where the sun sets
I can see most of the spires in town—
chanticleers whose flat fossil bodies turn,
soldered to their masts.
Whims are but twists.
I get along well with postal clerks
and shopkeepers.

Come dark, the roosters settle.
Their calls will ruffle,
something of a surprise.

44

[PICTURA]

     At the Mardi Gras gallery the feather man
parts the plumes of my new duster,
its handle of oak lathed to the hand.
"Ostrich. These suckers are sturdy."

I point to a bone on the highest shelf,
bolt of white among the peacock.
"Cow bone," the feather man says
now atop the creaking ladder,
"a friend brought it back from Baja."

I weigh its heft in both hands, tracing
the curve of hip, smooth spatular flanges
to either side of two fist-sized holes.

[SUBSCRIPTIO]

     The feather man lectures me.
Do I know that Libra rules the pelvis,
bone of square balance,
gravity's seat? Every sign
lodges in my own medieval corpus.

He pauses, reaches for the bone,
lifts the hip to his face,
looks at me through empty sockets.
His touch turns mask
to magnet.

     How to make of oneself a sail

     The roof is going nowhere

Bed of Leaves and Likenesses

as when a man saves the seed of fire

Odyssey, Book V

Out of the seawater into the salt air
he musters, biding,
his very valves
swollen with brine.
Dust work, suspension, dusk.

He makes rakes of his fingers,
mounding the brittles —
mat of shuckings and rushes
for his salty sorry limbs
and what parts of me he will have.

His face, lop-stunned by swell and break.
My veil is down the beach,
a rag washed up, shifting
as the windrow shifts.

Here now, the smolder,
torch blackened still warm,
a smudge traced from earlobe
to that hollow he moans into.

Valentine

When he goes away I build spice racks
and bookshelves with my Makita drill.
I schlump around in the Carhart pants
I found for free. I scratch myself.

I love my teal drill, free of rust, with key
leashed fast to the cord so I can never lose it.
That was his father's touch, the one who stored
the first aid kit and the flares, tarp and tire iron
in the back of the Ford, the car I now drive
to the lumber store when he goes away.
I walk down to the bend in the river and stare.

I style my hair when he returns. I show my work, I say, "See!
Now there's a place for the garam masala and the zatar!"
His face is the door
thrown open,
and I am home.

FOUR

Logic of the Senses

About the skin I expected jaundice
but not the tang saffrons of these eyes,
room ringing of failure.

I leaned to kiss the cheek,
his head turned slightly to meet
me, his lips another breed.

The chapping grace note
of a touch was —
                    The chapped
and glancing brush was subsumed
by sulfur oxide, warmer now,
battery acid. I leaned in to gasp
the pale
exhales,
                    paper wicking sepia.

I fell in again,
                    bit through litchi,
                    splintering,
brought to my nose
cheap necklaces and my handling fingers,
tie irons, pennies,
shards of the oldest living thing.

Each Parting

is preceded by a join,
your voice on the phone
steadying outward,
an arm to either side
of poise.

I reach, I fly

This is safety, in small numbers:
two sisters and one infant promised for another.
We spend the day changing, feeding,
holding the one you will leave behind,
never unsaying what you've said all along.
The orderly glares and huffs at *what a white girl*
will do to keep her damn selfish self to herself.

On the fourth morning
I walk with you down the corridor,
away from all you're leaving
to the couple in the next room.
They will lift her, comfort her
before the toy runs out of song.

He Went So Far as to Confess that He

is secretive, has ever
been so.

Onto my fork I wind the new
datum, raise it to my open mouth,
bird hungry.

He chews, I swallow.

Tares sprout,
dense as knot-weed,
each doubt tendrilled
to its truth.

I rake the laundry
in piles.

I didn't see it coming —
the uses of burdock,
King Weed,
each nick in the infinite root
another spite
of tangledom, of burrs.

Now if only —

I dig it up,
pare it dry,
pestle with linseed,
rub the salve into my thinning skin,
wait, watch for the glow —

Or make a tea with which
to wash down the abject
fruits, and while I'm at it

eat this tree house
(two months since, sprung
by my leaving), unladdered.

All the flintknapping and pothunting
in the shatter of those middens I've happened upon,
have helped to mound or founded —
I give him this, my carbon self.

In Memoriam

You want to fault the tree
for flagging down the car that night,

run your finger through the grooves
naming who loved whom. Grieving,

you want relief. Every cell of your body
you yourself have made, something

is leaving, something will always
be leaving.

This is how I think about the dead:
the winds that brought them to me

brought also their air of being here to stay,
their gravity, its levity.

That they left was in every case surprising,
that I surprise easily is my distinction.

The sacrum fountains upward
and so the spine sways.

Winds blow through me, winds
blow through me — I can do nothing

A Change of Phase Will Always Entail a Change of Heat

Oh this new town must be
proud to have a road so new,
so quiet

For a mile my heart glides,
opening to the other nameless town,
that of ruts and potholes

The way in certain mountain counties where towns meet
as do fluids, the one carrying into itself
a long bead of the other's claim

Swirl of pasture disavowed
as pasture or moved on from

       I find myself a tractor
       who don't do reverse.

How in regions where borders so form
the switchback road will welcome you again
and again to the same town

       Entering M--------

You not knowing
you had left, nor whose
shifting turf you were
in the act of passing from

       He said, *This cake cannot be unbaked.*

At that line where surface changes,
the frictionless feel of tar laid even
just last week perhaps, I always think,
always —

       One fact dredged up,
         heat is not temperature.

I stand at roadside, a cube
no colder than the puddle of my melting

The bones between molecules breaking
nothing quickens
nothing happens except:

Anniversary

That's what pumpkins do,
he said. *They grow.*

Why my surprise, why joy
or any of the enthusiasms
I can't suppress?
Listen around,
people assuring one another
how much they'll like Y,
they've got to try Z,
Taste this isn't it great —

forkful thrust across the table
in something like love
of the chanterelles
and the mouth of the one
who made the mistake
of not ordering the special.

Neuropathology

Into my ear
she introduced a few mL's of icy water,
provoking the recoil
and eye shimmy,
the *nystagmus*.

Serum as both marrow
and marrow-spoon,
each answer sleeved to its question
as beak to trumpet blossom,
as tube of tongue in turn to beak and bloom.

She wanted
the truth. She arched and sharpened
the angle of her hover,
     Tell me something good!
My nurse, my provoker,
my ruby-throated mother.

I fold and refold the map
along its softening seams,
saying now what then
I had no thought
to name:
     Neglect.

This half of the flower,
undrawn because
   unseen.

A Crescent Still Abides

Our circular breathing sphered,

    sheered,

        toroidal,

such that every region
touched every other.

Our regions totaled a number
diagrammable, if not by us.

I can just now supply the night code
behind the seven colors,
bend my mind to it,

    manifold,

        mantle between crust and core.

Her black you breathed in, unremittent.
You, the breather, brinking,

    reeling,

        with keens into yourself.

The unknown want,
both rock and hurtle.

How could she but surface,
flower, billow,

    the stun —

        what follows

ENVOY

When, as one sheds
not tears but skin,
you shed the last, specific tear,
it will sit, precipitate
on my tongue.

Within 30 days or
10,000 brushstrokes or
if applicable —

       [interval, unspecified]

Whereby that tiny moon,
grief, mooted, morphed,
is lifted up into what seems its inimical ether,
joy.

Where will it go,
the sublated,
what neither this mouth
nor that lash can singly

admit? More than residue
and less, it rests
so deep into the new
as to be the new.

NOTES

"Chiasmus"
After Karl Blossfeldt, *Working Collages* (MIT Press, 2001), and after Maurice Merleau-Ponty, "The Intertwining — The Chiasm," in *The Visible and the Invisible, Followed by Working Notes,* translated by Alphonso Lingis (Northwestern University Press, 1968).

"Macondo"
The code name given to the offshore oil prospect near the Louisiana coast, site of the British Petroleum oil spill in 2010. A BP employee had come up with the name (borrowing from Garcia Marquez's *One Hundred Years of Solitude*) as part of a BP company contest. This poem is based on the experience of the 1969 Union Oil spill off the coast of Santa Barbara, California.

"Good to Go"
Adapted from George Plimpton's *New Yorker* profile of Larry Walters, a Darwin Award winner; fragments from the Book of Ezekiel in the Bible appear at end of poem. In memory of John Reichert.

"Showdown"
The final lines are from Samuel Beckett, *The Unnamable* (Grove Press, 1958).

"Project Grizzly"
Inspired by the life and work of Troy Hurtubise of North Bay, Ontario, as reported in the documentary film *Project Grizzly,* directed by Peter Lynch (National Film Board of Canada, 1996).

"Five Lessons"
Lines are quoted from F. M. Alexander, *The Use of the Self* (Methuen, 1932), and William Pleeth, *Cello* (Schirmer, 1982).

"Ransack"
Epigraph is from Lewis Henry Morgan, *The American Beaver and His Works* (J. B. Lippincott, 1868).

"Four Weathercocks"
Title (originally "Four Weathercocks, Six Meanings") is from the book *Emblematic Exhibitions at the Brussels Jesuit College* (1630–1685) by Karel Porteman (Royal Library, Brussels, 1996). The poem is set in Key West—especially on Thomas Street, home of Blue Heaven and Maskerville Feathercrafts.

"A Crescent Still Abides":
Title taken from Emily Dickinson, #1605: "[Each that we lose takes part of us;]."

ACKNOWLEDGMENTS

Thank you to editors of the following publications for publishing poems or earlier versions of poems.

Cider Press Review: "Five Lessons"

The Common: "At the Riverbank" and "To St. Hubert, Wonder-worker of the Ardennes, Patron of Hunters and Mathematicians, Protector from Rabies"

New Orleans Review: "A Change of Phase Will Always Entail a Change of Heat"

Paris Review: "Anniversary," "Chiasmus" (as "*Wundergarten*"), "Good to Go," and "Ransack"

Poetry International: "Emperor Select"

Prairie Schooner: "Milagro"

Seneca Review: "Each Parting"

Western Humanities Review: "Anchises, Aeneas, Ascanius," "Bourrée, from the Third Unaccompanied Suite," "The Marmiton," and "Showdown"

Yale Review: "Four Weathercocks" (as "Four Weathercocks, Six Meanings")

In addition, "In Memoriam" was produced as a letterpress broad-side by Greenware Press of Chicago, Illinois.

"Envoy" (as "Warrantee") was produced as a letterpress broadside
by Yes Press of Minneapolis, Minnesota.

The poems "Bourrée, from the Third Unaccompanied Suite,"
"Five Lessons," "In Memoriam," and "Project Grizzly" are
included on the audio-CD recording *Merge* (2006), performed
by Cassandra Cleghorn with Erik Lawrence, Allison Miller, and
Rene Hart.

For their love and encouragement, I thank my children, Oliver,
Ripley, Eve, and Jasper, whose dear lives span the writing of these
poems, and my mother, Freda Campbell, whose sudden loss
marked this book's final stages. For their attention to my writing,
I thank Sally Prine, Bill O'Neill, Rodger Dawson, Laura Slatkin,
Seth Schein, Tilly Shaw, Richard Howard, John Ashbery,
Robert Creeley, Michael Bell, Shawn Rosenheim, Jim Shepard,
Karen Shepard, Paul Park, John Limon, Marsha Recknagel, Erik
Lawrence, Marie Gauthier, and Karl Mullen. For their support of
this book, I thank Ilya Kaminsky, Robert Pinsky, Lee Sharkey, Dan
Beachy-Quick, Brenda Shaughnessy, the Dean of Faculty at
Williams College, Patricia Malanga, Mariela Griffor and the staff
of Marick Press, Barry Goldstein, Ann Aspell, and Jim Schley,
editor par excellence. And finally, blessedly, I thank my husband,
Jeffrey Levine, who shares in every poem I know by heart and
every poem I've yet to write.